Psychodiagnostics A Diagnostic Test Based On Perception

HERMANN RORSCHACH

PSYCHODIAGNOSTICS

A DIAGNOSTIC TEST BASED ON PERCEPTION

INCLUDING RORSCHACH'S PAPER

THE APPLICATION OF THE FORM INTERPRETATION TEST

(PUBLISHED POSTHUMOUSLY BY DR. EMIL OBERHOLZER)

TRANSLATION AND ENGLISH EDITION BY

PAUL LEMKAU, M. D.

THE HENRY PHIPPS PSYCHIATRIC CLINIC, BALTIMORE

AND

BERNARD KRONENBERG, M. D.

NEW YORK

FIFTH EDITION, WITH A NEW BIBLIOGRAPHY

VERLAG HANS HUBER, BERNE, SWITZERLAND

Distributors for the U S.A
GRUNE & STRATTON INC.
381 Fourth Avenue — New York, N.Y

PREFACE TO THE ENGLISH TRANSLATION.

The widespread and growing interest in the Rorschach test among English-speaking workers has made apparent the need for a more easily available source of information concerning Rorschach's original and basic work than the German Editions supply. This English Translation is presented in the hope of filling that need. We are aware that this need has been met sporadically by various unauthorized translations, but these have been available to but few of those interested in the test. None of these translations was at hand during the preparation of the translation presented here.

The task of translating Rorschach's German is doubly difficult. One wishes to present his ideas adequately and at the same time preserve as much as possible of the personality of Rorschach as it is revealed in his choice of words, his sentence structure, and his delicate shadings of meanings. The first attempt yielded a too literal translation which did not present the ideas clearly enough. This first effort was completely rewritten and carefully checked to make sure that the sense as well as the flavor of the original was preserved to the greatest possible extent.

We are especially grateful to Dr. Adolf Meyer who encouraged us to take up the task and who has continued to be interested in our progress. Many individual points have been discussed with colleagues at the Phipps Clinic, and we are grateful to them for their help and stimulation. To Mrs. Florence Halpern of the Staff of Bellevue Hospital in New York, and Miss M. R. Caine, also of New York, we also owe our thanks for help with particular problems arising in the course of the work. Other colleagues have generously considered our questions with us and have encouraged us; these friends are too numerous to mention but all may be assured that their help was appreciated. Especial thanks are due to Dr. Christopher Tietze for time-consuming labor in checking the manuscript for those finer shadings of meaning apparent only to one whose original language is German. The intelligent and co-operative criticism of Miss Helen Kaste as she typed the manuscript has resulted in the elimination of many errors which would otherwise have marred the work, 2nd Lt. H. L. Siple, AUS, was helpful in the preparation of the index'.

Bernard Kronenberg.

Paul Lemkau.

CONTENTS

IV. Results.

V. The Use of the Form Interpretation Test in Diagnosis.

Examples.

HERMANN RORSCHACH.

1884—1922.

Hermann Rorschach was born in Zurich. November 8, 1884. His youth was spent with the younger children in the family in Schaffhausen. It was originally his intention to study natural science, but the death of his father, a teacher of drawing, precipitated a situation in which the young man turned to Ernst Haekel for advice, and it was suggested that he go into medicine. He followed the advice, studied in Neuenburg, Zurich, Berne and Berlin, completing his studies and qualifying in 1910. The same year he married a Russian colleague who soon became his comrade and collaborator. He became an assistant physician, first in the insane asylum at Muensterlingen, then at Muensingen. He accepted a position in a private sanatorium in Moscow in 1913 but returned to Switzerland after one year. From June, 1914, to November, 1915, he was physician in the psychiatric clinic and asylum at Bern-Waldau, after which time he became assistant physician in a hospital in Herisau. While still holding this position he died, April 2, 1922, after only a few days illness due to appendicitis complicated by peritonitis.

Only those who knew Hermann Rorschach's versatility can understand what his death meant and still means to Swiss Psychiatry. He was not only a congenial co-worker, an extraordinary colleague and comrade, and a kind person; he possessed as well outstanding qualities as a practical psychiatrist and as a research scientist.

Flexibility of character, rapid adaptability, fine acumen, and a sense for the practical were combined in Hermann Rorschach with a talent for introspection and synthesis. It was this combination which made him outstanding. In addition to this rare nature, which tempered personal emotional experience with practical knowledge, he possessed sound traits of character most valuable in a psychiatrist. Most important of these were an unerring tendency to search for the truth, a strict critical faculty which he did not hesitate to apply to himself, and a warmth of feeling and kindness.

These few remarks will make it possible for those who could not know Rorschach to imagine what he was, and what he might have become. Bleuler fittingly expressed this when he said, «Hermann Rorschach was the hope of an entire generation of Swiss Psychiatry».

Dr. W. Morgenthaler.

PREFACE TO THE SECOND EDITION.

Hermann Rorschach himself considered his Psychodiagnostics a mere beginning. He worked indefatigably toward its completion until death intervened.

With the need for a new edition the question arose whether the work begun by Rorschach could not be continued by someone else. This meant that the first edition should be changed, improved and completed so that it would contain the results that have been evolved since his death and certain gaps might be filled.

Anyone acquainted with Rorschach's method and who has worked with it to any extent will recognize how difficult it would be for another to prepare a new edition. Rorschach's method is an expression of his own personality so that method and the personality of its author are inextricably interwoven. It will, therefore, be apparent to those who possess the clinical foundation necessary to work with the method successfully in psychopathology and psychiatry, that even the most skillful revision and completion of this rather personal method would result in the inclusion of some foreign influences, thus disturbing the unity of the work. Such revision would probably prove damaging.

We decided, therefore, to leave the first edition entirely unchanged except for a few corrections of the text. This was done for the practical reasons mentioned above and not merely out of respect for the deceased author. We have added the only other work on this subject, aside from the Psychodiagnostics, which the author left to us. It has been published posthumously by Dr. Emil Oberholzer under the title «Zur Auswertung des Formdeutversuches» in the number of the «Zeitschrift für die gesamte Neurologie und Psychiatrie» which appeared in honor of Prof. Bleuler. It is an important addition to the Psychodiagnostics since in it he discusses how he would like to have his method of diagnosis of the personality conceived and interpreted, and illustrates with concrete examples. In this paper, also, we have limited ourselves to editorial corrections.

— 12 —

We are exceedingly thankful to his widow, Dr. Rorschach, for supplying
us with material for comparison and for aid in correcting the proofs. We wish
to thank Dr. Emil Oberholzer for his many valuable suggestions, and the
publisher, Hans Huber, for the fine appearance of the new edition, in spite
of difficulties.

Bern, January, 1932.

The Editor,
Dr. W. Morgenthaler.

INTRODUCTION.

The following pages describe the technic of and the results thus far achieved in a psychological experiment which, despite its simplicity, has proved to be of value in research and in general testing. At the outset it must be pointed out that all of the results are predominantly empirical. The questions which gave rise to the original experiments of this sort (1911) were of a different type from those which slowly developed as the work progressed. The conclusions drawn, therefore, are to be regarded more as observations than as theoretical deductions. The theoretical foundation for the experiment is, for the most part, still quite incomplete.

It must also be noted that there has been constant checking of the observations on normal subjects against observations of patients, and vice versa

Hermann Rorschach.

LIST OF SYMBOLS AND ABBREVIATIONS.

R   =   Total Responses.

W   =   Plate Interpreted as a Whole (Whole Answer).

DW   =   Plate is interpreted as a whole secondarily, the answer based primarily on a detail.

D   =   A normal detail of the plate (Detail Answer).

Dd   =   An unusual or small detail (Small Detail Answer).

S   =   White intermediate figures (Space detail).

Do   =   A detail is interpreted in the place of a whole Example· in Plate III, only the heads are seen.

Apper.   =   Apperceptive Type. Relation of the apperceptive modes. W, D, etc

Sequence   =   Sequence of W, D, etc, in the individual plate.

F   =   Form Answers. Interpretation is determined primarily by the form of the blot.

M   =   Movement Answer. Interpretation is determined by kinaesthetic influences

FC   =   Form-Color Answer The interpretation is determined primarily by the form and secondarily by the color of the blot.

CF   =   Color-Form Answer. The interpretation is determined primarily by the color, secondarily by the form of the blot.

C   =   Color Answer. The interpretation is determined by the color of the blot alone.

Experience Type   Relation of M to C answers· $\dfrac{M}{(FC + CF + C)}$

H   =   Interpretation of Human Figure.

A   =   Interpretation of Animal Figure.

Hd   =   Interpretation of Part of the Human Figure.

Ad   =   Interpretation of Part of Animal Figure.

Obj.   =   Interpretation of Inanimate Object.

Ldscp.   =   Interpretation of Landscape.

A%   =   Animal Percent. $\dfrac{A + Ad}{R} \times 100$

Orig.%   =   Percent Original Answers (Answers occurring no more than once in 100 Tests) of Total Answers.

I. THE METHOD.

1. Apparatus.

The experiment consists in the *interpretation of accidental forms,* that is, of non-specific forms. A reproduction of the figures in their present form is issued as a supplement to this book and should serve not only for illustration but as available apparatus.

The production of such accidental forms is very simple: a few large ink blots are thrown on a piece of paper, the paper folded, and the ink spread between the two halves of the sheet. Not all figures so obtained can be used, for those used must fulfill certain conditions. In the first place, the forms must be relatively simple; complicated pictures make the computations of the factors of the experiment too difficult. Furthermore, the distribution of the blots on the plate must fulfill certain requirements of composition or they will not be suggestive, with the result that many subjects will reject them as «simply an ink-blot» without consideration of other possible interpretations.

Every figure in the series has to fulfill certain special requirements as well as these general ones, and each, as well as any whole series, must be thoroughly tried out before it can be used as apparatus for the test. (The individual requirements of the plates and the construction of parallel series is discussed on page 52.) The construction of a suitable series of ten figures is not so simple as might appear at first glance.

From the method of preparation it will be apparent that the figures will be symmetrical, with very little difference between the two halves. Asymmetrical figures are rejected by many subjects; symmetry supplies part of the necessary artistic composition. It has a disadvantage in that it tends to make the answers somewhat stereotyped. On the other hand, symmetry makes conditions the same for right- and left-handed subjects; furthermore, it facilitates interpretation in certain inhibited and blocked subjects. Finally, symmetry makes possible the interpretation of whole scenes.

Figures which are asymmetrical and show poor composition could add new factors to the results of the experiment but would require testing on normal control groups. But the problem cannot be further discussed here. The examination of individual sensibility to composition is a problem in itself.

The order of the plates within the series is determined by empirical results. This subject is discussed on page 53.

2. Procedure.

The subject is given one plate after the other and asked, «What might this be?» He holds the plate in his hand and may turn it about as much as he likes. The subject is free to hold the plate near his eyes or far away as he chooses; however, it should not be viewed from a distance. The length of the extended arm is the maximum permissible distance. Care must be taken that the subject does not catch a glimpse of the plate from a distance, since this would alter the conditions of the experiment. For instance, Plate I is frequently interpreted «the head of a fox» when seen at a distance of several meters; at a closer range this answer is almost never given. Once the subject has interpreted the plate as the head of a fox it becomes very difficult for him to see anything else when it is brought nearer.

An attempt is made to get at least one answer to every plate, though suggestion in any form is, of course, avoided. Answers are taken down as long as they are produced by the subject. It has proved unwise to set a fixed time for exposure of the card. Coercion should be avoided as much as possible.

Occasionally it becomes necessary to show a suspicious subject how the figures are prepared, ad oculos. In general, however, rejection of the test is relatively rare, even among suspicious and inhibited patients.

3. Interpretation of the Figures as Perception.

Almost all subjects regard the experiment as a test of imagination. This conception is so general that it becomes, practically, a condition of the experiment. Nevertheless, the interpretation of the figures actually has little to do with imagination, and it is unnecessary to consider imagination a prerequisite. It is true, however, that those gifted with imagination react differently from those not so gifted. On the other hand, it makes little difference whether one encourages the subject to give free rein to his imagination or not; the results will be little changed. Those who have imagination show it, those who do not have it may apologize for the lack, but the results may be compared without taking richness or poverty of imagination into account.

The interpretation of the chance forms falls in the field of perception and apperception rather than imagination.

«Perceptions arise from the fact that sensations, or groups of sensations, ecphorize memory pictures of former groups of sensations within us This produces in us a complex of memories of sensations, the elements of which, by virtue of their simultaneous occurrence in former experiences, have a particularly fine coherence and are differentiated from other groups of sensations. In perception, therefore, we have three processes; sensation, memory, and association.—This identification of a homogeneous group of sensations with previously acquired analogous complexes, together with all their connections, we designate as «apperception». It also embraces the narrower term of perception.» *(Bleuler,* Lehrbuch der Psychiatrie, p. 9. Verlag Springer. Berlin 1916; Translation from A. A. Brill's Authorized English Edition, p. 13.)

If perception can also be called an associative integration of available engrams (memory-pictures) with recent complexes of sensations, then the interpretation of chance forms can be called a perception in which the effort of integration is so great that it is realized consciously as an effort. This intrapsychic realization that the complex of sensations and the engrams are not perfectly identical gives the perception the character of an interpretation.

All answers given by the subjects are not interpretations in this sense, however. Most organic cases (senile dements, paretics), epileptics, many schizophrenics, most manics, almost all the feebleminded subjects, and even many normals are not aware of the assimilative effort. These subjects do not interpret the pictures, they name them. They may even be astonished that someone else is able to see something different in them. We deal in these cases not with an interpretation but with a perception in the strict sense of the word. They are as unconscious of the associative-assimilative performance as a normal person is of the process of seeing a familiar face or in perceiving a tree. From the above discussion, we conclude that there must be a kind of threshold beyond which perception (assimilation without consciousness of assimilative effort) becomes interpretation (perception with consciousness of assimilative effort). This threshold must be very high in cases of senile dementia, in manic states, in feeblemindedness, etc.

Where this threshold is low, it is to be expected that even the simplest, most commonplace perception brings with it the consciousness of assimilative effort. This is the case in certain pedants who demand an absolutely exact correspondence between sensation complex and engrams for their perceptions. It is even more apparent in some depressed subjects. Here the assimilative effort may have become so great that it can no longer be overcome and everything they perceive seems «changed» and «strange». Pedantic and depressed subjects show just this in the test; they search for those details in the figures that happen to have distinct counterparts in nature, frequently going on to say: «I know that I am interpreting and that actually it must be something else».

Normal subjects frequently speak of the «interpretation» of the figures spontaneously.

Cases showing congenital or acquired defects of intelligence want to «recognize» the pictures.

These different ways of handling the figures indicate that the difference between interpretation and perception lies in associative factors. Furthermore, reactions of subjects in elated moods show more of a perceptive character, while in depressed moods the reaction is more interpretative. Finally, it is apparent that the difference cannot be said to be due only to associative processes; emotional factors may also shift the boundary between perception and interpretation.

In summary, we may conclude that *the differences between perception and interpretation are dependent on individual factors, not on general ones; that there is no sharp delineation, but a gradual shifting of emphasis; and that interpretation may be called a special kind of perception.* There is, therefore, no doubt that this experiment can be called a test of the perceptive power of the subject.

The significance of the imagination in interpreting the figures is discussed on page 102.

II. THE FACTORS OF THE EXPERIMENT.

1. Statement of Problems.

In scoring the answers given by subject, the content is considered last. It is more important to study the *function* of perception and apperception. The experiment depends primarily on the pattern [1].

Protocols of the experiment are examined according to the following scheme:

1. How many responses are there? What is the reaction time? How frequently is refusal to answer encountered for the several plates?
2. Is the answer determined only by the form of the blot, or is there also appreciation of movement or color?
3. Is the figure conceived and interpreted as a whole or in parts? Which are the parts interpreted?
4. What does the subject see?

Other questions arise in connection with 2, 3 and 4 above, and will be discussed later.

The conclusions in this work are based on experimental observations which have been obtained with the series of plates accompanying this book. The following table gives a summary of the material collected:

	Male	Female	Total
Normal, educated	35	20	55
Normal, uneducated . . .	20	42	62
Psychopathic personality .	12	8	20
Alcoholic cases	8	—	8
Morons, Imbeciles	10	2	12
Schizophrenics	105	83	188
Manic-depressives	4	10	14
Epileptics	17	3	20
Paretics	7	1	8
Senile dements	7	3	10
Arteriosclerotic dements .	3	2	5
Korsakoff and similar states	3	—	3
Total	231	174	405

---

[1] German = Formale.

In addition to this, many experiments have been conducted using earlier, but now discarded, figures. These cannot be considered here because comparative scoring is possible only when observations are obtained with the same series of plates, or with a parallel series (see page 52).

The totals indicated above are far too small, especially in the groups of uneducated normals and the common psychoses. The small number of the common psychoses studied is partly due to the fact that an institution serving a country canton offers little variety of material. Before the printing of the plates the number of experiments was limited because the figures were damaged by passing through hundreds of hands [1].

---

[1] Since the material which appears in this publication is intended for a wide circle of readers, I am adding, for the sake of clarity, descriptions of the more or less well known psychoses.

Schizophrenia (Kraepelin's Dementia Praecox) is the most prevalent mental disease. Two-thirds of the patients in most institutions are schizophrenic. Bleuler considers the basic symptom a disturbance of associations: dissolution of the normal thought combinations, strange mental processes, the connection and condensation of the irrelevant, the splitting of valid relationships, absurd generalizations, the use of symbols in the place of the original concept, the incapability of thinking with a purpose. The result of this is scattering and disunion of many associative processes on the one hand; on the other, of perseveration, that is a constant sticking to the same mental processes, flight of ideas in the first case, paucity of ideas in the second. Furthermore, a striking symptom of schizophrenia is the defect in the ability to modulate the emotions, the emotional rigidity, the loss of emotional rapport In severe cases this increases to «emotional dementia», to an apparent lack of emotions Hallucinations, delusions, absurd movements, actions and mannerisms, etc., may occur as accessory symptoms. The accessory symptoms may become the prominent features of the disease in some cases.

Schizophrenia has four sub-varieties which in themselves do not form exclusive aspects of the disease but interchange and overlap in the same patient.

1 Paranoid: Delusions and hallucinations prominent Most superiority and persecution complexes fall in this group.
2 Catatonic Catatonic symptoms predominant. absurd movements, posturing, mannerisms, negativism (characterized by doing the opposite of what is expected, frequently the opposite of what is desired), impulsiveness. The schizophrenic «autism» of Bleuler is particularly evident in this group, the shutting out of all contact with the outside world. In addition, hallucinations and delusions are frequently seen.
3. Hebephrenic. Schizophrenics with accessory symptoms of all sorts, often showing motor excitement. Cases which cannot be classified as paranoid or catatonic are generally included here.
4 Simple dementing form (Schizophrenia simplex) Schizophrenia the course of which is gradual and slow with especially marked «emotional dementia», and without accessory symptoms.

Manic-depressive Insanity includes depressive and manic states as outstandingly contrasting symptom complexes.

1 Depression: characterized by depressed mood, slowing of thinking, inhibition of the centrifugal functions of decision, of action, and the psychic component of motility.
2 Manic States· characterized by elated mood, flight of ideas, the urge to be active and to talk, abnormal facilitation and acceleration of those centrifugal functions which are inhibited in depression.

2. Number of Responses.

Normal subjects generally give from 15 to 30 responses, rarely less than 15, often more than 30. The number depends principally on emotional rather than on associative factors. Depressed, sullen or unobliging subjects often give less than the average number of answers. Subjects ambitious to give answers of the highest quality occasionally choose to give but ten excellent interpretations, and consequently fall below the average number. Subjects in a happy frame of mind, those in a good humor, those who enjoy phantasy, and subjects who are especially interested. give a larger number of interpretations than the average. as do subjects who are anxious to do well, the «model pupils» and those of similar personality make-up.

For different reasons feeble-minded subjects and epileptics almost always show a larger number of answers than the average. this is largely because they enjoy performing a task that appears easy. The number of responses given by organic cases is usually within the average range, usually toward the lower border, except in the case of the confabulators. the Korsakoffs and paretics, where the number may be much higher than average. Manics usually give a few more than the average number of answers while in depressed subjects the number is usually within the normal range.

The number of answers is very inconstant in schizophrenic subjects. Inhibited cases often give less than ten; indolent cases settle the matter with ten mediocre answers. The better preserved[1] cases, as well as others, are frequently within the normal range; however, many also give high numbers of answers. Some cases which appear to be totally demented, having been psychotic for decades, produce surprisingly numerous and varied responses.

As may be seen, the study of the number of answers reveals nothing characteristic in the different groups of cases.

3. Reaction Time.

As a rule, 20 to 30 minutes are required to complete the experiment. If 20 answers are obtained in 30 minutes, the average reaction time is 1.5 minutes. Obviously, this is not an exact reaction time; in the strict sense, reaction time could be obtained only by means of a series of control ex-

---

Korsakoff Psychosis: Psychosis due to alcoholism usually beginning with delirium tremens, characterized by marked memory deficit. The patient attempts to cover up the defect even to himself by confabulation of all sorts of experiences to fill the gaps.

Organic Psychoses Those mental illnesses which are due to a diffuse reduction of brain substance This groupe includes the Korsakoff Psychosis mentioned above, senile dementia (dementia of old age), arteriosclerotic dementia, and paresis.

(All after Bleuler, Lehrbuch der Psychiatrie, Berlin, 1916)

[1] German = Geordnete

periments. It goes without saying that the reaction time is greater in epileptic, organic, and depressed cases than it is in manics.

The reaction time in schizophrenic subjects is notably shorter than in all other groups, including normals. Some scattered[1] schizophrenics find four or more interpretations for the same picture in perhaps five seconds. The more scattered the patient, the shorter the reaction time. provided he has been able to focus his attention on the test.

4. Failure to Answer.

Normal subjects almost never fail to give a response for the several plates. Occasionally neurotic subjects fail to answer; this is caused by inhibitions due to complexes. Feebleminded hysterical subjects often reject the figures because they are afraid they will give stupid answers; we deal with an «intelligence complex». Failure frequently occurs in a typical manner in schizophrenics, even in latent or practically recovered cases; they suddenly refuse to answer, even though they have been giving many and good responses all along. The refusal may come with figures not ordinarily considered difficult. The blocking may be insurmountable although in all other kinds of cases an answer may be obtained on coaxing.

5. Form, Movement and Color Responses: Their Relation to the Perceptive Process.

Most interpretations are determined by the form of the blot alone, both in normal and abnormal subjects. The subject searches among his visual memories for that one which in form, especially in outline, most closely resembles the entire figure or one of its details. In accomplishing this, he does not visualize the object «seen» as moving, but as a fixed form. Such *Form-answers* will be designated hereafter as F.

In contrast to these, we have «Movement» and «Color» responses. The *Movement responses, designated* M, are those interpretations in which it can be established that *kinaesthetic* engrams (visual memories of movements observed, imagined or executed previously) have had a determining influence in addition to the consciousness of the form of the blot. The subject imagines the object «seen» as moving. *Color responses,* designated C, are those interpretations in which it can be established that the color as well as the form, or the color alone, of the figure has determined the answer. The frequency with which these three types of answers occur, and especially their relative proportions to each other are very important. They show characteristic, typical variations which are significant in normals as well as in the various illnesses.

---

[1] German = Zerfahren.

a) Form Responses (F).

Most interpretations are determined by the form of the blots. This is the case generally as well as in each individual test. The evaluation of these form responses thus becomes a significant problem; in order to avoid subjective evaluation statistical methods were used. Form answers given by a large number of normal subjects (100) were used as the norm and basis. From this a definite range of normal form visualization could be defined, and a large number of frequently recurring answers were collected. These were called «good forms» (F+). In this process, many forms which would not. on subjective estimation, have been called good, were so designated. Those answers which are better than these, are called F— also; those which are less clear are F—. Even though the normal range is statistically fixed, judgment of what is better or worse than the good normal response remains a matter for subjective evaluation to a certain extent. However, this evaluation can be made with relative certainty. The form answers having been evaluated, 5 % more or less F+ should not be considered significant in calculating the F+ percentage, since the evaluation is purely empirical and not absolutely objective. Nevertheless, the F+ percentage provides useful leads in the study.

Table I is a summary of the empirical relationships found in the cases. Only rough averages are given. Naturally, the perception of form by a schizophrenic depends on what it was before he became ill. Furthermore, the adjective «intelligent» is used loosely; as is demonstrated below, however, the test is capable of evaluating the individual components of what is called «intelligence». One of these components is sharpness of form visualization. The Table requires no special comment except to call attention to a few points. It is noteworthy that depression improves the sharpness of form visualization, while elation dulls it. Certain groupings already seen earlier in the study are repeated in the table. Those subjects who were most conscious of the assimilative effort in interpreting, namely the pedants and mild and severe depressions, are all to be found in the group which saw forms most clearly (see page 17). On the other hand, those whose interpretations were simply perceptions occupy the lower half of the table; these are the manics, the epileptics, the feebleminded, and the organic cases. Thus, acuteness in the perception of objects and a marked consciousness of assimilative effort in the experiment are seen to go hand in hand; the converse of this statement is also true, that lack of acuity in the perception of objects goes with freedom from a sense of effort in the test. Probably only in schizophrenics can this relationship be disturbed

*

Table I.

Form Responses

	Normal	Feebleminded	Schizophrenic	Manic-Depressive	Epileptic	Organic
100—80 % F+	Intelligent Pedantic Depressive	—	Apparently well preserved paranoid cases, latent and recovered	Depressed	—	—
80—70 % F+	Intelligent but careless Mod. intelligent	—	Relatively well preserved	—	—	—
70—60 % F+	Unintelligent «normal» elated mood	—	Scattered	—	Epileptoid	Korsakoffs, arteriosclerotic dements
60—50 % F+	—	Morons	Very scattered, originally morons	Manic	Epileptic	—
50—30 % F+	—	Morons Imbeciles	Originally morons, abulic	—	Demented epileptic	Paretic
30— 0 % F+	—	Low grade imbecile	—	—	—	Senile dements

b) Movement Responses (M).

Movement Responses are those interpretations which are determined by *form perceptions plus kinaesthetic factors.* The subject imagines the object interpreted to be in motion. For instance, in Plate I he sees two angels with fluttering wings: in Plate II, two carnival clowns dancing with each other, their knees bent; in Plate III, two waiters bowing to each other, etc. Frequently the gestures of the subject during the test will indicate whether or not kinaesthetic influences are in play. He makes the movements which he is interpreting or indicates them by involuntary innervations.

One should not be misled, however, into considering each movement described or even demonstrated by the subject as indicating that the answer is kinaesthetically determined. There are subjects who indicate not a few animated objects but whose answers, nevertheless, may not be considered as determined by movement. Responses such as «a duck going into the water», «a dog snapping at a butterfly», «a bird in flight», «an airplane in flight», a «volcano in eruption», etc., are not M answers in many cases. These are form answers, determined by the form alone, and the indication of motion is often only a rhetorical embellishment of the answer, a *secondary* association. This may be the case even if the movement is demonstrated in some way. We deal here not with movement sensed in the figure, but with an association of the movement designated. A point which will be intelligible only after further elaboration must be mentioned here. The motility observed in a subject is not a measure of the kinaesthetic influences playing upon him while interpreting the figures. On the contrary, the individual who is influenced by kinaesthetic factors in the test is stable in his general motility; the energetic person is influenced little by a sense of movement in the figures. Such empirical results of the experiment can be reproduced at any time, though they lack theoretical foundation.

The following may be taken as a rule. answers may be considered as kinaesthetically determined practically only when human beings or animals capable of motion similar to that of human beings (monkeys, bears) are seen in the figures.

Interpretations involving human beings are not always M answers. The question always is, does the movement indicated play a primary role in the determination of the answer? Do we deal with an actual *sensation of motion,* or simply the conception of a form that is secondarily interpreted as moving? Plate III is important for this consideration. It is usually interpreted as «Two waiters carrying a champagne bucket», or something similar. In this interpretation the black fish-shaped forms below and laterally are thought of as the legs of the waiters, and the legs are, as may be seen, separated from the body. Primary kinaesthetic factors are very probably necessary to make it possible for the subject to overlook this separation. Such answers are, then, to be considered as kinaesthetically determined. To be sure, very many subjects will give the answer «two men», but they do not indicate the fish-like figures as the legs, but tend rather to point out the «arms» of the waiters carrying the champagne bucket. These subjects are interpreting primarily by form alone; they perceive the heads and necks of the men, and fabricate the rest without the participation of kinaesthesias.

Other subjects frequently answer, «a sketch of men», or «caricatures». Such answers are almost never M's. «Skeletons» is the answer given by others; this also is not an M answer according to my experience.

Sometimes it is difficult to determine whether an answer is F or M. Intelligent subjects can generally say with reasonable certainty whether or not kinaesthetic factors have contributed to the response; one should wait until after the completion of the test before asking the question, however; otherwise attention is drawn to kinaesthetic factors too strongly. Occasionally unintelligent subjects and patients will give clues on careful questioning. In other cases, comparison of the interpretation under question with answers clearly F or M will make differentiation possible. (An M answer, the designation of which is definitely established, is compared with the interpretation in question, and the same procedure is carried through with an F answer.) There are some subjects who can perceive movement not only in human figures and animals with certain human characteristics but in all kinds of animals, plants, geometric figures, and even in single lines. In such cases the differentiation is usually not difficult, however, for the subjects are nearly always good at self-observation and can give the necessary information.

The experience and practice of the examiner using the same series of test blots counts heavily in scoring the M answers. Apparently the speed and certainty with which experience is acquired varies widely from individual to individual. If the observer himself has a personality too inclined to make kinaesthetic interpretations or lies at the opposite extreme, it will be difficult for him to judge properly. At any rate, the scoring of the M answers is the thorniest problem in the entire experiment. The personal equation of the observer, dependent upon his «imagery-type», can warp the results most easily here. Some statistical method might be introduced to avoid false subjective conclusions based on analogies. If there be too much schematization, however, many correct subjective conclusions will be stifled at the start.

There are considerable differences in the number of M answers given, in normals as well as in patients. The number ranges between 0 and 15, is rarely higher. See Table II.

Table II is a rough compilation which nevertheless allows certain conclusions to be drawn. In normals, the number of M responses rises in proportion to the «productivity of the intelligence», the wealth of associations, the capacity to form new associative patterns. Stereotyped and feebleminded subjects have no M's. The rule is the same for schizophrenics; the more pro-

ductive the associative life of the patient, the more M's; the more stereotyped the thinking, the fewer M answers. Elated mood increases, depressed
mood decreases the number of M's, so that in psychotic depressions, there
are no M answers. In depressions in a schizophrenic setting, a few M's appear; in psychogenic depressions, the number may remain rather large. More
M's occur in hypomanics than in manics, but in the hypomanic states of
organic cases, there is little or no increase. Depressed and pedantic subjects are again found together, showing few or no M's.

The results with epileptics are extraordinary. The most demented of
them show the highest number of M answers, while cases in which the dementia has developed slowly, over the course of many years, produce the
least.

Comparison of tables I and II shows a few clear relationships. In normals,
the number of M's is, in general, clearly proportional to the acuity of form
visualization. Pedants and depressed subjects do not conform to this proportion; they can combine the most acute clarity of form visualization with
no M's at all. No definite conclusions can be drawn from the rough compilation in the case of schizophrenics, and this would be possible only if individual symptoms were the basis of comparison. Such a study would go
beyond the plan of this treatise. In organic cases, the results are identical
with the normals; the poorer the forms, the fewer the M's. The fact that
arteriosclerotic patients do not react as do the normals in this respect is due
to emotional factors.

The normal relation, i. e., the better the forms, the more M's, is entirely
inverted in all cases in which there is mood disturbance. In elated or depressed moods of normals, in manic-depressive insanity and in arteriosclerotic
depressions, the proportion reads, the better the form, the fewer the M's.
The reverse of this is also true in these cases; the poorer the forms, the more
M's. Epileptics show this inverse proportion also.

The answers determined by kinaesthetic factors can, as was the case in
the form answers, be divided into good and poor M's (M+ and M—). Those
answers which correspond poorly to the form of the figure are to be considered M—. Many of these M— answers occur in the protocols of manics
and epileptics but are rare in schizophrenics. A few M— answers may occur
in elated normals and in subjects with Korsakoff's psychosis. M— answers
are practically impossible in normal tests; however, M— responses may occur
in a normal subject who knows the test and is ambitious to produce as many
M's as possible; this ambition is betrayed by a few M— responses.

The movement answers are further divided into primary and secondary.
In most M answers it appears that the form and kinaesthetic engrams have
mixed very rapidly in the assimilative process, so that the form and motion
of the objects seem to reach perception simultaneously (primary M). In other
cases, it appears that first the form and later the motion of the figure reaches

Table II.

Movement Responses

	Normal	Feebleminded	Schizophrenic	Manic-Depressive	Epileptic	Organic
More than 5 M	Good, productive intelligence. Imaginative. Intelligent + «normal» elated mood.	—	Most inhibited catatonics. Most productive paranoids.	Manic	Epileptics with early dementia.	Korsakoff
3—5 M	Average intelligence. Unintelligent + «normal» elated mood.	—	Inhibited catatonics Productive paranoids.	Manic	Epileptics with slow dementia	—
1—2 M	Intelligence predominantly reproductive.	Morons + «normal» elated mood.	Unproductive catatonics + hebephrenics. Depressive.	—	Epileptics with later dementia Epileptoid	Paretics
0 M	Unintelligent Pedantic. «Normal» depressive mood.	Morons, Imbeciles	With simple dementia. Stereotyped. Some querulous cases.	Depressed	Epileptoid	Arteriosclerotic and Senile Dements.

perception (secondary M). For example, an epileptic may see a human form in Plate III and begin to maneuver his body, bending and stretching until his position conforms to the lines of the figure. Then he gives his answer; it may be well or poorly visualized.

Is this reaction in epileptics different from that of normals because of an inherent slowness of associative processes in epilepsy? Manics show the same sort of reaction, but with much greater rapidity. They, too, may give well or poorly visualized M answers. In the manic there is no slowing of the associative process to account for this, so that it must be concluded that there are other factors at work. Suffice it to say that there are differences which must be examined more fully, and will be expressed in terms of «primary» and «secondary» M answers for the present.

Frequently the responses of morons and delirious patients are similar to these secondary M's. They often describe movements that they simply imagine, and the forms they use do not correspond to any part of the figure. Subjects of these groups may see a human head and then imagine a body, or even a whole story full of movements. Such answers are not to be considered as M's, but as F's, or entirely separately, as «confabulatory F—M's».

In conclusion, it is instructive to examine the movement answers, especially in normals, to see whether they indicate flexion or extension. Subjects who usually see extension movements are fundamentally different from those who see only bent, burdened or twisted figures. In Plate V, held vertically, one of the first type saw a danseuse stretching herself upwards and backwards, making passionate movements, while one of the second type saw a bent old woman carrying two umbrellas under her arm. Subjects who see extension movements are active individuals with strong drive toward self-assertion, though they often show neurotic inhibitions. Those who see flexion movements are passive, resigned, neurasthenic individuals. Control experiments made with plates selected so that extension and flexion movements could be perceived with equal ease would be helpful in this case.

c) Color Responses (C).

On examination of the influence of color on the interpretations, various possibilities are apparent. These are:

1. The interpretation is based primarily on the form but is also influenced significantly by the color. Such an interpretation is designated FC, form-color answer. Examples are: The brown parts of Plate IX interpreted as «deer», the blue rectangles in Plate VIII as «flags», the medial green figures in Plate X as «caterpillars».

2. The interpretation is primarily determined by the color of the blot, but the form is not entirely disregarded. This is called a CF, color-form answer. Examples The blue rectangles in Plate VIII as «blocks of ice»,

Plate IX (the red up) as «a bouquet of flowers», Plate X as «a modernistic fly-leaf».

3. The interpretation is determined by the color of the figure alone without any significant consideration of form. Such an answer is called a primary color answer and designated C. (The fact that the sign «C» indicates both color answers generally and primary color answers is of no practical importance.) Examples of primary color answers: the blue rectangles of Plate VIII as «the sky» or as «forget-me-nots», the green of Plate IX as «Russia» (Russia usually being colored green in maps), in Plate X, the large red figures as «roses» or «rosewater».

The differentiation of the three groups of color answers is quite important, and frequently assignment to one or the other group is open to question. Naturally, the primary color answers, those which completely neglect the form, are the easiest to recognize. The other two groups can usually be differentiated from pure form answers by asking whether the interpretation would have been the same if the figure had been black. The question may be answered by the subject, or by the examiner, using other answers given by the subject for comparison. In time a statistical method may be evolved on the basis of the frequency of those answers which allow positive designation.

If the subject cannot settle whether an answer is FC or CF, comparison with the clarity of form vision when interpreting black figures is helpful. If the clarity of form visualization in the color answers is less acute than when the subject interprets black blots, it is probable that we deal with a CF rather than an FC. It is also true that cases which give primary color answers usually give CF's as well. Experience with as many different types of subjects as possible facilitates the scoring.

Epileptics, especially deteriorated cases, show an almost specific type of color answer. They simply name the colors, «black and red» or «blue and red», as the case may be. One such case called Plate X simply «a motley of colors». Very occasionally a scattered schizophrenic will react in the same way. Answers in which black and white are spoken of as colors must be noted separately. They are equivalent to the other color answers only when they occur in epileptics and in some completely scattered schizophrenics. When scored as color answers in diagnostic control experiments they proved to be a source of error. Whether they have any specific significance has not yet been shown.

The number of color answers of all types varies widely in normals as well as in patients. Because of this, Table III is even more crude in its summation of results than has been the case for the preceding tables, and it indicates only the most generally significant results for the different groups of cases. The table shows that all cases where depressed mood is a factor are in the group with few color answers, while those with elated moods fall in the group with numerous color answers. Few color answers are received from depressed subjects, whether they be manic-depressive, arteriosclerotic, or even psychogenic depressions. Color plays an important role in the interpretations of manics and subjects in elated moods. Furthermore, it is found that *subjects characterized by stable emotions give few or no color answers.* Depressed and pedantic subjects, indolent or stereotyped cases, especially old stereotyped schizophrenics, and simplex types, give few or no color answers. *Subjects characterized by affective lability give many color answers.* In this group are found the subjects in elated moods, «neurotic» individuals, artists, morons and imbeciles, scattered schizophrenics, epileptics, organic cases, and the manics.

Comparison between Tables I and III shows almost complete parallelism. *The more stable the emotions, the better the form visualization; the more labile the emotions, the more inexact the form visualization.* This parallel relationship breaks down only in the case of a single group of normals, the neurotics and artists. This group does combine good form visualization with unstable emotional tone. Occasionally schizophrenics, especially productive paranoids, react similarly.

The relationship between movement and color answers will be discussed more fully later, but a superficial comparison of Tables II and III shows certain facts. There is a direct proportion between the number of M and C responses in epileptics and manic-depressives, that is, there are either many of both M and C answers, or none of either kind. In feebleminded and hebephrenic subjects, the proportion is inverse, that is, there are many C with no M answers. The remaining inverse proportion, many M but no C answers, is found in the psychogenic depressions and in paranoics. There is a certain similarity of reaction between normals and the majority of schizophrenics as shown by the tables, though this similarity does not hold in all cases. This material will be taken up again later.

The three categories of color answers must be discussed separately. Primary color answers, C's, are missing in the upper part of the table. These answers are absent in all normal subjects and in patients who are emotionally stable, be they depressed, emotionally stereotyped, emotionally impoverished and outwardly calm, or more or less well preserved. C answers are seen, first, in the irritable and sensitive, and increase in number in manics where irritability and instability are features. Irritable and impulsive patients show large numbers of C's as does the group of schizophrenics which shows the most emotional and associative scattering; epileptics, also impulsive and irritable, fall into this class.

From this summary it can be deduced *that the primary C answers are the representatives of impulsiveness.* The more C's, the greater the tendency to impulsive actions. Most of the deductions of this section are based

Table III.

Color Responses

	Normal	Feebleminded	Schizophrenic	Manic-Depressive	Epileptic	Organic
0 FC, 0 CF, 0 C	Pedantic. Indolent. With «normal» depressive mood.	—	With simple dementia Stereotyped. Capable of rapport.	Depressed	—	With Arteriosclerotic dementia.
1—3 FC 0—1 CF 0 C	Most common normal values	—	Well-preserved, capable of rapport. Depressive.	—	(Epileptoid)	Korsakoff
0—1 FC 1—3 CF 0—1 C	Irritable. Sensitive.	—	Less capable of rapport. Indifferent Unstable	—	—	—
1—2 FC 2—3 CF 1—2 C	Hypomanic mood. «Good humored» Impulsive neurotics.	Morons	Unstable Irritable	Manic	With late dementia.	Parotic
1—3 FC 2—3 CF 2—6 C	—	Imbecile	Scattered catatonics.	—	With rapid dementia.	With senile dementia
1—2 FC 3—4 CF 5—10 C	—	—	Most scattered hebephrenes and catatonics	—	Imbecility + Epilepsy	—

on statistical methods. As many protocols as possible from as widely diversi-
fied clinical material as available were obtained and the results analysed
according to the individual factors (C, M, FC. etc.). Thus it was discovered
that those subjects giving the most primary color answers were exclusively
epileptics, manics, imbeciles, paretics, scattered schizophrenics, or notoriously
hot-headed and hyper-aggressive and irresponsible «normals». From this it
was concluded that C answers have a «symptom value», that is they represent the common trait of all these cases, namely, the tendency to impulsive
emotional discharge.

The sources of error of such a method were compensated as far as possible
by the following means:

1. Comparison of the clinical symptoms in the respective psychoses with
the conduct of the normals concerned. This is done by statistical study and
consideration of etiological factors.

2. Statistical and etiological comparison of the assumed «symptom value»
of a factor with that of a related factor similarly established (e. g. comparison between C and CF).

3. Examination of the diagnostic value of the respective symptoms. As an
example of this method, the diagnostician would attempt to read records of
unknown subjects on the basis of the C answers.

CF answers prove to be analogous to pure C answers, but occur in a
larger number of subjects. CF's are almost always found when C's are given,
but the inverse of this does not hold. CF answers are frequently found in
normals whereas C's are not. CF's are more frequent in women than in men.
They have proved to be the representatives of emotional instability, irritability, sensitivity and suggestibility.

The form-color answers, FC, are proportional neither to the C or to the
CF answers. FC's are most common in normals and slightly less frequent in
manics and epileptics, though in the latter they are accompanied by CF and
C answers. The number of FC's shows wide individual variation. From studies
as indicated above, it was found that FC answers may be regarded as representative of that emotional instability biologically necessary and basic for
the ability to achieve emotional rapport and to make emotional approach to
the environment. The C and CF answers express the more egocentric affective responsiveness, while the more adaptive affective responsiveness is expressed in the number of FC's. Completely stabilized subjects, the depressed,
the indolent and the pedantic, show no C, CF or FC answers whatever.

Several spheres of psychic function must combine in the form-color answers which take up the form first and then the color. In the interpretation
of form, associative factors come into play; in the interpretation of color,
emotional factors are influential. The form-color answer is, therefore, an
associative as well as an emotional response; it is an assimilation of external
stimuli. It also proves to be an expression of the capacity for getting into

rapport, of the ability to adapt, and this can be shown by either the statistical or the etiological method of study.

A better way of saying this is that the FC answer is the expression of the *desire* to adapt, for the FC may be poorly visualized. This would mean that only the emotional adaption was effective, the associative being insufficient. The poorer the visualization of form in the FC answer, the nearer it approaches the CF group, and, thereby, the appearance of egocentric emotional responsiveness. Egocentric affectivity may show a definite «will to emotional adaptability», but the associative component is insufficient, so that the affectivity usually, perhaps always, becomes egocentric.

These conclusions must be subjected to corroboration by the means noted above. Many FC answers are given by normal, epileptic and manic subjects. In normals the form visualization is good, in manics and epileptics unclear. The conclusion from this is that only normals can make entirely satisfactory adaptions, adaptions satisfactory in both associative and affective spheres. In manics and epileptics the adaption would be frustrated by the fact that no matter how strong the will to emotional adaption might be, the associative component could not produce it. This is the case in fact. When a normal person wishes to make a gift to me, he will look for something *I* would like; on the other hand, when a manic gives a gift, he gives something *he* likes. When a normal person says something, he tries to adjust it to *our* interest; a manic graciously tells things that interest only *him*. Both of these examples appear egocentric because they both lack the right associative adaption.

The form-color should be separated from the color-form answers as clearly as possible in order to differentiate this apparent affective egocentricity conditioned by the failure of the associative component from actual egocentricity. Form-color answers are to be considered representative of the capability for rapport when the form of the answer is clearly visualized.

The logical conclusion to be drawn from this discussion is that the relationship of the three types of color answers in a given protocol is significant. FC (capability for formation of rapport), CF (affective lability), and C (impulsiveness) may be united in widely varying proportions. These variations are great even within the range of normal. 3 FC, 1 CF, and 0 C are probably the most usual values. Male subjects show fewer color answers than female, corresponding to the greater emotional lability of the female. The greater the preponderance of FC's over CF's the more stable is the affect and the greater is the adaptability and the capacity for the formation of rapport. The closer the number of CF's comes to the number of FC's, the greater the moodiness, instability and egocentricity of the subject. Table III shows clearly that this holds in the psychoses as well.

The complete affect-picture is, furthermore, dependent on the number of M answers Just as the CF answers are stabilized by a large number of FC's, the sum of all the color answers, representing the total affectivity, is stabilized by the M answers when these occur in greater number than the C's. To the same extent that the number of M's preponderates over the number of C's, is it certain that the affective tonus of the subject is stable, be he normal, neurotic or psychotic. The less the number of M's, that is, the greater the preponderance of C's over M's, the more affective lability is in evidence.

Finally. it has proved practical to consider the unit M balanced by the unit CF. This can easily be justified theoretically, since in both CF and M the form is considered. FC was scored as one-half, and primary C answers as one and one-half M-balancing units. Though this method of computation is quite artificial, it has, nevertheless, proved to be very useful.

A phenomenon encountered frequently in connection with the color an: swers must be mentioned. Some subjects experience an unmistakable shock, an emotional and associative stupor of varying length, when the colored Plate VIII appears after the preceding black ones. These subjects suddenly become helpless though previously they had been interpreting very well. They find the colored plates more difficult to interpret than the black plates, and they react with astonishment or vexation. Such subjects are always «emotion-repressors», neurotics of varying grades of severity. «Emotion-controllers» show the phenomenon to a lesser extent, not showing shock but scant production with the colored plates. Subjects who are timid in showing their emotions are found between these two groups; interpretations of the colored plates occasionally become hasty and more fantastic after an initial indication of helplessness before the problem. «Emotion-controllers» show a preference for the blue and green figures which is peculiar to this group, and they avoid the red in a striking way.

The expression «color shock» best sums up these phenomena. The presence of them reaffirms the internal relationship which must exist between color perception and the dynamics of affectivity.

d) Incidence of M and C in the Same Interpretation.

Now and then interpretations are seen which appear to be conditioned both by kinaesthesias and color, either with or without consideration of form. These occur quite rarely It usually happens that most answers which appear to be in this group at first glance, show, upon closer examination, that either M was primary and C secondary, or vice versa. In Plate IX, for example, a subject may say, «Two dwarfs fencing» (upper brown) and later add, «Yes, they are brown like dwarfs». Another subject interprets the large red figures in Plate X as «cardinal purple», and later sees two cardinals walking toward one another. In the first example the movement was primary; in the second, the color.

Those rare answers in which movement and color appear to influence the answer simultaneously may be called MC's. Plate X, the whole interpreted,

«Expressionistic picture of a country fair », and plate IX, as «Witches' Sabbath», are examples of the type. Such answers are given by very talented subjects, especially painters, more rarely by subjects in euphoric mood, and finally by catatonic schizophrenics. These same subjects will be found associated again later on, but in a different connection; it is these in which a large number of M answers appear with an equal or almost equal number of C's.

In schizophrenics interpretations may be influenced by very absurd factors as well as form, movement and color. Such factors as the *number* of items is one of these; any two symmetrical blots may be called «father and mother», or any three blots, «the three confederates». *Position* may influence the interpretation; a point in the middle of the plate may be called «the abdomen». A negativistic catatonic may simply call the plate a rectangle, not seeing the figures at all, but only the form of the card itself He may even look around the figure and say, «There is nothing next to it».

6. Mode of Apperception of the Figures.

a) Statement of Problems.

The third question on Page 19 reads: «Is the figure conceived and interpreted as a whole or in parts? Which are the parts interpreted?» A few other questions may be added here.

The normal subject goes at the experiment in somewhat the following manner. He first tries to interpret a given plate as a whole, searching his store of visual memories for something which coincides as far as possible with the entire figure on the plate If his search is successful, we have a «Whole Answer», hereafter designated as W. This done, he goes on to the separate parts of the figure. He keeps to those parts which are most prominent because of their arrangement. We then have one or more «Detail Answers» (D) When the most striking details are exhausted, he goes on to the smallest details of the figure and gives, perhaps, one or more interpretations of these «Small Detail Answers» (Dd). The next figure is treated in the same way and the sequence W-D-Dd is repeated, and so on through the entire series as regularly as possible. A normal subject interpreting the plates in this schematic manner would give, perhaps, ten whole answers, twenty detail answers, and thirty small detail answers; a total of about sixty interpretations Every plate would be conceived in the sequence W-D-Dd.

If there were a subject who would react exactly in this way, he would be so «normal» that he could no longer be considered normal at all in any practical sense. Among my many subjects not one has reacted in this «normal» manner. It is possible that some day such a subject will turn up. Basing my conclusions on observations of subjects most closely approaching the fictitious (normal , this man would have a psychological make-up something like this: – He would be a know all, have a large store of available associations, and would show a logic far beyond the range of anything that might be called healthy common sense. He would constantly impress one as tyrannical, grumbling, impatient and pedantic. He would also be very proud of his power and stamina of thinking, especially of his logical reasoning ability, but he would show no originality of reasoning nor sense for practical things. He would be original only in his desire to know and do everything. He would have almost no capacity to form rapport, would be empty of any temperament, but full of self-righteousness and pride. In fine, he would be a proud but sterile technician of logic and memory. Such would be this «normal» individual

Actually the problem is more complicated. There are many associative and emotional factors which tend to modify this fictitious normal type.

Nevertheless, the following questions may be drawn from this schematic case:

1. How may W. D. and Dd be determined?
2. How many W. D and Dd answers are given by the subject?
3. How strong is the tendency to maintain the normal sequence of W, D, Dd? Is the sequence disciplined and orderly or irregular and confused?
4 What factors determine the relationships indicated under questions 2 and 3 above?

b) Scoring the Mode of Apperception.

The scoring of Whole answers (W) is self-evident. Examples of this type of answers are: Plate I interpreted as a butterfly or as two angels giving aid to a woman, Plate V, as a bat; and Plate VI as the skin of an animal or a leaf: Plate IX (inverted) as a volcano. Further differentiation among the W answers is necessary, however, for there are *primary* and *secondary* answers of this type The examples given above are of the primary type. The differentiation can best be explained by comparison of the two types. There are, moreover, further differentiations within the secondary whole answers.

The «confabulated» whole answer is the most common type of secondary W. In this type of answer a single detail, more or less clearly perceived, is used as the basis for the interpretation of the whole picture, giving very little consideration to the other parts of the figure For instance, in Plate I, the small claw-like figures (medial top) lead many subjects to call the whole figure a «crayfish». The primary whole answer interprets the figure primarily as a whole, using as many and disregarding as few details as possible. Between this type and the confabulated secondary W there are many intermediate types. When the phenomenon of confabulation is as clear as in the example above, it is advisable to score the answer, not W, but DW, DW indicating that the Whole is arrived at from a detail. Naturally the result of DW visualization is unclear conception of form. These answers occur in many unintelligent normals, in morons, in epileptics, in organic cases, and in schizophrenics.

There are, in addition, *successive-combinatory answers,* also secondary Wholes. In these the subject first interprets a few details and then combines them into a whole answer. In Plate I, for example, the subject may say, «Two men (sides) and a woman (middle)», adding, «The men are quarreling about the woman».

In contrast to these successive-combinatory answers, there are *simultaneous-combinatory* Wholes. The latter differ from the former only in the greater rapidity of the associative process, and should be added to the primary W's in scoring. Plate I interpreted as «Two men taking an oath on an altar» furnishes an example. Both types of answers are characteristic of imaginative subjects and are very frequently F+ or M+. Successive-combinatory answers of varying degree appear also, of course, in protocols of Korsakoffs, manics, etc.

In the psychoses, *confabulatory-combined* whole answers are more common. These are amalgamations of confabulation and combination in which the forms are vaguely seen and the individual objects interpreted are combined without any real consideration for their relative positions in the picture. An example is Plate VIII interpreted as «Two bears climbing from a rock, over an iceberg, onto a tree trunk». Here the forms are F+, but the position of the objects in the picture is neglected. Such answers are frequently given by unintelligent normal subjects. Confabulating morons, Korsakoff cases, and delirious patients are able to invent whole stories in this way. Less frequently such responses are seen in manics and schizophrenics.

Contaminated whole answers are found only in schizophrenics. A catatonic subject sees in Plate IV, «The liver of a respectable statesman». This response would be incomprehensible had not many other experiments furnished the key to it. The plate is not infrequently conceived as a degenerated organ, perhaps a liver or a heart, but it is also frequently seen as a broad man sitting on a column-like stool. The schizophrenic interprets the figure twice, once as a liver and once as a man, and then contaminates the two with each other, at the same time tossing in the associated ideas, «respectable» and «statesman». Schizophrenics give many interpretations in which confabulation, combination and contamination are mixed in together. Thus, an old paranoid catatonic tells the following story in interpreting Plate IX: «This is Weinfelden (lower red = spilled wine = C answer). It was there I was married. At that time the Bodensee reached to Weinfelden. There is the Bodensee (greenish-blue = C), and here is the door of the hotel where we stayed (indicating a tiny section of the middle line). There were two men sitting and drinking wine from a bottle (the brown figures at the top = M), and here is the cup from which we drank, too (the intermediate figure, center, between the brown and green) and here is the wine that they spilled (back to the lower red again).»

Detail answers (D) must be separated from the small detail answers (Dd). The differentiation carries with it certain difficulties, but it is important since D is the normal detail. Dd, however, whenever occurring in large numbers, is more or less abnormal. The normal is generally finished with the plate when he has given a few D; he rarely goes on to give Dd answers.

D's are those details which, because of their position in the figure, are the most striking. One can define them statistically, as was the case with the forms, but the procedure is unnecessary because after the test has been given to 50 normals one knows most of the normal details. The final theoretical differentiation between D and Dd answers rests on factors not yet fully studied. The principal research indicated is examination of the individual sensitivity to spacial rhythms. It is certain that factors of this sort are effective in the experiment. Certain small details have to be considered normal because of the frequency with which they are interpreted; this is the case with the black points above the middle white part in Plate II and the intermediate figure between the blue squares in Plate VIII. Both these lie in the midline about the same height on the card.

The D's are by far the most frequent answers. Primary and secondary answers—and various classes of the latter—may be distinguished among the D's as was the case with the W answers, but in practice the differentiation has proved superfluous.

The small-detail answers are those which remain after the statistically common D's are subtracted from the total. Occasionally large parts of the figures have to be designated Dd; this is the case where very unusual sections of a figure are picked out, or where an ordinary detail is interpreted peculiarly and with unusual associations. However, Dd's are usually the smallest details of the picture almost always overlooked by normal subjects. Classification of these would add nothing. It is only necessary to do a test with a scattered schizophrenic or a notorious grumbler to understand very quickly what is meant by a Dd answer.

There are only two special forms of Dd diagnostically important enough to be distinguished and scored separately. These are the *intermediate form* (S) and the *oligophrenic detail* (Do).

Intermediate forms (S) are those answers in which the white spaces are interpreted rather than the black or colored parts of the figure which surround them. If there occurs more than one S in a protocol gives reason for suspicion. S are most common in stubborn, eccentric normals and in negativistic, scattered schizophrenics. They are seen less frequently in epileptics, and tend, in this group, to be changed to color-form or form-color answers. S answers always indicate some sort of *tendency to opposition*.

Oligophrenic (oligophrenic = feebleminded) *small detail answers* (Do) are those interpretations in which only a part of the body is seen by a subject, though others see the whole body clearly in the same part of the figure in question. In Plate I, for instance, the central figure is frequently called a female body; if a subject interprets only hands or legs we deal with Do answers. In Plate III the same applies if only heads or legs of the figures are pointed out. Do answers are found primarily in morons and imbeciles less frequently in anxious or depressed subjects. They are almost invariably present in protocols of compulsion neurotics.

c) Number of W. D, Dd, etc.

The absolute number of W. D, and Dd is of less importance than the proportions in which they occur. The absolute number is significant only in the case of the W answers. Table IV indicates the significance of the number of W's. Counts of four to seven whole answers are by far the most frequent, both among normals and patients. There is a difference between male and female subjects, the average for males being from 5 to 7, for females, 4 to 6. Only subjects with great freedom and wealth of associations produce more than 7 W's; intelligent or hypomanic normals, and previously intelligent but now introspective. withdrawn schizophrenics are found in this group. Artists and subjects who enjoy reverie attain the highest number of W answers. Least W's are produced by feebleminded subjects, depressed cases (excepting psychogenic depressions), and, finally, cases of schizophrenia showing simple dementia. Elated mood increases, depressed mood decreases the number of W answers.

Comparison of Table IV with those given previously shows that there is no definite relationship between $F+^0/_0$ and the number of W's, or between the number of C answers and the number of W's. Only when dealing with mood disturbances is any relationship apparent. Comparison of Tables II and IV, however, shows that a *direct proportion exists between the number of M's and the number of W's,* and that this may be traced throughout the tables.

The number of D answers shows no significant relationships, and the same is the case for Dd, S and Do. It may be noted in the case of the small detail answers, however, that the more grumbling and pedantic the subject, the more Do in his protocol. The same is true for factors of scattering and impulsiveness in schizophrenics. S's indicate oppositional tendency whether they occur in large or small numbers. In normals they indicate argumentative, willful, obstinate and querulous types; in schizophrenics they indicate blocking, negativism and eccentricity. Do answers, when they occur concomitantly with better types of answers, indicate inhibition of thought processes conditioned by depression; this is particularly the case when the visualization of

forms is good. Do's associated with many F— interpretations indicate a
dearth of associations (feeblemindedness).

d) Apperceptive Types[1].

A series of *apperceptive types* may be differentiated according to the
relationships of W, D, and Dd to each other as they occur in the protocols.
To do this mathematically would require a larger amount of material than
I have available, but even from this relatively small amount the types are
rather clearly distinguishable.

There is, first, a pure W type. Subjects of this type go through the whole
experiment giving a round number of ten whole answers, or approach this
closely. They go on to the details rarely or not at all. These interpretative
efforts are artificial feats; the ability to make them presumes a considerable
wealth and availability of engrams, though it rests primarily on emotional
factors. This pure W type is usually seen in intelligent subjects, who do not
take the experiment as a «test of imagination», the usual assumption, but
rather as a test of the ability to make abstractions and combinations On the
basis of this they seek to distinguish themselves by a brilliant score; they are
in the mood to break records in the experiment. Because they are attentive
and conscious of the goal, and because of their ambition, they are able to
produce good forms. This type can be designated the «W+» type. Imaginative subjects who are capable of constructing a combined W for each plate,
may also be of this type, especially if the associative processes are facilitated
by their being in a particularly good humor.

In contrast to this W+ type, there is a W— type. Subjects of this type
give ten W answers but the form is poor, F—. This situation probably never
occurs in normals. On the other hand, it is seen occasionally in abulic, indifferent schizophrenics who simply call every figure a «butterfly» or a
«mangled butterfly». The type is also seen in very scattered, excited schizophrenics who give 10 DdW answers, that is, they pick out some small unimportant detail and name the whole figure according to it, neglecting other
parts of the figure. Such a patient may call Plate X «a mountain landscape»
after having interpreted a minute detail as «the knee of a chamois». Another
patient called Plate VIII «a session of the Swiss parliament» because the red
and white coloring reminded him of Switzerland and its government.

I have never seen a pure D or a pure Dd type. These are always mixed.
The type depends on how rapidly the subject shifts from the W to D, from
D to Dd, etc., or, conversely, how long the patient persists in trying to see
as many W's as possible, as many D's as possible, etc.

---

[1] German = Erfassungstypen Variously translated in English as «mode of apperception», «type of attack», etc

Table IV.

Whole Responses

	Normal	Feebleminded	Schizophrenic	Manic-Depressive	Epileptic	Organic
More than 10 W	Imaginative. Abstract.	—	Scattered.	—	—	—
7—10 W	Intelligent «Normal» elated mood	—	Inhibited catatonics. Paranoids. With abulia.	—	Epileptoid	—
4—7 W	Average normal.	«Normal» elated mood.	Most better preserved cases.	Manic	Most epileptics	Korsakoff Paretic With Senile Dementia.
0—3 W	Pedantic. «Normal» depressive mood.	Morons, Imbeciles.	With simple dementia. Depressive. Very stereotyped.	Depressed	Originally morons.	With arteriosclerotic dementia.

Table V indicates the distribution of the main types in the diagnostic groups.

In normals. the most common apperceptive type is W-D, with more or less definite supremacy of W's. the subject shows some perseverance in the tendency to give at least one whole answer for each figure. The more definite this tendency, the more certain it is that the subject is theoretically inclined; the less this tendency makes itself apparent. the more practical the intellectual life of the subject. The latter is especially common among women The different types of intelligence indicated here will be discussed more fully in connection with a fuller discussion of that subject later.

e) Sequence in the Modes of Apperception.

The idea of conceptive types would be defined most clearly if the strictness or laxity of the succession of W's, D's, etc., could be expressed simultaneously in a single formula. This could not be done without undue complications, and the type had to be fixed simply according to the number of W's, D's, etc., produced by the subject. Consequently, the problem of succession of the various modes must be discussed separately. It is possible that distinct types dependent on sequence could be established, but this is not necessary. It suffices to differentiate between rigid, orderly, inverse, loose and scattered successions.

Subjects who take the experiment very seriously show the most rigid succession; they come closest to the fictitious «normal» described on page 36. These subjects take everything they do seriously, not excepting the experiment. Their highest law is logical reasoning; they are logicians to whom the form is more important than the content. Pedantic and «school teacher» personalities are found in this group, as are, on the other hand, depressed subjects with ideas of inferiority, anxious subjects. and psychotic depressions.

The average subject shows an optimum rigidity of sequence. This is to be distinguished from the maximal rigidity just described; it does not sacrifice the content for the form as was the case there. Well-preserved paranoid cases and most of the organic patients react like the normals in this respect. This type of sequence may be called «orderly».

Inverse sequence is seen most frequently in careful, timid subjects, also in those who are imaginative and show fabulation and combination in their answers.

Loose succession is seen in unintelligent or feebleminded subjects, in manics and epileptics, in Korsakoff cases, and, finally, in many schizophrenics. Euphoria or labile mood tends to make the succession loose. Many neurotics, imaginative people. artists also show this though otherwise their results are excellent.

This looseness of succession may go so far as complete scattering, as is the case in many schizophrenics. This occurs in latent cases, and even in

Table V

Apperceptive Types

	Normal	Feebleminded	Schizophrenic	Manic-Depressive	Epileptic	Organic
W	Abstract W+ «Good humored», Imaginative W+	—	Abulic W-.	—	—	—
W̱ - D	With theoretical intelligence W+·D+, «Normal» elated mood W±·D±	—	Well preserved, especially Paranoids. W↑·D+	—	—	With dementia senilis W-·D-, Paretic DW-·D-
W - Ḏ	With practical intelligence. W+·D+	—	Well preserved. Catatonica in interval. W+·D-	—	—	Korsakoff W↓·D↓
D - Dd	Unintelligent D+·Dd±, Grumblers D+·Dd+	—	Less well preserved cases, all types. D±·Do+	—	—	—
D - Do	Pedantic D+·Do+	Morons D∓·Do±, Imbeciles D∓·Do∓	Anxious Depressed D∓·Do±	Depressed D±·Do'	—	With arteriosclerotic dementia D'·Do'
DW̱ - D - Dd	—	Morons in manic excitement DW+·D∓·Dd	—	Manic W∓·D±·Dd±	Most epileptics DW∓·D∓·Dd↓ *	—
DdW̱ - Dd	—	—	Scattered DdW+·Dd∓	—	—	—

+ Predominantly good forms.
+ Predominantly good, but numerous unclear forms.
∓ Predominantly unclear, but some good forms.
− Predominantly unclear forms.
* German gives this formula DGD∓·Dd∓. This is apparently a typographical error and is corrected.

cases where there has never been the slightest suspicion of latent schizophrenia. A scattered schizophrenic may interpret only a minute detail in
Plate I, give several answers which are quite normal in sequence and all other
factors for Plate II, see only a small white intermediate figure in Plate III.
give three W's for Plate IV one of which may be normal and the other two
absurd. He may fail to answer on Plate V. etc.

7. Content of Interpretations. Percent Animal Responses.

We now arrive at the fourth of the questions posed on page 19, namely.
«What is seen?»

All sorts of imaginable (and in the case of the schizophrenics, unima-
ginable) answers are given. A few principles can be established in spite of
wide individual and pathological variations in the content of interpretations.

Animal forms are seen the most frequently. Almost all intelligent subjects, regardless of education, gave from 25 to 50% animal forms in their
answers. Furthermore. only imaginative subjects gave less than 35%, while
subjects showing any kind of stereotypy gave more than 50% animal answers. This observation gave rise to the idea that the percent of animal responses could be used as an indicator of stereotypy in the subject; this proved
to be generally correct. The «animal percentage» actually is quite a reliable
indicator of stereotypy both for normals as well as for patients. Table VI
gives a summary of the findings.

In a few cases, and these are rare. the animal forms are replaced by some
other object as the indicator of stereotypy. This is especially the case in the
oligophrenics, particularly imbeciles. In these, parts of the body may replace
the animal form, so that the subjects see fingers, hands, feet, noses, eyes, etc.,
everywhere. In many morons with «complexes» [1] dictating that they try to
show «intelligence», especially morons with hysterical features, anatomical
forms replace parts of the body as indicators of stereotypy. Such subjects
may interpret the same items throughout the experiment: «lobes of the lung».
«the spinal column», «intestines», and so forth. Epileptoid and traumatic
neurotic cases react similarly.

Comparison with the other tables requires little commentary, though
attention must be drawn to one fact, that percent of animal answers is always inversely proportional to the number of kinaesthesias. The smaller the
animal percentage, the more answers in which the factor of movement has a
part; the fewer of the latter, the greater the animal percentage and the less
variable the answers.

Characteristic relationships appear when we study the interpretations of
human forms, quite apart from the animal answers. This is clearly seen on

---

[1] German = Intelligenzkomplex.

Table VI.

Animal Percent

	Normal	*Feebleminded*	*Schizophrenic*	*Manic-Depressive*	*Epileptic*	*Organic*
10—20 % A	Artists almost exclusively	—	The most scattered catatonics	—	—	—
20—35 % A	Imaginative, Intelligent, «Good humored»	—	Somewhat scattered, productive paranoids	—	The most demented.	—
35—50 % A	Average. «Normal» elated mood.	—	Less productive catatonics and paranoids	—	Less demented	Korsakoff
50—70 % A	Less intelligent. Stereotyped. «Normal» depressive mood.	—	Stereotyped. Hebephrenics. With simple dementia.	Manic	—	Paretic
70—100 % A	Very stereotyped Pedants.	Morons, Imbeciles.	Completely stereotyped, especially with simple dementia and old paranoids.	Depressed	·	With senile and arterio-sclerotic dementia

comparison of the number of answers in which whole figures are seen as opposed to the interpretation of parts of the human figure. Most normally intelligent subjects and the scattered and inhibited schizophrenics interpret more whole figures and almost no parts. Hypomanic normals. confabulating morons, epileptics, most schizophrenics, and most organic cases, interpret more complete figures than parts. More parts of human figures than wholes are seen by unintelligent normals, mildly depressed individuals, anxious and pedantic subjects, hebephrenic and stereotyped cases. Non-confabulating morons, imbeciles, cases of simple dementia, the psychoticly depressed, and arteriosclerotic patients show almost exclusively parts of human figures rather than wholes.

Inanimate objects are frequently indicated in the interpretations of very scattered schizophrenics and of oligophrenic epileptics. They are occasionally seen in the tests of rather scattered normal subjects, especially women, and also in the protocols of manic-depressive patients.

In schizophrenics, especially in cases showing scattering, and in some epileptics, answers which interpret a blue spot as «sky», a brown one as «cough mixture», are not infrequently seen. Abstract interpretations are numerous in schizophrenics. Examples of this are seen in Plate I interpreted as «resurrection» because the female figure in the middle is «rising from the grave», and in Plate X, as «a color benefit». Interpretations in which subjects refer to themselves deserve special mention and have not yet been examined sufficiently to do more than note that they are especially common in protocols of schizophrenics.

8. Original Responses.

The last item to be separated from the mass of answers concerns the *original responses.* These must be counted and converted to a percentage figure. Answers which have occurred but once in 100 tests are scored as original. These are separated into Original + (O+) and Original— (O—) according to the quality of the M, F, or FC of the respective interpretation. When the designation of the answer is CF or C, and it cannot be determined whether it is O+ or O— these answers are best subtracted from the totals before the percentage of original answers is computed.

O+ and O— responses are frequently found in the same set of results, but, in general, one or the other predominates. In schizophrenics, most absurd and very appropriate answers are found following one another. The relation of O+ to O— is, of course, not without importance. Table VII is an attempt to give orientation as to the significance of the original answers. The number on the left indicates the quantity of answers. The quality is indicated by symbols in the body of the table, ± indicating that O+ predominates over O— though both are present, and ∓ indicating the opposite relationship.

Table VII

Original Responses

	Normal	Feebleminded	Schizophrenic	Manic-Depressive	Epileptic	Organic
0—10% Original	Of average intelligence, practical +. Pedantic +. «Normal» depressive mood +.	—	With simple dementia ±	Depressed +	—	—
10—20% Original	More intelligent +. Less intelligent —	—	Stereotyped ±. Catatonic cases in remission ±	Manic +̄	—	Arteriosclerotic ±
20—30% Original	Intelligent + «Normal» manic mood +̄	Morons —	Hebephrenics +̄. Well-preserved paranoid ±	Manic +̄	Some few cases with slow dementia	Korsakoff +
30—40% Original	Imaginative +. In «Good Humor» +. Flighty +̄	Morons —	Relatively well-preserved cases +. Scattered ±	—	Average case +̄	Korsakoff +
40—50% Original	Artists +	Imbeciles —	Scattered +̄	—	With early dementia +̄	Paretic - With senile dementia —
50—70% Original	Those «apart from the world» ±	Imbeciles —	Most Scattered +̄	—	Feebleminded epileptics —	With senile dementia —
Over 70% Original			Rare negativistic cases +			

9. Summary.

All the factors of the protocols of the experiment subject to counting and computation have now been covered. There are others which might be mentioned, but which are omitted in order to avoid complicating the problem unnecessarily.

Logically one should discuss the interplay of the factors extracted above in the various types of normals and in the psychoses, as a summary of this section. Such a study would, however, go beyond the scope of this work, and the limited amount of material does not allow the necessary analysis. I therefore content myself by presenting Table VIII, which is, in a sense, a condensation of such a summary. Table VIII is in fact a summary of the preceding tables, and like them, therefore, can present only rough averages of results.

Two methods suggest themselves for orientation of the further discussion, first a more general attack on the problems; secondly, one based on differential diagnosis, a psychographic approach. For the present, we must use the first method of attack in order to clarify some of the heterogeneous and ill-defined concepts, such as «intelligence», which have already been used.

A few further details on the method of the experiment are in order before proceeding to this discussion.

Table VIII

Summary

	F	M	C	W	Apper Type	A %	Original %
Normal							
Artists	90—100 %	Over 5	1—2 FC, 2—3 CF, 1—2 C	10 & more	W—(D—Dd)	10—20%	30—90%+
Intelligent	80—100 %	5 & more	1—3 FC, 1—2 CF, 0 C	7—10	W—D	20—35%	20—30%+
Average Intelligence	70—80 %	2—4	1—3 FC, 0—1 CF, 0 C	4—7	W—D	30 55%	0—20%±
Unintelligent	60—70 %	0—2	1—3 FC, 1—3 CF, 0—1 C	3—4	DW—D	50—70%	0—70%+
Depressed mood	80—100 %	0—2	0 FC, 0 CF, 0 C	0—3	D—Do	60—80%	0—10%+
Manic mood	60—70 %	3—5	1—2 FC, 2—3 CF, 1—2 C	8—10	W—D—Dd	40—50%	20—30%+
Oligophrenic							
Morons	45—60 %	0	1—? FC, 2—3 CF, 1—2 C	1—3	D—Do	60—80%	30—40%-
Imbeciles	0—45 %	0	1—2 FC, 2—3 CF, 2—3 C	0—2	D—Do	70—100%	40—70%-
Schizophrenic							
Well preserved	70—90 %	3—5	1—3 FC, 0—2 CF, 0 C	4—7 & m	W—D—(Dd)	35—50%	10—40%-
Stereotyped	60—80 %	0—2	0 FC, 0—2 FC, 0 C	2—4	D—Dd	50—80%	10—20%+
Scattered	40—60 %	Over 5	1—3 FC, 2—4 CF, 2—8 C	10 & more	DdW—Dd	40—70%+	
With dementia simplex	60—90 %	0	0 FC, 0 CF, 0 C	0—3	D—Dd	50—70%	0—20%-
Manic-Depressive							
Depressed	80—100 %	0	0 FC, 0 C	0—3	D—Do	70—90%	0—10%+
Manic	50—70 %	5 & more	1—3 FC, 2—3 CF, 1—3 C	4—7	DW—D—Dd	50—70%	10—30%-
Epileptic							
In late dementia	50—60 %	1—2	1—2 FC, 2—3 CF, 1—2 C	4—7	DW—D—Dd	35—50%	20—40%-
In early dementia	30—50 %	5 & more	1—3 FC, 2—4 CF, 2—6 C	4—7	DW—D—Dd	20 45%	40—50%-

III. FURTHER OBSERVATIONS ON THE METHOD.

1. Prerequisites of the Individual Plates.

As was noted at the beginning of this discussion, the series of figures used in the test gradually developed on the basis of empirical observations. The particular qualities shown by the several plates are as follows:

Plate I. Black. Failure is almost never encountered. Stimulates form and movement responses equally. Easy to interpret as a Whole and in Details. There are a number of small Details which frequently give rise to answers.

Plate II. Black and Red. Kinaesthesias more easily seen than in I. Contains a prominent intermediate figure. Color is introduced and occasionally induces a suggestion of «color shock». The red runs into the black.

Plate III. Black and Red. Kinaesthesias' easiest to see. The red separated from the black.

Plate IV. Black. Form and movement answers both comparatively difficult. More difficult to interpret as a whole than in details. The figure is generally considered «beautiful» but the interpretation difficult.

Plate V. Black. The easiest form to interpret. Almost always interpreted as a «bat», or «a moth». Schizophrenics frequently fail to answer on this figure, or they see, for example, moving people in it.

Plate VI. Black Generally called the most difficult of the figures.

Plate VII. Black. The essential part is the white intermediate figure, a rather obvious oil lamp, rather than the black figures. This Plate presents the converse of Plate V, in that normals rarely see the lamp while schizophrenics frequently do.

Plate VIII. Multicolored. Harmonious color and form. Color shock apparent in neurotics. Easily interpreted, at least in detail

Plate IX. Multicolored. Discordant color and form. Kinaesthesias easily aroused. In addition, a definite intermediate figure.

Plate X. Multicolored. Disparate blots. Whole answers almost impossible.

Further work with the test, be it corroborative or simply the examination of large numbers of cases, can only be accomplished in a definitive manner with the plates accompanying this book. While I do not mean to claim that this series is a «non plus ultra», nevertheless, I must emphasize that results, if they are to be comparable to those here presented, must be obtained with identical plates or with an analogous series suitable standardized.

2. Parallel Series.

Two or three parallel series have proved necessary. Frequently occasion arises when the test must be repeated with the same subject. Such situations appear when one wishes to test normals in various moods. manic-depressives in different stages, schizophrenics in various conditions, or in testing patients before and after psychoanalysis, etc. Or a control test on a normal may be desired. If the test is repeated with the same plates, conscious or unconscious memory enters to warp the result. Analogous series of plates, different from the usual ones but satisfying the prerequisites for the individual plates of the basic series, are necessary for these situations.

These parallel series are obtained by selecting those which satisfy the prerequisites of the basic series from a large number of blots prepared as described above. This done, the plates must be tested to see that they are accepted by the majority of subjects and are not simply rejected as blots. After this, standardization is taken up.

Normal subjects of different degrees of intelligence and education must be used for the standardization. The standardization process consists in testing whether the new series is analogous to the original in that movement and color answers are aroused with equal ease. It must also consider whether the possibility of seeing wholes and intermediate figures is the same in the two series. In other words, it should neither be easier or more difficult to interpret the various factors from either series, and the number of answers should compare favorably. Plate I of the new series should give approximately the same number of F's and M's as Plate I of the original, etc. Plate V of the parallel series should present an object equally easy to recognize; Plate VII should have an intermediate figure that is not too obtrusive but easily recognizable. It is most important that the figures should not be more irregular and complicated, for the more complicated the figures, the more difficult the computations.

The production of such parallel series is not as difficult and time-consuming as it at first appears. I speak here from my own experience with them.

3. Control Tests.

The use of special series of plates as controls, special tests for M, C, etc., serves to widen the scope of the test significantly. Two examples will be given.

The original test has shown that color has a remarkable influence in the perception of epileptics, especially cases showing dementia. This phenomenon was studied further by the use of a control series of three pictures. The first represented a cat colored like a frog, the second a squirrel in the colors of a rooster, the third a frog in the colors of a chaffinch The result was that only epileptics, and only demented cases, particularly those which were originally feebleminded, called the green cat a frog, etc. The color was, in them. more influential than the natural, exact form. This has not been observed in any feebleminded subject to date. A similar answer was given by a scattered schizophrenic, but this was observed but once

Another control test was made by showing subjects two drawings, both of which depicted a mower in the position of mowing. No grass or scythe, etc., were shown in the picture. One of these two drawings was traced from the other, so that both had the same position and form, but the traced one showed the mower as left-handed. The subjects were asked, «What is the man doing», and then, «Which of the two is, in your opinion, drawn correctly?» The result was remarkable. Those subjects who gave a large number of kinaesthetic answers in the usual experiment recognized the mower as a mower. but were at a loss to answer the second question. In more than half the cases, they finally designated the left-handed figure as the one drawn correctly. (Left-handed subjects indicated the right-handed figure.) On the other hand. those subjects who gave no or few M answers immediately answered both questions correctly. Imbeciles in most cases were able to say which figure was drawn correctly, the right-handed indicating the right-handed figure, and the left-handed the left. Schizophrenics, when an answer was obtained, reacted similarly, though they also frequently said that the figures were equally correct. On the whole, this test was found to be far less applicable to schizophrenics than is the usual interpretation experiment.

Such problems need much further study.

4. Recording Technique.

The record of the experiment should contain more than the answers given. Facial expressions, voluntary and involuntary movements, signs of possible color shock, etc., should be included.

The symbols used as abbreviations above are used in the computations: by using them the essential factors of the answers may be summarized quite easily. The following are examples of the method:

Plate I. «Butterfly». Interpreted as a whole = W. Answer frequently given by intelligent subjects, therefore, a good form = F+. Animal Figure = A.   Signum: WF+A

Plate X. «Two caterpillars». Green medial. Detail answer = D. Form considered first, color secondarily, form good = FC+. Animal figure = A.   Signum: DFC+A

Plate I. «Two angels with streaming robes floating in the air». Detail answer = D. Kinaesthetic motif = M. Good F+ and M. Whole human figure = H.   Signum: DM+H

Plate   I. «Crab». Secondary, confabulated whole answer = DW. F poorly
        visualized = F—.   Signum: DWF— A
Plate IV. «A castle». A small but well-visualized detail lying in the depres-
        sion on either side between the head of the figure and the inser-
        tion of the lateral projection.   Signum: DdF÷ Landscape
Plate X. «A collection of butterflies». Whole answer determined primarily
        by color but form is not entirely disregarded.   Signum: WCF— A
Further examples will be found in the last part of the book.

It is unfortunate that long descriptions are often necessary to indicate
what part of the plate is interpreted. This difficulty is apparent only in
publications, however, for in practice it is possible to locate unusual answers
by tracing the part of the plate in question. An even better method is to
allow the subject himself to do the tracing.

IV. RESULTS.

1. Intelligence.

Thus far in the discussion the concept «intelligence» has meant nothing more than an empirical estimation of the subject. The figures given in the tables are averages and the number of subjects is large (about 120 «intelligent» normals); it should be possible to draw conclusions from the figures given. Since the entire experiment is a test of perception and conception, these averages should give information as to how the perception and conception of normal, intelligent subjects may be distinguished. At the same time, it should be possible to establish «symptom values» for the experimental factors on an etiological basis; thus far, this has been possible only on statistical bases.

Protocols of intelligent subjects are characterized by the following findings:

1. A large percentage of clearly visualized forms.
2. Many kinaesthetic influences acting in the perceptive process.
3. A large number of whole answers.
4. Good conceptive types; W, W—D, or W—D—Dd
5. Optimum rigidity of sequence of mode of apperception («orderly»).
6. Small percentage of animal answers. In other words, increased variability of interpretations.
7. Neither too large or too small percentage of original answers.

(The color answers alone show nothing characteristic for the group.)

These seven factors may vary considerably from the average in individual cases. These variations express the mixture of a number of the faculties composing what we call «intelligence», or, better, «the various types of intelligence».

A high percentage of good forms presumes, first, the ability to maintain attention throughout the whole of the test, that is, a real ability to concentrate; only when this ability is present are clear perceptions possible. Subjects in which the span of attention is shortened show hazy form visualization in at least part of the experiment. Such is the case in «flighty» or fatigued subjects, in manic or delirious patients and in organic cases. Secondly, the engrams must be clear, for if the memory images are not definite, accurate form visualization will be impossible. This is the case with confabulators, many morons, and organic cases. Third, a high percentage of good forms presumes the ability to recall into consciousness, to bring to mind , clear memory images. This is an associative process which may be disturbed by fatigue or by organic disease. Fourth, there must be an ability to select the most fitting of the various similar images which arise. This ability is, in itself, a complex associative process which depends upon the attention which must now focus, not only on the external stimuli, but on the memory images arising as well. This function must, at the same time, furnish a control of the perceptive processes, controlling criticism of the interpretations.

When all these abilities are present to the maximum, the best forms should be seen in the protocols. Accordingly, we find the best forms in the pedants and depressed subjects. especially in psychotic depressions. These subjects take the test very seriously. They search laboriously for good forms, bringing to bear all their attention and faculties of self-criticism so that they achieve an F + percentage of almost 100, though the answers are extraordinarily stereotyped, showing a poor range of variation. The maximum and the optimum of these four abilities are, therefore, two quite different quantities.

Pedantic and depressed subjects sacrifice almost all the other factors of the experiment in payment for the privilege of having the best forms. So far as form goes, they outstrip the normally intelligent subject, but in other factors they are far behind so that they approach the reaction shown by imbeciles. The exaggerated propensity for clear form visualization makes their answers stereotyped and the content suffers. Furthermore, a number of other formal principles of the perceptive process are curbed by this propensity. It is these pedantic and depressed subjects who experience the interpretations as painfully uncertain and who become most acutely critical of the perceptions, of their own functions, as it were. This is a part of their general self-criticism. (See page 23.)

Judging from the total data from intelligent subjects, the optimum clarity of form visualization is to be found when engrams and perceptions are clear and there is control of the assimilative process, but these faculties must not be present to such an extent that they cripple all other functions.

In summary, it may be concluded that the F percentage is an indicator of the clarity of certain—perhaps all—associative processes, and of the length of the span of attention and the ability to concentrate. The optimum F+ percentage, that is, the optimum of the faculties listed above, is expressed in from 80 to 95 % F+. This is, then, the first component of intelligence. Only pedants show 100% F+, the maximum.

The situation is the same in the case of the second factor. The sequence of the mode of apperception shows an optimal rigidity in the intelligent subjects, but is more or less loose in unintelligent and «flighty» subjects, and in manics and epileptics. Maximal rigidity is shown by pedantic and depressed subjects. (See page 43.)

The tendency toward a very rigid succession of W, D, etc., for each of the ten figures has its basis in the same ingrained attitude that the best visualization of forms has. It is that conscious and almost painful attitude of self-criticism in regard to the form of logic in thinking. For this rigid succession the same stable attention and great precision of the associative process is required as for the form vision. Again, the content and many other principles of perception are sacrificed to some extent for the sake of the form of thinking. When the sequence is rigid to the maximum, we usually deal with «poor» types of apperception such as D—Do, or almost that. Rigid sequence and a better type of apperception such as W—D, may be found chiefly in two situations.

The first of these is in the case of certain «schoolmaster» and bureaucratic types, where daily exercise supports and emphasizes the attitude. Here the precision of self-control and the pride in consistency gives rise to ideas of superiority, overcompensating the feelings of insufficiency in the individual. The second instance in which rigid succession and a «good» apperceptive type can occur together is when labile affectivity is stabilized by conscious attention to the form of thinking, as is the case in many compulsion neuroses. The number of M's and W's remains too small, the animal percentage too large, and a few Do answers, otherwise characteristic of feeblemindedness, creep in, reducing the quality of the type of apperception in these cases.

The optimum rigidity of sequence and clarity of visualization of form characteristic of the normally intelligent subject occurs with no consciousness of effort; it is automatic, a result of habitual tendencies in the individual. The logical function is also automatic, like the control of the nervous impulses involved in riding a bicycle. This function is preserved even in the cases of organic brain disease, probably because it is an ability which became automatic early in life.

The sequence becomes loose and scattered when there is flattening of the affect; the effect is even greater when the affect is unstable. Sequence is also disturbed when the span of attention is too short, or the ability to direct the attention is interfered with as in the case of manics. In schizophrenia, where the complex associative processes are constantly vague, interrupted and scattered, the sequence is, again, loose and scattered.

The automatic, unconscious ability to discipline the thinking to logical ends is, then, another component of intelligence. It is expressed in terms of optimal rigidity of sequence of W, D, etc., and is dependent upon stability of attention.

Intelligent subjects produce 7 to 10, or more, whole responses, usually clearly visualized F's or M's. This undoubtedly demands the availability of many visual images in memory, and also a considerable degree of that freedom of association which allows the right engram to be recalled at the right moment. In short, it demands a considerable store of available engrams. There are some subjects, however, who give only 5 or 6 W's though their answers clearly indicate a wealth of available engrams. While a goodly number of W's is unlikely without a wealth of engrams. it is equally true that this factor alone is not sufficient to produce the large number of W's. Those subjects who are ambitious to produce a test of the best quality, who take the experiment as a test of the ability to make abstractions and want to make an excellent record by giving only W answers, the W types described above, together with those in elated mood, produce the most W answers. Among intelligent subjects, pedantic and depressed cases give the least W's. Therefore, we conclude that the more vivid the affect, the more W answers produced by the subject. Evidently the production of a large number of W's requires a certain affective coloring. a special sort of volition, in addition to the wealth of engrams.

This must be a «willing» attitude, its goal to conceive «the whole»; not infrequently, this attitude is combined with a strong antipathy for details. The act of the will may be toward combining details into wholes. Sometimes the subject is quite conscious of his attitude of striving to set a record, again, it is an habitual tendency which is not consciously realized. It may be an entirely unconscious tendency. It is always the expression of associative activity, this activity being increased by the affective charge (the state of «willing»). The energy of this charge must not be confused with diligence in carrying out the test; the pedants and depressions never give large numbers of W responses, even with the most assiduous diligence. We deal with a «will to produce», a disposition set toward producing, and this is intensified in the experiment by the desire to set a record.

Manics show less W responses than do intelligent subjects in hypomanic mood, and organic cases in manic phase do not give large numbers of W's. These facts will be explained in a later section.

The number of W responses is to be considered primarily as an indicator of the energy of associative activity, dependent on a dispositional set of the subject. Frequently the number of W's is an indicator of a conscious or un-conscious «willing» in the direction of achieving complicated performances, such as abstraction or combination in the interpretations. Thus we find that subjects with philosophic interests produce many good primary W respon-ses, and the imaginative show many good combinatory W's. An optimum ability to produce W answers is another component. Study of the apper-ceptive types will indicate where this optimum lies.

The intelligent subject usually has a W—D conceptive type, with more or less emphasis on W or on D, and with more or less inclusion of small details, Dd. Individual variations among intelligent subjects are much larger with this factor than in the case of F and W. The various apperceptive types are associated with very different types of intelligence. Subjects producing many W's and a few or no D's are abstract thinkers, or are persons given to phantasy. They have strong self-assertive tendencies, and are ambitious to produce the best. They dislike the small, concrete details of daily life. Subjects who, in addition to a large number of W's, also produce an even larger number of D's, but few Dd's, are more plastic. They are better able to direct the attention to a given problem. While less abstract than the group last discussed, they are still oriented more toward the theoretical rather than the practical, more concerned with the problem than with the absolute facts. Subjects producing an average number of W's (6 or 7), and with them many D's but only a few Dd's, are definitely more practical than theoretical, do not dwell on abstract subjects, but reach for tangible things. They prefer cleverness to wisdom.

Subjects who combine the findings of the last group with many Dd (W—D—Dd), are confined to details in their work and have little ability to make combinations and abstractions. They may possess good powers of observation, but they get stuck in the unimportant details. The subject who responds with many W, few D, but many Dd, is certainly impractical and actually avoids practical things. His ideas may be original, but their development is faulty, now chasing an abstract idea, now stuck on a tiny, curious detail. He is a tyrant and a grumbler in all his judgments.

A combination of W's, D's, and Dd's which indicates neither a cramping tendency to think abstractly nor too great a concern with petty details, is characteristic of that form of intelligence usually called the «common-sense type of mind».

All of these types occur in the finest nuances of variation and all within the «intelligent» group. The capacities of the subject in any particular field are not indicated, but much is indicated about the ways and means the subject will adopt in bringing his capacities to bear on any subject.

What component of intelligence is represented by the apperceptive type? Table VII shows that elated mood improves the apperceptive type (neglecting the other factors for the moment), while depressed mood tends to make it poorer. If we neglect all the other factors, it is seen that the apperceptive type characteristic of normal, intelligent subjects is also approached in organic cases (excluding depressed arteriosclerotics), by epileptics, by scattered schizophrenics, and even by imbeciles and feebleminded subjects, provided they show confabulation. At the opposite extreme there are the pedants, some compulsion neurotics, also the depressed, the apathetic imbeciles and the stereotyped schizophrenics. From the comparison of these extremes, it may be concluded that the quality of the apperceptive type is determined primarily by emotional factors.

A rich apperceptive type includes a goodly number of whole answers. Energy of associative activity, evidenced by the large number of W's, must, therefore, be present if a rich apperceptive type is to be produced by a subject. This energy of associative activity is not sufficient to produce a good apperceptive type: the pure W type subject with all his will to set records for the experiment demonstrates this point. A really good apperceptive type must not be so one-sided. A good type also requires good form visualization, that is, clarity of associative processes and ability to concentrate. If form visualization is not clear, and the attention cannot be directed properly, the apperceptive type may be rich, but never good.

A further faculty is necessary to produce optimal rigidity of sequence, namely the ability to discipline the logical functions. This has been discussed previously, and is, it will be recalled, dependent largely on the capacity to direct the attention.

In summary, it may be said that a good apperceptive type is dependent upon an almost incalculable number of associative and emotional factors, regulating, facilitating or inhibiting as the case may be. A good apperceptive type is impossible without a certain lability of the will which allows direction. without the clarity of associative activity which leads to good form visualization, and yet not too intense clarity in this respect.

The regulation to which all these factors must be submitted if a good apperceptive type is to result, is again, dependent on still more factors. The basis for any given apperceptive type is probably the individual type of intelligence springing from the constitution of the subject. This may be abstract-theoretical, combinatory-imaginative, practical-concrete, grumbling, or some other combination. This way of reacting, which has its roots in the constitution, is modified by the mood, and, on the other hand, by conscious direction of the attention. These factors influence the distribution of associative energy in various ways. The intraindividual variations in different experiments demonstrate the range of variation in productivity within a single individual; the inter-individual differences indicate the variations of the constituent parts of the «intelligence», and these are significant.

Another component of intelligence may now be defined It is the ability to distribute affective and associative factors so that there is a drive towards logical arrangement, so that important and unimportant things are in logical relationships and in proper logical sequence. The presence of a goal idea gives rise to the ability to concentrate which makes possible, in turn, the distribution of affective and associative factors as indicated above. An optimum of urge toward associative activity then arises, and makes possible a maximum number of W responses as well as the optimum clearness of associations on which visualization of good forms depends. This activity shows wide variations in subjects within normal range.

Average intelligence is characterized by 20—35—50 % animal responses. This indicates a certain optimum variability for interpretations. Because of the great number of possible forms, the animal figure is generally appropriate, and arises most easily during the interpretation. Because of this there is an associative acceptance of animal engrams which exerts a stereotyping influence on the interpretations. In consequence, the percent animal responses becomes the indicator of the tendency to produce stereotyped associations. In the case of imbeciles, however, it appears to be more difficult to recall animal figures, while parts of human figures are called up in associations more easily.

The opposite of this stereotyping tendency is freedom of associations, the ability to withdraw from associative acceptances which lead to stereotypy. Both situations are expressions of the concept «looseness of associations», which must neither be too constricted nor too free in normal thinking. Too marked looseness of associations inevitably leads to unsteadiness, scattering and flight in the associative process; too little freedom (looseness), to stereotypy, confining to one category of engrams.

20—30 % animal answers are observed in protocols of imaginative subjects, artists, persons who turn away from reality to a greater or lesser degree. Only scattered schizophrenics see as few as this. (In epileptics, other factors of the experiment may replace the animal percentage as indicator of stereotypy; usually the factor is the kinaesthetic answer.) In the normal group, the practical sort of person stands in contrast to the artist. Subjects in the definitely practical occupations almost always have a high percentage of animal answers. Furthermore, percent animal responses rises with age, so that a subject over 40 rarely has less than 50 % animal responses, and above 50, rarely less than 60 %. We may conclude, then, that age increases the tendency to stereotyped associations and decreases the freedom of associations.

Depressed mood, especially psychotic depression, and dulling of the emotional reactions as in dementia simplex, markedly increase stereotypy. Hypomania (within the range of normal moods) increases the range of variability in the answers; this is less outspoken in real elation.

The optimum of variability in the answers is not the same for all types of intelligence. The business man with too little stereotypy in his make up would be hampered in his business routines. The theorist with a strong tendency toward stereotypy would slip into dogmatism easily.

It must be emphasized that this tendency to stereotypy is entirely independent of the ability to concentrate. The creation of the associative attitude is of unconscious origin and is, primarily, in the associative category, whereas concentration is fundamentally an emotional, conscious phenomenon

Still another component of intelligence is now apparent. It is the optimum ability to form stereotyped associations, or, in other words, neither too great nor too little freedom (looseness) of associations.

To a certain extent, the same factors determine the number of good original answers, but others also enter in. A large number of good original answers is another characteristic of intelligence. These responses are also based on the clarity of the engrams, etc.. which make possible clear visualization of forms. and on optimal variability or freedom of association of the engrams.

The average tradesman does not produce as many good original answers as does the educated subject or, particularly, the creative artist. The original answers alone are sufficient to indicate the extent of the subject's education. The number of good original answers as well as their content enters into consideration. The number of original responses reveals certain peculiarities of the associative life of the individual, while the content of the answers frequently reveals whether this peculiarity is a result of his specialized training or is actually the result of broad education. If the O responses all fall in the same group, if they all originate in the same associative «set», the individuality is determined primarily by the subject's technical education. Examples may be found in the medical man who interprets many anatomical objects in the test, and in the botanist, who because of his special knowledge unknown to laymen, produces a large number of O+ responses. If the original answers themselves are highly variable, however, they demonstrate strikingly the individual's broad, general education.

The rule, «the maximum is not the optimum», is valid for the original answers. A subject who produces no original responses will be unoriginal in living as well; more than 50 % O responses is, however, beyond the optimal range. If the original answers are all of one sort, stereotyped, the subject is one who «talks shop». If they are real original responses and are based on a very marked loosening of association, the subject is «in the world but not of it» [1]. He lives more in his problem—more likely, even in his fantasies—than in reality; he has separated himself from the perceptive and apperceptive mode of his fellows to such an extent that he has lost the ability to adapt intellectually.

Another component of intelligence is indicated. It is the possession of an optimal number of «individual engrams». The number of these must not become so large that because of them the subject loses the ability to adapt to the apperceptive type of his fellow men.

Finally, intelligent subjects always produce at least a few responses determined by kinaesthetic engrams as well as those determined by form perception. It should be possible to deduce a further component of intelligence from this fact. The groups which showed the least whole answers, i. e. those with poverty of ideas, the stereotyped and the depressed, produce no M responses whatever. Artists, imaginative subjects, and abstract thinkers interpret the most M s. Two other categories lie between these extremes: practical subjects who are more imitative produce few M s; a larger number are interpreted by theorists, the more «creative» subjects. These findings would

[1] German = «Weltfremder».

tend to indicate that M responses are characteristic of subjects who function more in the intellectual sphere, whose interests gravitate more toward their intra-psychic living rather than toward the world outside themselves.

On the whole, there is a direct proportion between clear form visualization and the number of M responses. Disturbances of mood alone disrupt this proportion, making it inverse. Because of this finding, however, it cannot be said that any more than an indirect relationship exists between F's and M's. The findings are the same when the number of M's and the rigidity of sequence are studied for their relationship to each other.

There is a definite incompatibility between the state of being aware of the clarity of associations and the production of M s. Subjects who consciously wish to produce movement responses will produce hazy interpretations. This is the case with manics and epileptics who give secondary M's In conclusion it is found, furthermore, that the subjects possessing the clearest associations. the pedants and the depressed, those who produce the best forms and the most rigid sequence, have no movement responses in their protocols.

The number of M's is, however, directly proportional to the number of W's. Disturbances of mood do not reverse this relationship, but fit in with it. (See Table VIII.) There are, of course, exceptions in which large numbers of W answers occur with relatively small numbers of M's, and few W's with relatively many M's, but these exceptions do not invalidate the usual direct proportion, and nowhere do they reverse it. Furthermore, it never happens that very few W's occur with many M s, and almost never are very large numbers of W's seen without large numbers of M's accompanying. There must, then, exist a direct, or at least a relatively direct. relationship between whole and movement responses.

Since there is an incompatibility between kinaesthetic factors and the state of being aware of the clarity of the associations, the relationship above cannot be founded on the factors which produce a large number of W's, namely, a conscious willing to make complicated performances (see page 41). Furthering this line of thought, the kinaesthesias naturally are not associated in any way with the performances of abstraction or combination.

Therefore, the basis for this relationship must lie in another field. It is based on the emotional and disposition-associative factors of W-formation, i. e., on the energy of associative activity in the disposition (constitution) of the subject. The prominence of emotional origins for this relationship is supported by the fact that mood disturbances do not invalidate the direct proportional relationship between W's and M's, but rather fit in with it, or tend to make it more apparent. The same dispositional energy which is the origin for large numbers of W responses must also be the origin for M answers.

This must be demonstrated in the relationship between the percent animal responses and the original answers In fact, the number of M's shows the most definite direct proportion to the variability of the answers: that is, there is an inverse proportion between the number of M's and the percent animal answers. The direct proportion between the number of good original answers and the M responses is even more clear. These proportions are most constant—they are even supported in cases where mood is a factor. M's must, therefore, depend in some way upon the freedom of association which prevents stereotyped associative patterns. When the capacity to dispense with such stereotyping influences is great, the number of M's is large. This capacity may become too great as it does in hypomanics and imaginative subjects. When stereotypy is too marked, on the other hand, few or no M's are produced. The tendency toward stereotypy increases with age in general: the number of M's decreases with age.

M responses represent, then, a component of intelligence which parallels the freedom of association, parallels the number of individual (original) responses. This component is increased in force by elated mood; its effect is decreased in depression and dulling of emotional reactions. From these facts it may be concluded that this component of intelligence must be intimately bound up with the emotional processes. This component is not increased in force by conscious effort or by consciously focussing attention upon it; these efforts tend rather to injure its functioning. It must be identical with emotional energy (more unconscious than conscious), and with the energy of associative activity inherent in the disposition of the individual subject.

This component of intelligence can be nothing other than the ability to create new, individual productions, the capacity for «inner creation». In its finest development we call this artistic inspiration, religious experience, etc. Kinaesthesias must, therefore, be some sort of instrument for «inner creation» and for the ability to show introversion (see discussion below). Thus we arrive at the same conclusions that were deduced earlier by statistical means, namely, that M responses are characteristic of those subjects whose interests gravitate more to their own intrapsychic life than to the world outside.

So far as they are deducible from our experiment, then, we would have to differentiate the following components of intelligence:

1. Capacity for continuous, active attention (F+ and sequence).
2. Optimum clarity of perception, of engrams, and of associative processes in assimilation (F+).
3. Optimum of ability to discipline the logical function; this is an automatic function arising in the individual
4. Optimum of «dispositional» energy of associative activity, i. e., a conscious or unconscious «willing» to produce complicated performances (W).
5. The ability to distribute the emotional and associative factors by means of a goal idea which maintains direction of attention.
6. Optimum ability to form stereotyped association sets, and, in contrast.
7. Optimum freedom and ease of flow of associations from sets which

otherwise would tend to stereotype associations markedly (Percent Animal Responses).

8. Optimum number of individually determined engrams, optimum originality or ability to form original associations. These faculties must be optimal in the sense that they do not interfere with the capability to adapt to the associative scope of others (Percent Original Responses).
9. Wealth of associations (Variability, Original Responses).
10. Availability of associations (Particularly W).
11. Capacity for «inner creation» (M).

All of these components may be more or less developed so that there may be an incalculable number of variants, partial and total, of «intelligence». Further components of intelligence will be found later in this study.

It may be stated definitely that the form interpretation test makes possible a finely differentiated examination of intelligence. This test examines on a very broad basis and is almost entirely independent of education and memory. Fundamentally, it examines the «pattern» [1] of the intelligence.

It must not be forgotten that some components of intelligence are differently developed at different ages. It is obvious that these components will be quite different in a five year old child from those in a ten year old, but there will be variations in the interplay of the components even after the 20th, 30th or 40th year, etc. The material available at the present time does not allow the construction of a more definite picture of these intra-individual variations of the components of intelligence.

2. Influence of Volition on the Factors.

The experiment, representing a process of free choice in its usual form, can be altered to be one where the choice is conditioned by «helps» [2]. In the usual test, subjects focus on the content of the interpretations. (The W-type is one of the rare exceptions to this statement.) They choose the formal components of perception according to constitutionally individual peculiarities. With parallel series, the experiment may be repeated in such a manner that this complete freedom of choice is limited. For instance, subjects may be asked to try to interpret as good forms as possible, or as many moving figures as they can. Such control tests give rise to the following questions:

1. How does the focussing of attention on a factor influence the findings concerning that factor?
2. How are the findings in the other factors influenced when attention is focussed on one?
3. How large are the individual variations that may result in all these possible control experiments?

---

[1] German = Formale
[2] W. Stern, Differentielle Psychologie Leipzig, 1911. P. 83

To answer the many other questions arising from these would require
a very large amount of suitable material obtained with different parallel
series of blots. The material of this study was not collected with this problem
in mind, and the findings stand in need of confirmation The results are
given. nevertheless.

If the subject is asked to interpret as clear forms as possible. the F+
percent is raised. there is, however. very large individual variation. Factors
necessary for good visualization of forms are facilitated by the setting up of
the conscious goal idea implied in the request. These factors are stabilization
of attention, clarity of perceptive and assimilative associations and self-control. It is, in fact, the function of directed thinking to make these factors
more effectual. Concomitant changes include a significant decrease in M and
W responses. loss in quality of apperceptive type. increase in the percent
animal answers, and a decrease in original and color responses; in each case
the individual variations are large. In general. it may be said that the whole
quality of reaction approaches that characteristic of depressives and pedants.

The results are similar if we demand the most rigid sequence of W. D,
etc . possible for the subject. The sequence does become more rigid, while
other factors suffer The loss in quality is not as marked as when good forms
are demanded, however, and it is found that with increasing rigidity of
sequence, clarity of forms decreases. Since we are dealing with the ability to
discipline the logical functions, it is obvious that a command to set up a goal
will carry with it improvement in sequence. The evident facility of improving
the sequence is supported by the fact that a certain amount of this sort of
discipline has become automatic in normals. The quality of the other factors
of the experiments suffers less than in the search for good forms, proving
that the command in this case calls upon a function already available in the
constitution of the subject. That the forms become poorer when the attention is drawn to the sequence can only mean that clarity of perception and
association are factors in which this constitutional availability plays a less
important role; it also signifies that for best performance undivided, uncon-
ditional, and very narrowed concentration of attention is necessary. If the
subject is commanded to interpret as many W's as possible, a different result
is obtained Subjects who interpret many wholes in the usual test are able
to increase the number by spurring on their «volition to make complicated
performances». On the other hand, those subjects who give few W's in the
usual test prove their inadequacy for this special one so that the result is
little different from the usual. Naturally, the result is similar if they are
urged to produce the finest apperceptive type possible.

The percent animal answers allows two types of investigation; the subject may be requested to interpret animal figures only, or to interpret no
animal figures at all, rather anything else. and as many other things as
possible. i. e., the widest variability of responses. The first of these tasks is

easily accomplished by normals. As before, the number of M's, W's, and original responses will be decreased by the establishment of a goal idea. Aside from this, the result differs little from that of the usual test, indicating that the request to interpret animal figures only touches upon a constitutional ability which is easily available to the subject. This is the ability to form stereotyped associative patterns.

The request for the greatest variability possible, and the exclusion of all animal figures frequently leads to a complete failure to answer at all. Only subjects who have a very small percent of animal responses in the ordinary test are able to complete this task with ease and without marked general changes in the results. This finding indicates that the freedom of associations, the fluidity of thought processes, represents a function which is amenable to conscious control only when it is present to a considerable degree habitually.

Original responses do not lend themselves to this form of testing. In the usual experiment each subject gives his personal ideas, and each considers his interpretations original. If «original» or «imaginative» responses were requested particularly, the subject would not interpret differently from what he would do in the usual test. At most, he might attempt daring combinatory responses, making an attempt to express originality.

There remain the M and C responses, and the problem of the correlation of M and W comes up for discussion. Those subjects who, in the ordinary experiment, give numerous M's, can increase the number of good kinaesthetic responses with relative ease. On the other hand, those who interpret few M's in the usual test, produce few or very poor ones in the control. Kinaesthesias represent, therefore, a function which can be increased in effect by the setting up of a goal only if present as a definite tendency in the personality.

As for the color answers, subjects who produce no color answers ordinarily, can produce them when requested to include color in their interpretations; they will, however, consist largely of FC's, only rarely will the impulsive C appear. The awkwardness of the depressives and the pedants, and the tension apparent in neurotic «emotion suppressors» when they handle color is quite remarkable. For them, this is an unpleasant task, and may even arouse feelings of inadequacy. The number of color responses is easily increased by those subjects who produce several ordinarily. The relationships with the other factors vary widely according to the individual subject in this test.

The task may be reversed in the case of both M and C. Subjects who produce numerous M's or C's may be asked to suppress them. Since many M's usually occur with a relatively large number of C's, we deal with the same subjects in giving this group of special tests. It is very difficult for these subjects to suppress M's and C's completely and they find the task irksome, though in a manner quite different from the reaction of depressives to the opposite problem. They feel restrained, hemmed in, under these conditions. The task is managed best when they suppress both M and C at the same time, turning their attention to the visualization of clear forms.

Color responses, therefore, probably do not represent an individual constitutional tendency in the same way that the M's were found to. They seem to represent, rather, a more general disposition which may be influenced, in some of the subjects at least, by the setting up of a conscious goal so that color answers may be aroused, increased, or inhibited. This «general disposition» is the total affective pattern, the affectivity. Interpretation of kinaesthesias and the affectivity are peculiarly bound together. It is difficult to suppress either alone; it is easier to suppress both at the same time This suppression is accomplished by means of those factors which make possible consciously directed good form visualization, namely, the subject's maintaining a conscious, sharp control over the associative processes.

The components of intelligence respond to conscious influences as follows:

I. Increase in productiveness:
   1. Ability to give constant, active attention (F+, sequence).
   2. Clarity of perceptions and of associative processes in assimilation (F+).
   3. Ability to control and discipline the logical function (sequence and apperceptive types).
   4. Ability to form stereotyped associatives sets (A%).

II. Increase of productiveness absent, except when the conscious «willing» is abetted by individual constitutional tendency:
   1. Energy of associative activity (W).
   2. Freeing of associations from stereotyping associative sets (A%).
   3. Ability to produce original associations (Orig.).
   4. Faculty of «inner creation» (M).

As a general rule it may be said that a conscious, directed, increase in productiveness in respect to those general functions collected under I above, is followed by a significant decrease in productiveness in respect to those constitutionally determined functions—differential as opposed to general—gathered under II. In contrast to this, a consciously «willed» increase in those functions under II does not necessarily lead to a decrease in productiveness of those under I, although there is a tendency in that direction. Furthermore, the abilities of the first group can be learned, while those of the second are of the nature of talents.

The affectivity cannot be attributed to either group. It eludes all attempts at classification. In general, however, the conclusion may be drawn that the affectivity is stabilized by an increase in productiveness of the group I factors. «Attention is a form of expression of the affectivity» (Bleuler). Concentration is stability of affect to the highest degree. Where there is an increase of productiveness of the faculties in group II. the affectivity is usually more unstable.

3. Effect of Mood on the Components of Intelligence.

In general, the term «mood» or mood disturbance includes depression and states resembling depression, and elation and manic-like states. The material at hand is not sufficient to take up the many mixed and otherwise differentiated moods.' A single special case must be mentioned, however; it is the state of being in a «good humor»[1].

Depressed mood (see Table VIII) improves the visualization of forms. increases rigidity of sequence, decreases the number of W's, makes the apperceptive type poorer. diminishes the variability of answers, diminishes the number of original answers, increases the percent animal answers. The number of M's is diminished, frequently to zero or very near that level. Depressed mood causes the complete disappearance of color responses in practically every case.

Hypomanic mood makes the form visualization poorer and the sequence less rigid. The number of W's is increased, the apperceptive type is of better quality, the animal percentage smaller, the variability of the responses, the number of original answers and the number of M responses increased, and color responses are relatively frequent in this mood.

The observations on the effect of depressed mood on the test are applicable in psychotic depressions as well. It does not hold, however, that actual psychotic elation shows the same effect as that observed as due to hypomanic mood. In manic states the number of W's is smaller than in cases with hypomanic mood, the apperceptive type is of poorer quality, the variability less, and there are fewer original answers. The number of M and C responses is. however, increased somewhat in manic states, but the movements are likely to be poorly visualized. The percent animal answers is only a little lower than it is in depressed moods.

This means that in depressed mood, especially in psychotic depression all of those factors which are determined by an increase in the control of associations are most accentuated. In contrast to this, all of those factors dependent upon emotionally charged energy of associative activity and on freedom of association are very greatly reduced. In hypomanic mood even more than in actual elation, the reverse is the case. All of those factors which are favorably influenced by conscious direction and ability to concentrate are reduced. All of those factors which have their basis in increased energy of associative activity and in components which are resistant to conscious direction are increased in these moods.

---

[1] German = Wohlgelauntheit.

Those factors capable of being increased by conscious direction are found to be more reduced in actual elation than in hypomanic moods. Those factors not subject to conscious control, such as M and C, are more accentuated in elation than in hypomanic moods. The observations in elation are, to this extent, conceivable as the extreme of those seen in hypomanic moods. This does not conform with observations of other factors, however, for in elation the number of W's is smaller, the animal percentage is larger, the apperceptive type is of poorer quality, and the number of original answers is smaller than is the case in hypomanic moods. These latter factors should show the reverse relationships if elation were simply an intensification of hypomanic mood. (It is, of course, possible that my material does not represent all the varied types of manic states). The fact that the four factors indicated above do not show the same findings as do the others indicates that the energy of associative activity and the freedom of association (very closely allied phenomena) are prevented in some way from being accentuated as hypomanic mood is replaced by actual elation. The reason for this remains an unanswered question.

«Good humor», our special case of mood mentioned above, has many features in common with hypomanic mood. When this mood prevails, the animal percentage is greatly reduced and the variability of responses and the number of original answers is much larger, the number of W's is increased and the apperceptive type is of better quality. The number of M and C responses equals that observed in elation, but poorly visualized M's are rare.

Comparing the observations in elation, hypomanic mood, and «good humor», we find that both elation and the state being in a «good humor» are derivatives of hypomanic mood. Those factors which do not show the expected values in cases of elation, are present in expected values in «good humor». The energy of associative activity and freedom of association are greater in the state of «good humor» than is the case in hypomanic mood, while in elation these components are reduced below the level observed in hypomanic mood. Those components which are prevented from reaching their highest function in elation, namely, those which can be consciously controlled, are seen to be most effective in «good humor». The freedom of association typical of a subject in a «good humor» makes his experimental result more like that of a scattered schizophrenic than that of an elated subject.

Clinically, the main difference between psychotic elation and the state of being in a «good humor» is the absence of the push of physical activity in the latter. From this fact the supposition arises that it may be this urge to activity, the increased motility, which prevents the functions of freedom of association and energy of associative activity from appearing as expected in elation. The absence of this urge to activity in «good humor» allows full play of the functions in question, freedom of association, energy of associative activity. and ability for «inner» creation. (In a clinical sense, these functions give rise to clever ideas, wit, quick repartee, the ability to be emotionally responsive, and the ability to become enthusiastic, etc.).

The supposition outlined in the last paragraph above, leads to the assumption that the factors which are essentially «inner» or self-determined and are expressed primarily in sensations of motion in the test, are in some way opposed to physical motility, the actual execution of motion.

I would like to add an example so that this conclusion is not left simply hanging in air. Dreams are «inner» or selfdetermined productions and kinaesthesias play an important role in them [1]. On awakening, necessary movements, physical motion, begins at once. This movement sets the dreams aside. There is, however, a way to recall dreams: lie perfectly motionless on awakening in order not to cover up the kinaesthesias of the dream by present physical movement. This scheme works if it is not negated by an attempt to consciously direct the attention, for this would oppose the revealing of the more unconscious functions. That is, if one immediately on awakening sets up the goal to lie quietly by conscious effort, the kinaesthesias are likely to be cut out at once.

4. Interrelations of Movement and Color Responses.
«Experience Types» [2].
Introversion, Extratention, Coartation.

Certain conclusions and generalizations may be drawn by study of the relationship between movement and color responses. In the following discussion, the color answers are given values as described above, the unit being the CF responses: 1 CF = 1, 1 FC = $^1/_2$, 1 C = $1^1/_2$ units.

It was noted above that certain material in the discussion of M and C responses would be subject to later correction. The absolute number of M's and C's, important as this is as representing the «inner» faculty of creation and the emotional factors in a subject, is not, in itself, sufficiently representative of the actual conditions. The essential data concerns the relationship between M's and C's.

Table IX illustrates the findings concerning these two factors. It does not consider the form responses, but the various possibilities of relationship between M's and C's only. The absolute numbers of these factors increases reading from the top to the bottom of the table. The middle column comprises those cases in which M's and C's occur in equal numbers. At the top of this column are found those cases with 0 M's and 0 C's, that is, those who gave form answers exclusively. To the left of the central column is the field

---

[1] See Mourly Vold, Über den Traum. O. Klemm, Leipzig, 1910 and 1912.
[2] German = Erlebnistypus.

Table IX.

Relation of Movement and Color Responses.

1. Distribution of normals, oligophrenics, etc.

1 M 0 C («normal» depressives)	2 M 1 C 3 M 2 C Good average	0 M 0 C (Pedants and subjects in «normal» depressive moods)		0 M 1 C Unintelligent
2 M 0 C —	M 1 C 3 M 2 C	1 M 1 C —	1 M 2 C Average	0 M 2 C Moron
M 0 C —		2 M 2 C —	2 M 3 C 1 M 3 C Practical («Flighty»),	0 M 3 C —
		3 M 3 C (Compulsion neurotics)		
x M 0 C Psychogenic depressions	M » C M > C Abstract Theoretical Imaginative Artists	x M x C (Subjects in «normal» manic moods) Very talented subjects	M « C Practical Industrious	0 M x C Imbeciles

Those categories whose place in the scheme is conditioned by affective factors are enclosed in parentheses.

M » C = M's predominate greatly over C's.

M > C = M's predominate little over C's.

Movement and Color Responses.

Table X   *2 Schizophrenics*

		0 M 0 C Simple Demented		
1 M 0 C		1 M 1 C Frequently cata- tonics in interval		0 M 1 C Completely abulic
2 M 0 C	2 M 1 C	2 M 2 C Mild catatonics	1 M 2 C Somewhat scattered cases with motor excitement	0 M 2 C Hebephrenics
x M 0 C Paranoics	M > C Productive paranoids	x M x C Severely catatonic and blocked cases	M < C Scattered cata- tonics with motor excitement	0 M x C Hebephrenics Querulous

(2 M   1 C line: Stable, wellpreser-
ved paranoids*)*

Movement and Color Responses.

Table XI.   *3. Manic-Depressives*

		0 M 0 C Depressed		
1 M 0 C		1 M 1 C		0 M 1 C
x M 0 C	M > C	x M x C Manics	M < C	0 M x C

Movement and Color Responses.

Table XII.   *4. Epileptics.*

		0 M 0 C		
1 M 0 C		1 M 1 C		0 M 1 C
x M 0 C	M > C	x M x C Epileptoid	M < C Rapid Dementia with Epilepsy and Imbecility	0 M x C

(center column: Slow
Dementia*)*

Movement and Color Responses.

Table XIII.   *5. Organic Cases*

		0 M 0 C Arteriosclerotic Dementia		
1 M 0 C		1 M 1 C		0 M 1 C
x M x C	M > C Korsakoff Psychosis	x M x C	M < C Paresis	0 M x C Senile Dementia

in which movement answers predominate, reading from the middle to the left, the number of M's is seen to remain constant. while C's decrease, so that the outer left-hand column reveals 0 C's and only M's remain. The same is true in the right hand side of the table as regards color responses. The relative number of M's increases from right to left as the number of color answers decreases: the reverse is true. of course, in reading the table from left to right.

This scheme of presentation indicates four extreme possibilities:

1. Both M and C responses absent (Middle column, top).
2. Many M's matched by many C's (Middle column, bottom).
3. M's only. C responses absent (Left outside column).
4. C's only. M responses absent (Right outside column).

This scheme is to be considered as a sort of blank temperature chart, not as a pattern into which results are to be forced. Let us examine it to see how the actual observations do fit into this scheme

Tables IX to XIII illustrate the findings in normals (including several of the neuroses). in feeblemindedness, in schizophrenia, in manic depressive psychoses, epilepsy, and in cases with organic brain disease. I must repeat at this point that the findings, especially those of some of the psychoses, need further testing and review, since the series of cases at my disposal does not allow definite conclusions to be drawn. It is possible that upon such review, the observations as shown in this scheme would have to be shifted here and there.

Various methods of study present themselves for consideration in the discussion of the five schemes presented in Tables IX to XIII. Identical areas in each of the schemes might be studied to compare the types of normal and mentally ill subjects who show the same M—C relationship; Tables I to VIII might be examined to determine how the components of intelligence fit into the scheme. Or the study might be oriented around the etiology of M and C responses as discussed above. It is, however, of particular interest to study Tables IX to XIII first, leaving the correlation with previous findings for later discussion.

A glance at the tables shows the left half of each to be less filled in than the right. In the scheme for normals, the left side is occupied by subjects with intelligence differentiated on the basis of «inner» life, independent thinkers, creative individuals. (This is, of course, no criterion of value. The question of what these individuals in which M responses predominate actually produce is not pertinent at this time. It is simply a fact that something will be produced.) In the scheme for the schizophrenics, paranoids are found in the left half of the table. These patients have more or less systematized ideas of persecution and grandeur, but we must note that the delusions are «self-created». Paranoids are also found on the right side of the table, but these are invariably cases whose delusions are scattered and show no trace of systematization. The Korsakoff patients, perhaps not all of them, are also found on the left side of the table; these cases are characterized by the joy they find in confabulating. On the side of the schemes where kinaesthesias predominate are found, then, all those subjects, regardless of whether they are normal or ill, who would rather live in their thoughts, even more often, in their fantasies, than adapt to the world outside themselves. On the right half of the schemes are, among normals, the practical subjects, the light-hearted, the «flighty», those with more reproductive than creative intelli-gences. Feebleminded subjects and morons and imbeciles are also found on the right. The schizophrenics are represented here by the motor excitements and the scattered catatonic states, by hebephrenia and by perhaps all querulous schizophrenic patients. All epileptics are seen to be in the right half of the table, though it is possible that an occasional epileptoid might be found who would fall in the group on the left. All organic cases are found in the right half of the table with the exception of the Korsakoff patients and the arteriosclerotic dements.

But contrasting the two sides of the schemes is not such a simple matter. There are creative subjects who fall on the right, and subjects with repro-ductive intelligence whose results place them on the left. We will see many such exceptions in the further discussion of the matter. Some of these will be only apparent exceptions, for it must not be forgotten that when a sub-ject falls into the middle of the left half of the scheme, we deal not with the entire exclusion of color and complete dominence of kinaesthesias, but with a predominance of kinaesthesias. It is a more or less relationship, not an absolute, categorical «this» or «that».

Color responses have proved to be the representative of the affectivity and the rule is, the more color in the test, the greater the emotional insta-bility of the subject, the more kinaesthesias, the more stable the affectivity. This conclusion obviously agrees with the schemes which have been presented. On the left half of the tables, where kinaesthesias are predominant, we find more stable affectivity than on the opposite side. On the right are found the «flighty», the lighthearted, and normals who make emotional adaptions easily. Feebleminded subjects who react to their every passing emotion are found here, together with all epileptics and all organic cases except depressed arteriosclerotic dements and Korsakoffs. The latter two types of organic brain disease are accompanied by more stable affect than the group as a whole. In contrast, on the left are found those who are difficult to change in their emotional tone, who are more stable, more taciturn, more intro-verted.

One can see at a glance that the subjects with stable affectivity are on the left side of the tables, those on the right are more labile. Lability of affect must be considered here in its broadest sense, including the normal capacity for emotional rapport. On the left are those subjects who adapt with difficulty; on the right, those to whom adaptions are easy so long as excessive lability does not prevent it. and other functions necessary for adaptions to be made are not disturbed as they may be in organic and schizophrenic subjects.

It must be repeated again that the middle line does not represent a sharp demarcation between two entirely different types. It is, rather, a question of more or less; on the left more capacity for ‹inner life», less for adaptibility, and on the right, the reverse of this.

The concept «capacity for emotional rapport» which represents what may be called the normal affective lability, may be differentiated further by means of the schemes. One must distinguish between intensive and extensive capacity for rapport. This capacity for getting into rapport may be strongly intensive, very little extensive as it is in the shut-in individual who has difficulty in making contacts, but, once he has made them, shows that he is able to get into close personal rapport. There may be great capacity for extensive rapport rather than intensive, as in the case of the opportunist who is «everybody's friend», is a «hail fellow, well met», and is forgotten as soon as he is gone. Both intensive and extensive rapport may be possible, but this is rare, occurring generally only in very talented people and occasionally in hypomanics. Finally, rapport may be weak both intensively and extensively. This is the case in subjects in depressive moods, with single-minded business men, bureaucrats, pedants, and rigid, narrow individuals. These are capable of intellectual rapport only.

Those who are capable of more intensive than extensive rapport are found on the left side of the schemes. They have more stable affectivity and are, at the same time, subjectively oriented by nature. Also on this side are found as a clinical example, those paranoids who can get into very intensive rapport with a member of the family, a friend or a physician, though they appear inimical to the whole world. The fact that the delusions invariably shatter any intellectual rapport proves nothing as regards ability to get into emotional rapport. Normal life presents an analogy to this situation in the tendency of the introspective individual to idealize his friends. That is, he attributes qualities to his friends which they do not possess in reality, or at least not to the extent he gives them credit for. In his thoughts, the intellectual adaption is very defective, the affective response increasing the deficiency.

In the right half of the schemes are those who are capable of more extensive than intensive rapport. These are the masters at affective adaptions, the practical people, the skillful, the «light-hearted». Here, too, are the hebephrenic schizophrenics who are always ready to speak to whomever is about, and the querulous cases ever ready to tell whomever will listen the story of their legal battles. Also the epileptics who expect sympathy from everyone they meet, and the paretics and senile dements who greet each new face as an old acquaintance.

Capacity for intellectual rapport is reduced when lability of affect is too marked, just as it is when stability of affect is very great. In these cases the affect becomes egocentric. When the affect is extremely labile, the desire for adaption becomes, quite unconsciously, the desire for others to make the adaption, not the subject with the labile affect himself.

Capacity for simultaneous existence of both extensive and intensive rapport, whether the capacity be great or small, is only found in those subjects who fall in the middle column of the schemes. These possible situations will be taken up again later. Before doing this we must look for further differentiations between those subjects who interpret kinaesthesias principally, and those who tend to interpret color more frequently.

On the right of the schemes are found many subjects showing motor excitement. Closer examination reveals that subjects characterized by precise, calm, phlegmatic or awkward motility, motility stabilized in some manner, are grouped in the left half of the scheme. On the right, in contrast to this, are found subjects showing motor excitement, also the skillful, the «ready and willing» personalities, the quick, vivacious, agile subjects. These relations are easily seen in the scheme for normals, but this does not tell the whole story. Motility, like affective response, is, more or less, subject to conscious direction, and capacity for this direction may be acquired. The direction in which this control needs to be exercised is quite clear; calm motility needs a freedom from restraints, restless motility needs development of inhibitions. Undisciplined restless motility is seen in the constant push of activity in the manic, and in certain intoxications. Undisciplined «calm» motility is a sort of phlegmatic, awkward carelessness. Restless motility when controlled leads to skill; «calm» motility when disciplined, probably results in precision.

As a matter of fact, the skillful and adroit are found on the right in the schemes, the awkward and clumsy subjects on the left.

The following table furnishes a short summary of the findings:

Kinaesthesias Predominant:	Color Predominant
More individualized intelligence	Stereotyped intelligence
Greater creative ability	More reproductive ability
More «inner» life	More «outward» life
Stable affective reactions	Labile affective reactions
Less adaptable to reality	More adaptable to reality
More intensive than extensive rapport	More extensive than intensive rapport
Measured, stable motility	Restless, labile motility
Awkwardness, clumsiness.	Skill and adroitness

Here, again, we find two different types. Again they are not to be considered as absolutes, but as mixtures, with predominance of one or the other.

though they seem to appear in pure culture in some subjects. Nor do the separate characteristics of the two types show an absolute correlation with each other. The relationship is not that simple If a subject has 3 M's and 5 C's, for instance, we cannot say that any single characteristic is present in the personality to a definite degree. or that a certain degree of individualization of intelligence corresponds to a definite degree of affective stability. Each of the characteristics is influenced by other factors such as the mood, conscious logical functioning, and by the unconscious. automatic logical functioning gained through self-discipline.

A further caution must be indicated. The progression of qualities denoted in passing from the middle of the schemes to the left, i. e., the kinaesthetic side. differs from that on the opposite or color side. The types most vaguely defined are those in or near the middle. In passing from the middle to the left, the types of subjects encountered show increasing predominance of the qualities associated with kinaesthesias as outlined above. The nearer the proportion xM/0C (x = a large number) is approached, the more clear it is that we deal with the awkward, introspective type. The progression is arrested at xM/0C. Subjects who have many M's and no C's are quite different in some respects at least from those who have a few C's with the many M's. In passing from the middle column to the right side of the scheme, the type of subject who interprets colors predominantly becomes more clear; there is, however, the middle ground between the middle and outside column where the type is indistinct. It is rare to find color answers in greater proportion than 1M/2C (provided the number of M's is above 2) in the normal subject, and when this occurs it is usually a pathological finding.

For the present, I will designate the predominantly kinaesthetic group as the M type, the group with color predominant, the C type. While these groups may appear as contrasting types, it must be kept in mind that this is only true in a clinical. not a psychological sense. Psychologically, the types cannot be said to be contrasting, any more than one could speak of movement and color as antitheses. M type simply means that a certain group of functions is developed to a marked degree. The opposite of this would be poor development of these functions. This does not mean that it would become the C type, for C type refers to another group of functions entirely, and these functions may, like the others, be markedly or poorly developed. What appears clinically as antithesis, is, psychologically, simply variation.

A further conclusion may be drawn from the table of the qualities of the M and C types: the more kinaesthesias, the less motor activity, the more motor activity, the less kinaesthesias. This same observation proved to be true when the differentiation between elation and «good humor» was made earlier Elation, having the urge to physical activity as a component symptom, presents fewer M's than are seen in «good humor», where this urge does not exist. Kinaesthetic engrams, therefore, act as inhibitors of physical activity; motor activity inhibits kinaesthetic engrams.

There is a very close relationship between motility and affectivity. almost a parallelism. For illustrations of this point, one needs only to turn to emotional gestures. The same terms are used in both fields; one speaks of motor or emotional excitement. and «stable» and «unstable» may be applied to affective states as well as to motility.

Unstable affectivity, when disciplined and restrained, results in emotional adaptability and rapport. Unstable motility when controlled and restrained results in motor adaptability, skill. Optimum control of both affectivity and motility results in «social skill». This sort of restraint is made possible by the conscious self-control which is required in clear visualization of forms; it is not mere chance that we speak of «social forms». Too great a control of motility and affect changes emotional rapport into etiquette and motility into «stiffness». Kinaesthesias and color responses invariably disappear in such «super-productions» of conscious control, regardless of whether the state is consciously induced at the moment. or is the automatic result of long self-discipline. The individual who is completely controlled by rules of etiquette approaches the pedantic personality, which, as we have noted above, gives neither M nor C responses, but a maximal F+ percent.

Kinaesthesias stabilize the motility as well as the affectivity. This is a definite conclusion from this discussion. There are, however, some facts which appear to negate the conclusion. Many subjects of the M type makes gestures accompanying the interpretation of movement in the figures. Dreams, the origin of which would appear to be kinaesthetic engrams, very frequently lead to motor neural impulses. This is true in normal dreams, but is even more marked in somnambulism, in states of semi-consciousness, and in delirium. In all these states the movements may exhibit strong emotional coloring. In the situations listed here, then, kinaesthesias do not cause stability of affect and motility, but instability.

In all of the states mentioned there is one common factor, namely, the «fonction du reel», the practiced, conscious logic of adaptability is excluded, or is almost excluded. The factor represented by good forms in the usual test is entirely lacking under these conditions. This is also true in the case of the subjects who demonstrate the movements they are interpreting in their many M responses. It is these subjects who surrender quite passively to every whim during the test, regardless of whether they are or are not conscious of the constitutional energy of associative activity, of freedom of association, and ability in personalized creation. The C type. on the other hand, searches actively for interpretations. The constitution of the subjects of this type requires the inclusion of the utmost conscious control of associations. Subjects of the M type exclude this sort of control as far as possible, and thus approach the sort of reaction characteristic of dream states. For the M type. the test is play: for the C type. it is work.

We may summarize with several conclusions:

1. Kinaesthesias stabilize the affect as well as the motility
2. Consciously acquired reasoning and habitual logical functioning inhibit kinaesthesias as well as affective responses and motility.
3. Consciously acquired reasoning and maximal logical functioning suppress kinaesthesias completely and stabilize motility and affective response in the service of maximal concentration. This is seen in the muscle tension characteristic of concentrated attention.

The M and C types will. therefore. appear entirely different from each other, varying according to the effectiveness of conscious or habitual logical function These considerations will come up again in connection with the relationship of factors in the middle columns of the schemes.

The M type shows the following characteristics· 1 Predominance of personalized productivity; 2. Intensive rapport; 3. Stable affect and motility, awkwardness, insufficient adaptibility to reality and insufficient extensive rapport. Among many educated people the type is designated colloquially as «introverted»

This term «introversion» originates in psychoanalytical terminology. and was first used by Jung. The term then meant «introversio libidinis sexualis», in the broad sense indicated by Freud. It defined the situation in which «a part of the love which previously belonged to a real love object, and should still belong to it, was introverted, was turned inward, into the subject and there caused increase in fantasy»[1]. When Jung widened Freud's libido concept so that it comprised all manifestations of the will (in the sense of Schopenhauer), the concept of introversion changed as well. It now meant detachment from reality and submersion into fantasy; «The inner world gains in (personal) reality to the same extent that the (universal) reality loses in emphasis and determining power»[2] Up to this point, introversion was considered a pathological process.

More recently Jung has abandoned the position that all introversion is pathological. He now distinguishes two types of psychological reaction, the introverted and extraverted types. «The basis of the one (extrovert) is the affect. of the other (introverted). thinking.» Pathology appears only when the basic factor comes into conflict with the non-differentiated and largely subconscious accessory function (reasoning in the extrovert, affect in the introvert)[3].

[1] Jung, Über die Konflikte der kindlichen Seele. Jahrbuch für psychoanalytische und psychopathologische Forschungen, Vol. II, p 38 (1911).

[2] Jung, Wandlungen und Symbole der Libido op. cit, p 159 (1912).

[3] Jung. Die Psychologie der unbewußten Prozesse. Verlag Rascher Zürich 1917, p. 58 and 77

Meanwhile, common language has taken over the word «introversion». Some of the developmental ideas of the concept still stick to it, and these do not help in clarifying its meaning. In general, however, the introverted person is understood to be one who is turned in upon himself, who lives more within himself than in the outer world, and who has difficulty in his approach to the world outside himself.

To remove all possibility of misunderstanding, I wish to emphasize that I am going to use the concept «introversion» in a sense which has almost nothing except the name in common with Jung's. The clinical picture of the M type as it appears from the results of this test is not the picture of introversion as Jung describes it. It corresponds more closely to the concept as it appears in colloquial usage.

The tendency to turn in upon one's self, is, without doubt, a universal human characteristic As is the case with all other functions, this characteristic shows wide variations in importance in the inter-play of human functions. Aside from the importance in general functioning, it must be determined whether the introversion is active or passive, and whether it is fixed or mobile. It is active to a great extent in the poet. In the catatonic, who simply becomes a victim of it, this tendency is passive. In the normal the tendency to turn in upon oneself is mobile, short-lived, and quite within voluntary control. The normal can shunt aside the factors which inhibit introversion, and can always restore adaptive function by turning his attention to it. In schizophrenics the tendency to introversion is fixed so that they cannot achieve adaptation at all, or, at least, only by means of a compromise in the form of delusions.

The need to make these differentiations indicates the caution necessary in using the term «introversion». It has always had a double meaning, standing for, first, the process of «turning in upon oneself», and, second, for the state of «being turned in upon oneself». Distinction must be drawn carefully between the introversion process and the introversion state. The normal subject of the M type must not be said to be «introverted», but described as «capable of introversion», or «introversive» in order to indicate that this is not a fixed characteristic but a mobile trait. The state of being introverted means the rigid dominance of introversive tendencies over the non-introversive, and this condition is pathological. A subject whose responses are predominantly kinaesthetic, would, therefore, have to be designated predominantly introversive.

«Introverted» individuals are, colloquially, contrasted to «extroverted». The «extroverted» corresponds to the C type. There is a disadvantage in this terminology, however, in that it might be concluded that introversion and extroversion are really opposites; let me repeat again that this is not true. The psychological processes producing introversion and extroversion are not opposite, but different. They are as different as thinking and feeling. as motion and color

This difference should be expressed in the terminology used'. Yet, it would not be correct to contrast the introversive to the C type. designating the latter as the «adaptive type», for the introversive person can achieve adaptability in high degree through his conscious. logical function and by his consciously acquired ways of thinking. To call the extroversive the «feeling type is also not correct because, while the introversive may be more intensive than extensive, still there is not less emotion in this type. The subjects who definitely belong to the adaptive type, and those obviously in the «feeling» type, are actually also members of the C type, and simply represent variations within that group. It is more important to keep in mind the general characteristics of the C type These are:

1. the urge to live in the world outside oneself,
2. restless motility, and
3 unstable affective reactions

It is these characteristics which I would like to contrast to «introversivity» under the term «extratensivity». (Introversion-Extratension, calling, then. the C type «extratensive».) A subject with 2 M and 4 C would, therefore, have to be designated as being more extratensive than introversive.

We return now to Table IX on page 73 to settle the problems presented by the middle column of that Table. This column comprises those cases in which the number of C's and the number of M's are equal. It should. therefore, include those subjects in which introversive and extratensive features are in equilibrium.

The uppermost entry in this column shows cases having neither M nor C responses. This group comprises an occasional normal subject, a few pedants and cases in depressive moods. Cases of simple dementia. old paranoid cases which have long since become indolent, psychotic depressions, and depressive arteriosclerotics also fall in this area of the table. These must be conditions in which the introversive and extratensive features are reduced to the minimum.

The pedant has very good form visualization; he arranges his whole life according to forms. He abhors fantasy and all lability of emotional expression. In the experiment he repeats his usual life pattern—he demonstrates his ever-present mastery of his conscious functions over all his living, whether it be subjective life, or in the world outside himself.

Psychotic and other depressions are passively stereotyped, in contrast to this active stereotypy of the pedants Introversive and extratensive features are paralysed by the depressed, stable mood. The patients complain of «inner emptiness», of inability to think, of their stupidity, of the inability to love or to enjoy themselves, etc. They are always preoccupied with themselves exclusively, with a tormenting, constant control over themselves.

Cases of simple dementia and old, indolent paranoid cases are unimaginative, show poverty of ideas, are emotionally dull and without initiative or
perseverance. They are always the same. Their stability is due to emotional
dulling, to deterioration in the schizophrenic sense.

These illustrations confirm the observation that in the conditions noted
above the introversive and extratensive features are actually reduced and
narrowed down. In the pedant, they are subject to suppression, in the depressed cases they are constricted because of the stable emotional set, and
in the schizophrenics both extratensive and introversive factors are destroyed
by the disease. I should like to propose the expression «coartation» to describe these types of cases (from artus = narrow or few; coartare = to
narrow). The cases with findings 0 M and 0 C would be known as «coartated
types». Those cases, primarily those in the middle column with findings 1 M
and 1 C, 1 M and 0 C, 0 M and 1 C, and certain others, could be designated
«coartative types», i. e., types with a tendency to coartation. Except those
cases which fall on the extreme right or left of the schemes, all other combinations are called «broad» or «dilated» types, in contrast to the coartative.

The findings 0 M and 1 C, 1 M and 0 C, and particularly 1 M and 1 C.
are seen relatively frequently in cases with depressed moods. Such findings
are even more common in schizophrenics who have just recovered from a
catatonic attack and are still in that resistant, mildly depressed and at the
same time indolent mood which so frequently follows.

The picture changes very rapidly in passing further down the middle
column of the schemes. Hypomanics, elated cases, definitely catatonic pictures, the epileptoid and compulsion neurotic cases are found here together
with a few normal subjects. The latter are always very talented people.

Introversive and extratensive features should be combined equally here.
and both should be present to a marked degree.

The most varied clinical pictures may be found grouped together in this
area of the schemes. It is not easy to devise a name which expresses their
common characteristics, and it is perhaps simplest to designate them as
«ambiequal types».

It is noteworthy that distinctly coartative features may be observed in
ambiequal subjects with many M's and C's. Color shock occurs during the
test and the color responses are markedly confused and appear to surprise
the subject himself as he gives them. Similarly with the M answers which.
in some subjects, appear only after a number of pure form answers are given
for each plate. Both these situations doubtlessly represent suppression phenomena. The ruling function is that controlling good form visualization; the
kinaesthesias and the color responses are, as it were. smuggled into the
replies against the will of the subject. This is the case in compulsion neuroses
(see table IX) and would indicate that subjects of this class constantly check
marked introversive and extratensive tendencies by means of ever present

conscious control. Apparently they want to suppress emotional responses.
and in doing it coartate the affectivity generally, sacrificing the faculty for
introversion in the process. The control experiment described on page 66
showed that this was possible. A subject who interprets many M's and many
C's. told to suppress either M or C responses. must suppress both to suppress
either. and has to set himself to interpret only forms. The pedant, with
0 M's and 0 C's, is the completely coartated compulsion neurotic. The compulsion neurotic is the pedant whose introversive and extratensive faculties
are strong enough to resist total coartation.

The elated cases are found at the opposite extreme from the depressions,
both in the middle column. The psychotic depression complains of «inner
emptiness», and «deadened feelings», but the manic enjoys sensations of
«inner richness», of having a multitude of ideas. of being able to do any
and everything. He seeks emotional rapport with anyone at any time.

The introversive and extratensive features which in the manic fuse into
a harmony which the patient is certainly aware of, appear to paralyse each
other in the catatonic case. The fusion is lacking. The catatonic is ambi-
valent in respect to these tendencies; his attention is caught both within and
outside himself; it is as though he were wedged between his introversive and
extratensive tendencies.

Epileptoid cases falling in this area are too few in my material to allow
conclusions to be drawn: one of the cases is an epileptoid-ecstatic patient.

We come now to the group of normals in the lower part of the middle
column, the group with many talents. These are individuals in whom are
combined marked introversive features including creativeness, subjectivity,
and intensive rapport, with marked extratensivity. as shown by extensive
rapport, ability to make sympathetic reproductions, excellent emotional approach, and motor adroitness. These subjects could be no better grouped
than under the name «highly talented». Further clarification of this matter
will follow later. The genius would be found near this group in the tables.

I wish again at this stage to note the relationship between genius and
epilepsy, between genius and compulsion neuroses, and between the last
and manic-depressive insanity.

The two outer columns of the schemes remain for discussion. On the left,
in the section distinguished by a few or even several M's but no C's, are
found subjects with psychogenic depressions. A few climateric melancholias
and paranoids with late onset of their illness and who might better be diagnosed as paranoics, were also found to fall in this column. Completely color-
blind subjects should also appear here. No definite conclusions could be
drawn from the available material, but there was the impression that the
adaptability was purely intellectual, though exceedingly variable. Perhaps it
would be justifiable to classify these cases as «without extratension». It is,
however, also possible that we deal, in the depressions, with especially effec-

tive suppression of emotions, and in the paranoics, with particularly effective mastery of the affect; unfortunately, the question must remain open.

The groups of subjects giving the result 0 M's and x C's certainly cannot be designated «without introversion». Assuming that kinaesthesias represent the capacity for introversion, this association must be supported theoretically, even though all empirical results point in that direction. Also, the visualization of movement has, in this series of figures, been made somewhat difficult purposely, so that the number of M's is in some degree predetermined by the configuration of the plates. The significance of the number of M's is, therefore, relative. In the control experiments with the figure of the mower described above, even imbeciles recognized the movement: 0 M is only a relative measure of the capacity to see movement; if the task had been made easier, 0 M would occur more rarely

The left outer column of the schemes appears to represent a particular type The right, however, appears to be simply the logical extreme of extratension, i. e., egocentric extratensivity

The types established in this discussion are distributed in the scheme as shown in the following table.

Table XIV.

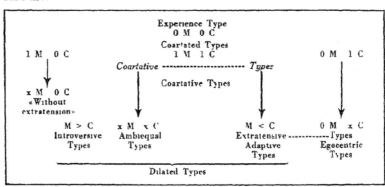

We have now available materials from which we can gather a great deal of information about our patient. We know how strong the introversive features are from the absolute number of M responses, and how strong the extratensive features are from the number of C answers. We know in what relation introversive and extratensive features stand to each other from the relationship of M and C responses We know the extent of coartation or dilation of these features from the number of M's and C's and a few other factors We do not know *what* he experiences, but, rather, *how* he experiences. We know many of the traits and characteristics with which he goes through life, be these of associative or emotional nature, or a mixture of the two. We do not know his experiences: we do know the apparatus with which he receives experiences of subjective or objective nature, and to which he subjects his experiences in assimilation of them.

The conclusion of all this is that kinaesthetic and color influences in perception represent the most essential components of the apparatus for experiencing. It is to be noted that these influences are not themselves the apparatus, but simply represent it in this test. The relationship of the numbers of M's and C's is, therefore, the expression of the experience type of the subject.

It is always daring to draw conclusions about the way an individual experiences life from the results of an experiment. To try it on the basis of the findings of so simple an experiment as this may, at first glance, appear absurd. In this case, however, the conclusions are supported by many diagnostic controls, and the experience types developed have been confirmed by clinical observations in the psychoses.

5. Experience Type and Living.

The introversive and extratensive features of a subject comprise independent groups of psychisms, the relations of which determine the experience type of the individual. These features must have an entirely different mental basis from the conscious, disciplined thinking of the subject. Disciplined thinking is an acquired faculty; introversive and extratensive features are not acquired, but are inherent, primary qualities of the constitution. Disciplined thinking can master and control both introversive and extratensive features; learning disciplined thinking is learning to control and regulate these features of the constitution. Disciplined thinking cannot ever replace the introversive and extratensive features, and when its control is exercised to the maximum, the apparatus on which experience depends becomes atrophied and damaged, the result being stereotypy and inability to experience fully.

The experience type of an individual is not his general psychogram. It indicates how the person experiences, but not how he lives, or toward what he is striving. An individual with very predominant introversive features may be decidedly extratensive in his behavior, though the extratensive features are less in evidence in the test than the introversive. Another person may have an extratensive experience type and appear to be introversive on observation, though this is a rare finding. These discrepancies between the experience type and actual living can only be explained by the fact that the «active energy», the effective energy at the moment, the will, the libido, or whatever else it may be named, is so oriented as to allow only a part of the faculties for experiencing to be in operation. It is instinct which transforms the constitutional features into active tendencies As will be apparent in later discussions, one can, under favorable circumstances, discover from the protocols which part of the apparatus for experiencing is principally activated.

The apparatus with which the individual is endowed for assimilating experiences is a much broader, more extensive instrument than that which he uses in living. A person has a number of «registers» with which he can experience, but he uses few in the ordinary run of living, sometimes so few as to leave him quite stereotyped

The experience type demonstrates the limits of the apparatus which the individual could call into the service of living. It cannot reveal, however—except under very favorable circumstances—what parts of the apparatus the patient actually puts to use in active living. This will become even more evident in the discussion of experience type and talents.

6. Experience Type and the Components of Intelligence.

What relationship exists between the components of intelligence and these experience types? Comparison of Tables I to VIII with Tables IX to XIV will give some information on this point. The following pages are a short summary of these matters. We begin with the movement responses.

The study of the variations in the number of movement responses has shown that these represent the capacity for «inner» creativeness The discussion of the relation between M and C answers has shown that predominance of M's indicates introversion. Both studies lead to the same conclusion, namely, that the kinaesthesias represent the tendency toward «inner» life, i. e., introversion. This would appear to be an argument arriving at identical conclusions in the two cases because it started with identical material. To disprove this, we must show that those factors of the experiment which show definite correlation with the number of M's are also identically correlated with the experience type.

There is a constant, direct proportion between the M's and the original answers. The latter indicate the ability to form numerous original associations specific to the person. At the same time, the number of O's indicates whether or not the subject can prevent these original associations from becoming so numerous that the common mode of associations is lost. All subjects, no matter what the type or the psychoses they suffer from, who give predominantly good original answers must fall on the kinaesthetic side in the schemes for presenting the experience types. The least number of original responses should be seen in the coartated types, the number should be somewhat larger in the extratensives who give M answers, and the maximum number of O's should be found in the strongly introverted subjects. This proves to be the case. Pedants and depressed subjects have the least original answers and the markedly coartated compulsion neurotics show very few. The intro-

versive group give far more numerous original responses. and the most are
seen in the most introverted. individuals shut up within themselves, incapable
of extensive rapport. and awkward in motility and impractical of mind. Only
subjects whom we have spoken of earlier as ‹ in the world but not of it · give
more than 50 % original interpretations. To say that a person is estranged
from the world in this way simply indicates in different words that he is
markedly introverted In egocentric extratensives the number of good original responses dwindles down to zero. and the responses are less and less
clearly visualized.

The percentage of animal answers is the resultant of two different psychisms, first. the ability to form stereotyped associative patterns, and secondly,
the ability to drop these patterns as indicated by freedom and fluidity of
associations. The first of these psychisms is present in all types of subjects:
it is only in the most scattered schizophrenics that the freedom of association
becomes so marked that stereotyped patterns disappear entirely. If this
ability to form patterns is so strong that it becomes a constant inclination
to indulge in particular series of associative ideas, whether by choice or un-
willingly. stereotypy immediately appears, and is expressed in the test by a
high percentage of animal answers. Introversive subjects show a small A percent, in the adaptative extratensive it is large, and even higher percentages
are seen in the coartated and coartative subjects. Egocentric extratensives
either show a high percentage of animal responses or some other figure than
the animal will act as stereotypy-indicator and be present in a high proportion.

There is also a correlation between the number of W responses and the
M's. This is best understood in terms of the energy of associative activity
which has its basis in the constitution of the subject. This energy of associative activity can be increased, as we have noted heretofore, by a conscious
or unconscious desire to perform in a complicated way. There are then two
factors, first, the energy of associative activity which is related to the freedom of associations which is also more or less constitutional, and. secondly,
a trend toward complicated performance which has emotional origins. Introversives have the most W responses; extratensives may have more under
certain conditions, namely, when the emotional set is particularly effective.
Coartated and egocentric extratensive subjects show the least W's.

Study of apperceptive types leads to similar conclusions. The results with
introversive subjects reveal a much richer apperceptive type than is the case
with the extratensives, and these subjects achieve the result with ease. In the
introversive subjects, the most common apperceptive type is W—D. with W
predominant; in extratensives, the most frequent type is W—D, with the D
more or less accentuated. In coartated and egocentric extratensive subjects,
the apperceptive type is of poor quality.

The case is different in the matter of sequence. The coartated and coartative show the most rigid sequence, and it is not unusual to find very rigid sequence in those cases which fall in the adaptative groups, but near the top of the scheme. where M and C answers are few. Optimal rigidity of sequence is found in all the dilated types across the bottom of the schemes. and mixed in with them in this area are found the excessively free and scattered types. The rigidity of sequence, dependent on the ability to discipline and properly distribute the «logical energy», is correlated with no factor in the test except the $F+^0/_0$. The rigidity of sequence has no regular distribution in the schemes of experience types; this corroborates the conclusion that it is more independent of the introversive and extratensive features of the personality than is any other factor thus far discussed

Clear form visualization as a factor shows similar relationships. Best visualization is seen in the coartated, and high $F+$ percentages are frequent in the introversive and, occasionally in the adaptative extratensives. The visualization is less clear on the · right side of the schemes where the egocentric extratensives are found. The clarity that the latter group achieves only after great effort. is easily accomplished by the introversive subjects by reason of their richer store of engrams. The greater availability of engrams is the reason the introversives are able to produce clearer forms than are the extratensives.

In the course of the discussion we have frequently mentioned the variation in the intensity of the perception on the part of the subject that he is carrying out an assimilative performance in interpreting the figures. This runs a parallel course with the findings concerning the visualization of forms. It is felt most strongly by the coartated, except that the simple dements of this group are less conscious of it. The adaptative extratensives are next to the coartated in perceiving that the task is an assimilative performance; they dislike interpreting the figures and consider the task tiresome. On the other hand, though they may be conscious that they are interpreting, the introversives nevertheless consider the task a pleasant one. The groups to the extreme right on the extratensive side of the schemes do not feel that they are interpreting, but believe themselves to be simply perceiving. These give very unclear form responses.

Thus far, I have said little about the ambiequal group because it allows no general conclusions. In the very talented group, the components of intelligence fall into the same relationships as is the case with the introversives; in manics, however, the relationships are like those of the extratensive group of subjects · and include many characteristics of the egocentric extratensives. Catatonics are in the middle, showing a mixture of extratensive and introversive features in the components of intelligence as in the other factors.

Table XV presents another summary of the findings. This Table is complete only if the classification of the components of intelligence into those capable of being increased by conscious effort on the part of the subject, and those not capable of such increase, is kept in mind while studying it (see page 69) Those components subject to increase by conscious volition are the following: 1. the number of good forms: 2. the clarity of form perception: 3. the accuracy of the associative process in assimilating (F): 4. the ability to discipline and distribute the (logical energy) (sequence and apperceptive type): 5. the ability to form stereotyped associative patterns (percent animal responses). Those components not subject to conscious volitional increase are: 1. the energy of associative activity (W): 2. the freedom of

Table XV.

	Coartated Type	
	M 0	
	Orig. 0	
	A°₀ large	
	W few	
	Apperceptive poor	
	Sequence rigid	
	Form · good	
	Interpretation recognized as such, with feeling of discomfort	
Introversive Type	*Extratensive Types*	
	Adaptative Type	*Egocentric Type*
M . many	M few	M : 0
Orig. many ⊥	Orig. few ⊤	Orig many —
A % small	A % . large	A ‰ : large
W many	W medium	W : medium or few
Apperceptive rich	Apperceptive usually poor	Apperceptive usually poor
Sequence variable	Sequence . usually good	Sequence : loose
F generally good	F often good	F : poor
Interpretation recognized as such. feeling of pleasure	Interpretation recognized as such, with feeling of displeasure	Interpretation not recognized as such
	Ambiequal Types	
Talented Group	*Catatonic*	*Manic*
M many	M : many	M medium
Orig many --	Orig · many ⊤	Orig . medium ⊥
A % small	A ‰ small	A % large
W many	W many	W . medium to few
Apperceptive rich	Apperceptive . rich	Apperceptive medium quality
Sequence variable	Sequence scattered	Sequence : loose
F usually good	F · good and poor extremes mixed	F · mixed, unclear
Interpretation recognized as such, feeling of pleasure	Interpretation usually recognized as such, with blocking	Interpretation frequently not recognized as such

associations from stereotyped patterns (A%); 3, the ability to make original associatiors (Original+); and, 4, the capacity for «inner creation» (M). We have noted, that these factors are subject to increase at will only in those cases in which the conscious direction of the will is abetted by individual constitutional predisposition. From this discussion. we are now able to deduce the characteristics of the various types of subjects

The coartated, and to a considerable extent, the coartative types are distinguished by the extreme predominance of those factors which can be increased by direction of attention to them. These are the groups distinguished primarily by logical discipline In achieving this discipline, however. introversive and extratensive features become atrophied; in other words. they sacrifice their ability to experience fully

The adaptative extratensives closely resemble them. Here. too, the logical functions are strongly predominant, frequently resulting in narrowing of the introversive and extratensive features, though there is not the degree of atrophy of these features seen in the coartated. In this group we find that the best performances of adaptability, both emotional and intellectual, are possible by means of conscious direction. Stereotypy, a mark of adaptability, also follows this general pattern more or less.

Introversive features in the test cannot be said to be introversive tendencies in actual living (see page 87); nevertheless, a case with introversive experience type would certainly fall in the group with introversive tendencies. Introversive features, extratensive tendencies, and conscious functions may be intermingled to a most extraordinary degree in the introversive subjects, so that many different personality constellations of character, intelligence, and modes of mentation result.

The normal ambiequal subject combines the introversive pattern with strong extratensive features and tendencies. Introversive and extratensive features, both quite strong, are combined equally in this group.

The normal ambiequal subject appears to fall more to the introversive side of the schemes, while the hypomanic (and manic) seem to fall more on the extratensive side. The latter combine an extratensive pattern with increased introversive activity. In general, hypomanics show fewer M and C responses than normal ambiequal subjects. Furthermore, the function of the factors subject to conscious control is more developed in the normal ambiequal than it is in hypomanics. One more point must be mentioned here Manics show motor excitement, but normal ambiequal persons do not. Catatonics, whose test findings place them between these two categories in the schemes, show blocking of motor function.

In the egocentric extratensive type the logical function is generally found to be rather weak. We deal in these cases with a condition in which affective reactions are not sufficiently controlled by logical functions. This is the case regardless of the reason this condition exists, be it damage of the introversive faculties as, for instance, in senile dementia, or the congenital weakness of the function as in the feebleminded. or destruction as in paresis or dementia senilis. or. finally, some sort of dilapidation as is seen in hebephrenic and querulous schizophrenics

7. Experience Type and Mood.

This topic has already been covered in the course of the discussion to a large extent. A glance at the schemes for classification of the experience types shows that those cases with elated mood, manics and hypomanics. excited hebephrenics and catatonics, and excited morons and imbeciles, all are found in the group of dilated types. All depressed subjects are found near the area of the schemes characterized by 0 M's and 0 C's, that is, with the coartated and coartative cases; only in the case of psychogenic depressions are the kinaesthesias maintained. Of this group, some subjects showed distinctly coartative tendencies in spite of having several M responses: it may be assumed that if tested at some other time they would have showed more M's than when tested while depressed. Subjects with depressions in the course of a schizophrenic illness, when tested during, before, or after a catatonic episode, are occasionally found to be color types, though they always show distinct coartative traits.

Depressed moods are, therefore. accompanied by a narrowing of the experience type; elated moods by a broadening of the type. Whether these changes are the cause or the result of the mood disorder is quite another question, probably not subject to solution by the test alone. It is probable that the question must be answered in different ways for each different mood

The coartated group also comprises the affectively dulled and indolent cases. Subjects with dilated experience type are never emotionally dull; they are always capable of affective reaction. Depressed and simple demented subjects, therefore, fall into the same experience type. The difference between these reactions lies in the form visualization and in the quality of the sequence of responses. In the depressed subject, the conscious thinking becomes sharpened as the experience type becomes coartated, but this is not the case with the simple dementias. The conclusion may be drawn that coartation with retention of the sharpness of disciplined reasoning shows depression, and that coartation with decrease of disciplined reasoning indicates indolence and dulling of the affect.

Common observation confirms these conclusions. Elated mood increases the feeling of capacity for experience. Depressed mood makes it impossible to enjoy anything; even the memory of former pleasures is rendered disagreeable by destructive contemplation as to whether they were really worthwhile. The joy of pleasurable memories is destroyed by means of this active

control of associations. The inability to work during depressions is of a
very particular nature. It is the opposite of the will to make complicated
performances, a persistent, insurmountable feeling of insufficiency. His own
ideas appear dull and trite to a depressed subject and he feels incapable of
producing anything creative; he believes himself capable only of imitation
at best.

The elated individual basks in a feeling of certainty as to his capabilities.
He marvels at his own ideas, not noticing that he is actually reproducing the
ideas of others. He dislikes any work which entails copying.

8. Temporary Variations in the Experience Type.

The results of the test provide a rather certain judgment about the experience type of the subject in question. It would, perhaps, be advisable to
repeat the test with two parallel series of figures, computing the results
separately and then averaging them, in order to make the conclusions even
more certain. Experience has shown, however, that practicable diagnoses are
possible using only the usual series.

It has been shown above that the experience type is dependent upon the
mood. A test made while the subject is elated gives different results from
those of a test made in a depressed period. For instance, a subject who, in
elated mood, has given 6 M's and 3 C's, may produce 2 M's and 1 C when
depressed. Another, when depressed gave 2 M's and 2 FC (1 C); when elated
he produced 4 M's and 2 C's. The absolute number of M and C responses
changes, but the proportion between them changes little or not at all. It is
not the mixture of introversive and extratensive features which changes, but
the breadth of the experience type. It appears to be a fact that the capacity
for narrowing and broadening the experience type varies widely among individuals. Very marked fluctuations are probably pathological. This material
all requires further confirmation by a large series of tests. Fatigue tends to
coartate the experience type markedly.

The experience type is, however, not an entirely fixed feature of the personality. Under proper conditions, it appears that it can not only be changed
in breadth, but completely displaced for a short time. The state of being in
a «good humor», for example, results in a normal ambiequal experience
type, not the ambiequal of the manic, but of the introversive sort. I must
note, however, that all my subjects in «good humor» were introversives; it
is possible that this mood in an extratensive subject would result in a manic
ambiequal kind of reaction. At any rate, «good humor» causes the experience
type to be shifted toward the ambiequal type.

We probably undergo a similar expansion of the experience type when
we exclaim after the performance of an opera, «That was an experience!»
(Erlebnis). A broadening of the experience type in the direction of extra-

tension we call a «pleasure»: when in the direction of introversion, this broadening is, depending on the degree, called «inner creation», or «inspiration», or even «a revelation». It is most probable that these temporary expansions of the experience type are not entirely independent of the habitual experience type, and are engulfed by it after a short time. After each expansion the experience type probably returns to its habitual state more or less rapidly.

The effect of other factors such as physical pain, various affects, mass suggestion, etc., has not, as yet, been examined.

9. Changes in Experience Type in the Course of the Life Span.

The results of the experiment thus far appear to justify the assumption that the experience type of an individual has a certain stability. The occasional expansions or contractions of it are temporary phenomena, so that the experience type returns to its habitual state within a relatively short time, a few hours, or at most days; only in mood disorders is the change more lasting. The changes in the experience type due to mental illness demand consideration also and will be covered in later discussion.

The development of the experience type and the changes which occur in it during the course of the individual's life span present a different problem. The experience type of a three year old child is different from that of a ten year old, that of an adolescent different from that of a thirty year old man, and that of a person of fifty is different from that of the very old. If the developmental changes in the experience type of a large number of subjects could be charted on the experience type schemes, each would show individual differences, but there would also very probably be parallel developments to be observed. It is, of course, impossible to examine the intraindividual development of the experience type; we must be content with conclusions drawn from inter-individual studies. For this purpose, we must develop a picture of the average changes with age, taking at least 100 observations in each group for the purpose. This would be an immense task, the more difficult because it would be complicated by questions concerning the comparison itself. This problem is taken up in the next section of the study.

The results now at hand allow us to glimpse only a few short periods of the average life span in relation to changes in experience type. We can guess at other parts of it, but for the most part, we remain in the dark.

The experience type appears to be ambiequal in the third to fourth year. Ambiequal phases appear to be present also in the period of puberty. After puberty the roads appear to separate; from this period on—or even earlier—introversive and extratensive types appear in larger numbers. An introversive tendency seems to be general about the thirtieth year. Thereafter, there is the greatest variability. It is quite probable that even after the thirtieth there

are certain critical years which bring with them a general tendency to introversion, as, perhaps, between the fiftieth and fifty-fifth After forty, perhaps even earlier, introversive features begin to diminish. The individual
loses the capacity for introversion and becomes more coartated with increasing age. Many appear to arrive at the adaptive extratensive type in this
process. After the sixtieth year, three things may happen. Coartation may
become more and more pronounced until the complete coartation indicated
by 0 M's and 0 C's is reached (results of very aged normal subjects of 70 to
80 years of age closely resemble those of cases of dementia simplex). Or the
coartation progresses more rapidly, as in the case of arteriosclerosis. Or the
type continues to change in an extratensive direction, reaching the egocentric-
extratensive type to eventuate in senile dementia. The extent to which capacity for introversion is retained in old age probably depends upon the
degree to which it was present in youth.

The work of H. Behn-Eschenburg is the first contribution in the systematic study of various age groups. He examined 220 school children from
the ages of 13 to 15 (see Bibliography).

10. Comparative Researches in Experience Type.

A large amount of experimental material allows comparative studies in
many directions. It would be ideal, of course, to have these studies based on
completed life histories, but routine material when in sufficiently large
amount and when carefully recorded, also can give rise to many new problems
in this field.

First, the comparison of the results in male and female subjects. The
differences are not so large that they demand notice of themselves. The number of W's is somewhat smaller, the number of C's somewhat larger in females
than in males. There are, however, many exceptions. It is practically impossible to determine the sex of the subject from the record of the test. Differences become apparent only upon examination of averages of a large
number of cases. The life curve of a woman doubtlessly runs a different
course from that of a man, though the differences may not be great.

Another problem in this field consists in the examination of whole families, perhaps such a study would bring forth striking results.

It would also be very interesting to examine groups from the different
trades. Many problems appear here which are not apparent on superficial
examination. One of these, the question of talent, will be taken up later.
Another important problem should be investigated, namely, do certain trades
and occupations speed the increase of stereotypy and cause the more rapid
loss of the capacity for introversion?

The experience type should be different in various peoples and races.
The average experience type of the forty-year-old Englishman is very prob-

ably quite different from that of the Russian, German, etc., of the same age. This difference should be even greater if the difference in race were greater. Large series of data would provide easily comparable and useful information. the number of experiments on which such comparative studies could be based would have to be very large to include all the problems mentioned above The test itself is technically so simple—it can be done through an interpreter—that it may be done with the most primitive Negro as easily as with a cultured European.

I can supply only one example in this connection from the material at hand. It has to do with the Bernese, especially those from the central part of the canton, and the Appenzeller. the people coming from the back and central parts of the area especially. The Bernese are more introversive in type than are the Appenzeller who are more extratensive. Of course, there are exceptions on both sides; nevertheless. the observations at hand indicate that the average life-configuration of the Bernese tends to the introversive, while that of the Appenzeller toward the extratensive. side of the schemes (The life-configuration may be considered to be the sketching in of the development of the experience types in the schemes as given above.) Kinaesthetic and original responses are more common among the Bernese. It is, of course, no new discovery that the Appenzeller is more adaptable emotionally, has a more extensive rapport and is physically more active than the reserved, stolid, slow Bernese; but it is worth pointing out that the test supports this piece of common knowledge.

Differences are seen in the schizophrenics of the two groups, also. A Bernese who becomes schizophrenic is more apt to fall into a profound catatonic state than is the Appenzeller. The Appenzeller, even though catatonic, shows some hebephrenoid traits and does not lose the ability to get into rapport as completely as does the Bernese. This dissimilarity between the psychoses of these two groups is apparent to all who have opportunity to compare them. The Bernese is more apt to show paranoid features in the development of the schizophrenic illness, and tends to construct more florid, colorful and myth-like delusional systems than the Appenzeller. In the latter group, the delusions are rarely original and they lack the mythical strain almost completely. There are other striking differences between the groups which will be noted later.

11. The Affectivity. The Personality[1].

«We gather together under the term `Affectivity' the emotions, the affects, the feelings of pleasure and displeasure.» (Bleuler.)

The test gives orientation as to the affective status of the subject. It gives information as to the stability or instability, strength or weakness of

[1] German = Charakter

Rorschach, Psychodiagnostics.

the feelings. the intensivity or extensivity of the affective reaction, the control of lack of control over the reactions, the suppression or freedom of reaction. The specific tone of the affect, whether pleasurable or unpleasant can be read only incompletely. It is frequently, but not always possible to say, in the case of the coartated type, whether there is depression in the picture, or whether the reaction is based simply on extreme fixation of attention. The problem in the dilated type is similar; it is hard to tell at times, whether the subject is experiencing pleasurable or unpleasant feelings (anger, irritability).

The absolute number of color responses is a good measure of affective lability. When considered in relation to the number of M responses, the number of C's indicates the amount of affective lability which the subject actually shows, or, in other words, the degree of stabilization of the affectivity. So far as experience types are concerned, the C responses represent the extratensive features of the personality, the ability to get into rapport, the capacity for emotional adaptions, both personal and situational. Avoidance of color in the test indicates emotional timidity. This may appear as conscious control of emotional reaction where there is preference for the blue of the figures, or as neurotic suppression of emotion shown by color shock.

It has been found empirically that the influence of colors in perceiving the figures may be taken to represent the extent of emotional excitability and actual excitement; the basis for this deduction is, however, quite insufficient to satisfy the demands of scientific logic. There is a definite correlation between the extent of emotional excitement, the extent of motor activity, and the number of responses influenced by color perception. The causes, the etiological sources, of this correlation remain to be discovered.

Why is it that the colors are not included in the perceptions of some cases? Is it a matter of diminished sensitivity? This would be to say that depressives are all color blind in a particular way. Frequently enough they say that everything is gray, and this is not only in the metaphorical sense, for they emphasize that all colors do not seem to have the same brilliance as before. Manics, on the other hand, always stress the brilliance of colors. Yet there must be a difference between color-blindness and the tendency to see everything as gray or all color-blind people would be emotionally abnormal; while this is contrary to ordinary experience, it might be worth while to investigate the problem. Or is it that the colors are perceived but are excluded from the perception complex? This exclusion may be demonstrated in the neurotic subject, and not infrequently in the cultivated individuals who «control» their emotions. Is there some kind of biological, or genetic, or anatomic relationship between the substrate on which color perception rests and that on which the affect is dependent? Or is the rejection of color simply a symptomatic change which is secondary to real changes in the affective substrate? The latter is probably the correct surmise since the findings with depressives and manics bear it out in one direction and the behavior of color-blind persons in another.

It has long been realized that there must exist a very close relationship between color and affectivity. The gloomy person is one to whom everything looks «black», while the cheerful person is said to see everything through rose-colored glasses. Black is the color of mourning: that other peoples have other mourning colors probably proves that they take a different attitude toward mourning than we do.

One cannot imagine a gay party without color, and a carnival without it is unthinkable. Colors draw people into extratension unless the affect is completely stabilized as in the case of depressed or phlegmatic persons. Music, especially strongly rhythmical tunes which induce rhythmical movements and thus cut off kinaesthetic perceptions, does the same thing. A veritable mass-action of extratensing factors appears in a parade where there are colored uniforms, sparkle and glitter of metals, and march music to which everyone is in step. Introversive tendencies are highly obstructive in armies. It was not without reason that the army clung to colored uniforms for so long a time. Investigation of the effect of field gray uniforms on the mental attitudes of soldiers would certainly uncover many interesting facts. General Booth's Salvation Army meetings are especially beautiful examples of the methods of drawing out extratensive features. Rhythmic, staccato speeches, «worldly» music with powerful rhythms, rhythmic flag-waving, and in the center the bright red blouse of the old general. This is certainly no «turning in upon one's self». Such examples could be multiplied many times.

The ability to blend colors and form them into a single engram is not a simple function but a composite one and it must be acquired. The form engram is the controlling part of the composite. An absolute memory for color is a rare finding; it is well known that few people are able to tell the color of the eyes of their nearest relatives.

It has become apparent in the test that the FC responses, the form-color responses, primarily determined by form, secondarily by color, represent affective adaptability. CF responses represent affectivity which is no longer capable of adaptation, though there remains a desire for adaptation. The C responses represent impulsiveness: here the desire for adaptability has been extinguished.

The relationships of these three types of color answers with each other when considered in relation to the number of M answers, naturally yields a much more complete scale of emotional tones than does the scheme of experience types with its rough calculation of the color responses. It is impossible to discuss or even describe all these variations systematically; only a few special types of general affectivity will be mentioned.

Empathy. Individuals capable of empathic relationships with others must include in their make-up certain introversive and extratensive elements This conclusion may be arrived at by theoretical deduction and is proved empirically Genuine empathy presumes that the two individuals in the empathic relationship are of similar type. A subject having the pattern, 3 M's, 2 FC's. 0 CF's and 0 C's, can have only partial empathy in his contacts with a subject who has 10 M responses: the former will be unable to follow the emotional reactions of the latter. A subject giving 10 M's will not be able to make a sound empathic relationship with one who gives 2 M's: the former will tend to accredit the latter with more introversion and individualism than he actually possesses. will idealize him. He who has no color answers at all is capable only of «intellectual empathy»; similarly, those subjects showing neither M nor C responses. As CF and C responses increase, especially when they outweigh the FC's in the pattern, a strong desire for empathy may be present in the subject, but the non-adaptable emotional components are so strong that they outweigh the adaptable, so that the subject, in his desire to adapt himself and to attain empathic relationship, actually demands adaptations and understanding from others. He is not capable of empathy, but is demanding. selfish, and egocentric. Such are those irritable and sensitive persons who frequently are found unable to understand irritability and sensitivity in others, the enthusiasts who cannot understand why others remain cool in the face of their enthusiasm, people in love who want to see the whole world happy because they are, the zealots and reformers who consider their own ideas of such great worth as to set the world on fire. Naturally the epileptics, who show. despite their overt friendliness, egocentric attitudes. and manics and senile dements also are of this type.

The capacity for purely affective empathy is limited in every direction, and is possible in spite of these limits only be means of intellectual components which tend to break through the emotional boundaries. The form-color responses are the expression of this mixture of components which makes possible adaptations on the emotional level. It is probably impossible to draw any sharp line between ability to get into empathic relation and the capacity for adaptation.

Suggestibility Affective suggestibility is represented in this test by the CF responses: M, FC and C answers may or may not be present; in any case there must be a predominance of CF's. either absolutely or relatively. Egocentric extratensive subjects are the most suggestible, and are particularly influenced by emotional suggestions. The greater the number of M's in the experience type formula. the less the suggestible is the subject, but if suggestive influences are at all effective in such individuals they are more lasting A fact already established is reaffirmed in this connection, namely. that the greater the capacity for conscious reasoning. the less suggestible is the subject, and conversely, the greater the affective lability, the greater the suggestibility of the subject. There is one exception to this rule, however, for when the lability exceeds a certain point. suggestions have insufficient time to become established, and are therefore ineffective. Coartated types generally are not very suggestible. Compulsion neurotics, for example, having conscious accentuation of disciplined reasoning as the outstanding characteristic of their psychic make-up, are very little affected by suggestion. if suggestibility comes into evidence at all it is likely to be in the form of the reciprocal reaction, negative suggestibility, together with doubts and a condemnation of their own «spinelessness».

Impulsiveness. In the following discussion, impulses are considered to be sudden discharges of emotion with simultaneous, sudden motor discharge The two discharges are related, as we have seen earlier, through the correlation established between the affect and motility. Impulsive outbursts represent the highest degree of affective lability. The situation in this regard is altered according to the presence or absence of M's or FC's in the record. If there are few M responses with many C's impulsive outbursts are less striking, and fit into the general picture of the subject's emotional and motor excitement. In this situation emotional discharges (and «abreactions») are continuous, the impulsive outbursts appearing as slight exacerbations of the usual affective behavior. The introversive impulsive person responds differently. In these individuals the emotions are stabilized, mostly by conscious control. When an impulse is released in such a person, it «explodes» the confines of his introversive stabilization in a manner quite different from the response of the extratensive. Ambiequal subjects are practically all impulsive; the various types of this group react in this respect in the same way they do in regard to other factors discussed previously: manics react like the extratensives do where impulsiveness is concerned; talented subjects, «good-humored» individuals, and catatonics respond like introversives. Compulsion neurotics can show either type of impulsive reaction, introversive or extratensive.

The capacity for rapport formation, for empathy, for suggestibility, and for impulsiveness, all vary according to the experience type of the individual and according to the relation in which various types of color answers appear in the test. This different shading is seen in all human characteristics. Such characterizations as benevolent, tyrannical, moody, or jealous, etc. describe very different situations which may have very different origins, according to the experience type of the individual. Tyranny in an introversive person is very different from tyranny in an extratensive. Examples of such differences are seen when Ludwig II of Bavaria or a personality such as Lenin's are compared with Wilhelm II or Louis XIV.

If all the languages of the world were used, it would still be impossible to express all the nuances of personality which are found to have their foundation in the experience type. The personality of an individual is almost entirely determined by his affective make-up, according to Bleuler. It is, therefore.

obvious that the experience type, especially when considered in conjunction
with the distribution of the three types of color responses, becomes significant in indicating the personality of the subject.

For the present, there is little more to add to the discussion of the various
moods and emotional states. Coartated types are the most attentive. The type
is invariably coartated in depressive moods; in cheerful states, dilated. There
is but one emotion which can appear in all experience types and that is
anxiety [1].

Since the personality of the subject may be determined to a considerable
extent by the experience type, study of the various characterological phenomena should result in a list of findings like that obtained from the study of
the combinations and variations of the experience types. Thus we should find
changes in the personality in the course of the lifetime, personality differences
among the various races, etc.

12. Imagination.

In the discussion thus far, there has been frequent occasion to speak of
«imaginative individuals» As it is usually understood, this means persons
with creative imagination; however, for the present, the question of recept-
ivity or productivity of imagination is of secondary importance. Many subjects believe that they have no imagination yet they admit that they enjoy
the productions of others; these react in the test in such a way as to make it
difficult to distinguish between them and subjects known to have productive
imagination. Such subjects' imagination functions only in a receptively crea-
ting imagination; as has been noted, the types are difficult to separate on the
basis of the test. The difference lies in the direction of the energy used in
the process of imagination. In the subjects with productive imagination, this
energy leads to productivity; in those with receptive imagination this energy
is dispersed to other, usually extra-personal ends, finding its direction toward
the extra-tensive side of the experiencing-apparatus. In the productive, this
energy is directed toward inducing action in that part of the experiencing-
apparatus which includes the disposition to be imaginative.

Szymon Hens, in 1917, published a study called «Testing the Imagination
of School Children, Adults. and Mental Patients by Means of Formless Blots»
Hens' studies were carried out with blots similar to those used in this study.
In his summary, he touches upon some of the problems which have arisen in
this research, but he could not study them completely because he addressed
himself to the problem of the content of the interpretations exclusively and
did not go beyond the concept of imagination, in a case where only perception can be considered as basic His conclusions, therefore, concern the con-

---

[1] German = Angst

tent rather than the pattern of perceptive process which has been my principle concern.

Individuals who enjoy losing themselves in the introversive sphere of their personalities, more or less actively eliminating reality, may be called imaginative. This reaction may be common or uncommon for them, of long or short duration, may vary in the extent volition governs it, but must not be entirely involuntary, and may be productive or receptive in varying degree.

In the test, these subjects are characterized by the interpretation of fairy tales, mythical pictures, and scenes from novels, so forth, but they are also characteristic in regard to the pattern of the factors of the test. They give very many M's, usually several, and frequently many color responses, though there is never a preponderance of color over movement. They show many whole answers, numerous original answers, and the animal percentage is low. Forms are, in general, clearly visualized, frequently exceptionally so. They are patient in the experiment, and surrender entirely to their ideas, so that, especially in the case of those with productive imaginations, they connect a series of ideas to produce combined whole responses, interpreting entire scenes.

The findings in these subjects indicate that the introversive factors are predominant as shown by the M responses, the good original answers and the percentage of animal answers. Wealth of associations and «energy of associations» on a constitutional basis, evidenced by the W's, are also strongly developed in these individuals. Sequence is neglected to the extent of extreme freedom or looseness. The affective make-up is extremely labile.

Confabulating subjects, another type of imaginative persons, react in quite a different way. The difference is best illustrated by an example. An imaginative woman—at times her imagination is productive in type—interpreted Plate VIII as «A fairy tale; a treasure in two blue chests is buried under a tree stump, and underneath there is a flame; there are two animals guarding the treasure». A confabulating subject gave the following interpretation: «Two bears, and the whole thing is round, therefore it must be the bear pit in Berne». The imaginative subject produces a complete picture from the plate without undue distortion of the individual parts, and, especially, takes into consideration the relative positions of the parts. The confabulating subject takes two parts of the Plate and combines them to the extent of contamination in some instances, disregarding the rest of the figure, and without regard to the relative position of the parts used. Interpretations given by imaginative subjects are made up of much more complicated associations than are those of confabulators.

The content of the first example above comes from the world of fantasy; in the second, the content has its source in reality. The first is the response of an introversive subject, the second of an extratensive individual. The first answer is marked by an emotional tone of pleasure which is typical of the introversive, while the second was given as though it were a triumph, in a manner typical of the extratensive-egocentric: the perceptive process is, however, more complete in the first than in the second interpretation.

The introversive-imaginative subject perceives reality more clearly than does the confabulating extratensive. His interpretations are made up of associative material characteristic of that which belongs to introversity, and the emotional tone is one of pleasure, the interpretations complicated. To him, the task is a game. The confabulating subject, on the other hand, does not perceive reality clearly. In producing his interpretations he employs the relatively small store of associative material, usually drawn from reality, characteristic of the extratensives, and the associative pattern is as simple as possible. There is little sense of pleasure in the process of interpreting; there is more the sense of triumph because of what he considers to be a brilliant performance. Finally, the imaginative subject is more conscious of the fact that he is interpreting than the confabulator; the latter frequently does not recognize that he is using imagination.

The differences between imaginative and confabulating subjects are, then, generally the same as those between introversive and extratensive ones. Introversive and extratensive features may be mixed together in the same individual as we have seen, and imaginative and confabulatory features may also occur together as is the case in elation or in pseudologia phantastica. In states of poetic inspiration in the ambiequal subject it may happen that the features of confabulation become predominant and overcome the consciousness of the unreality of the product of imagination. This is especially true when alcohol, which in itself increases confabulation, influences the picture; this may be seen in the works of E. T. A. Hoffman.

Delusions, whether schizophrenic or of other reaction type, do not allow direct comparison with imaginations of the normal person. The schizophrenic patient who was originally imaginative will, of course, produce different, richer, more colorful delusions than a patient originally unimaginative, just as in the test his interpretations are different from those of an originally unimaginative person. The function of imagination probably has little to do with the fact that the patient's delusions take on the same value as reality, become reality for him. This is dependent upon quite other factors having to do with the mechanism of projection.

13. Experience Type and Type of Imagery.

Imagery types, as set up by psychologists, are not clearly circumscribed, and are by no means well established, a fact that has been stressed by Stern[1]. In the earlier work visual, auditory and motor types were differentiated «ac-

---

[1] W. Stern, Differentielle Psychologie. Leipzig, 1911.

cording to the qualitative importance of one or another sensory field in the determination of the conceptive life—and thus also the higher mental functions of speech. learning, etc... (Stern, p. 193). The assumption that the preferred sensory field influenced activity in all phases of imagery life equally has proved to be untenable (Stern. p. 194).

Is the imagery type of an individual also his perceptive type? When a subject in the test shows kinaesthetic responses and visual images from memory, does this mean that this sensory field (the visual) dominates the imagery life? These questions cannot be answered at this time and will require control experiments. using the ordinary series of blots to obtain their answers.

It has been shown statistically that the «perceptive types» (using, for the moment. this term as analogous to the imagery type) fit into the experience type scheme in a quite definite way. This is shown in Table XVI.

Table XVI.   **Perceptive Types.**

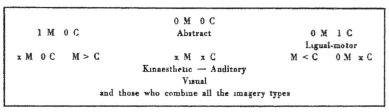

Introversives are predominantly kinaesthetic in «perceptive type» while extratensivies are predominantly auditory. Subjects of the visual type are found in the central column which is, as may be seen. quite broad and inclusive. In the center of this area are the subjects who are talented in many directions; these combine all the various imagery types. Introversive subjects may show auditory imagery type, but the extratensives are never strongly kinaesthetic in type. Adaptive subjects, especially if there are coartative features, generally fall into the speech-motor type (lingual-motor). Strongly coartative individuals can hardly be called anything other than «abstract»[1].

Exactly what is meant by the «motor type» remains unclear in psychology. From our data, we find that the individual who is strongly influenced by kinaesthesias is clumsy in the motor sphere while those who are skillful in motor performances produce few kinaesthetic engrams. In the classification above, motor skill is found in the same area as auditory apperceptive types. The lingual-motor type represents a special case of motor skill.

I do not deny that these statements stand in need of further research. Consideration of the problem of the talents lends support to the idea that the perceptive type and probably the imagery type as well are conditioned

---

[1] German = Begrifflıche.

by the experience type. If the perceptive and imagery type is conditioned by
the experience type, then everything which applies to the experience type
must also hold good for the perceptive and imagery types. The perceptive
type must, therefore, be subject to the same intraindividual variations as is
the experience type. The perceptive type should, then, show variation with
fatigue, change in mood, and especially, change in age. Variation according
to race should also be apparent.

The loss of capacity for introversion begins in men before the fortieth
year, and the experience type gradually approaches the extratensive thereafter. The perceptive and imagery types should show similar changes. A
quotation from Stern (p. 373) bears on this point.

«The visual qualities of Schiller's lyrics were compared with the same qualities in
Goethe's lyrics by Karl and Marie Groos, using Frank's computations on Goethe's works.
Certain similarities and differences were found in the comparison of the works of the two
men. It was found that, in his earlier works, Schiller used more than twice as many expressions referring to visual qualities (computed as rate in 10.000 words of text) as did
Goethe. In Goethe's works, the number of allusions to visual qualities increases with the
age of the writer, while in Schiller the number decreases considerably; this is especially
apparent in regard to expressions pertaining to brilliance glare, glitter. Similarities between the two authors appear. In both, the ratio between the number of expressions connected with vivid color and other optical qualities is 1.3, both in the early and the later
works. As both authors grew older references to red decreased in frequency and expressions involving green increased, in both blue was poorly represented, and both used yellow
hardly at all. In both there is an increase of expressions involving lighter shades as age
increases [1].»

In another section of his book, Stern quotes the same authors to the
effect that Schiller was more strongly acoustic (in imagery) than was Goethe
and was far more so than was Shakespeare.

The differences between the two authors and the trends shown in their
use of optical imagery may be explained by assuming that Goethe's experience
type was originally far more dilated than was Schiller's, that is, it originally
spread far more into the introversive sphere than did Schiller's. As both men
grew older, kinaesthesias decreased with the result that Goethe then fell
into the area of visual types, while Schiller more nearly approached the
auditory imagery type. This explains the decrease in expressions of optical
qualities in Schiller and the increase of them in Goethe.

The decrease of references to red with increasing age may be considered
as the expression of increase in emotional control. This finding would correspond with the results in the test, where emotional control was found to
increase with age. It is extraordinary that the use of blue does not increase
in frequency It may be that a preference for blue is a sign of definite emo-

---

[1] Literature as in Stern 1. L Frank, Statistische Untersuchung über die Verwendung
der Farben in den Dichtungen Goethes. Gießener Diss 90   2. Karl and Marie Groos, Die
akustischen Phänomene in der Lyrik Schillers Zeitschr f Ästh. 5, 545—70, 1910   3. Karl
and Marie Groos, Die optischen Qualitäten in der Lyrik Schillers. Zeitschr f. Ästh (Des-
soir) 4, 559—71. 1909.

tional timidity. So far as green is concerned, it may be that the test series as it is now used do not contain sufficient green to bring out the importance of that color

14. Experience Type and the Sense Hallucinated.

The effectiveness of imagery type in the determination of the sense in which an individual will become hallucinated should he suffer from sensory illusions cannot be definitely stated. In schizophrenics, the imagery type probably definitely determines the sense hallucinated. but in other hallucinatory states, such as delirium tremens for example, this is improbable.

The more extratensive schizophrenics almost always hallucinate in the auditory sphere. This group includes the hebephrenoid catatonics, stabilized paranoid cases of long duration and some hebephrenics. Introversive patients. however, very frequently show hallucinations in the realm of bodily sensations which often are quite indistinguishable from kinaesthesias. If voices are heard by patients of this type, these voices have kinaesthetic qualities and arise within the patient's own body rather than from outside. All the senses are hallucinated in the ambiequal patients, the catatonics and the catatonoid paranoics. Patients with simple dementia do not hallucinate at all.

The correlation between experience type and the sense hallucinated should carry through in all the other relationships of the experience type as described above. This problem must be left for later studies. Two observations will, however, serve as examples in this connection. It may be observed frequently that the sense hallucinated changes with increasing age in schizophrenics. Visual hallucinations may disappear with age, but «voices» remain. The opposite trend is observed extremely rarely except in cases showing exacerbations tending toward introversion.

Another example is afforded in the Bernese and the Appenzeller. The Appenzeller are extratensive even when schizophrenic and show auditory hallucinations practically exclusively. Visual hallucinations are rare in them, and kinaesthetic illusions occur infrequently. In the Bernese, however, kinaesthetic hallucinations and hallucinations of bodily sensations are among the most common symptoms. Visual hallucinations are also more frequent in this group than in the other, and auditory hallucinations are, of course, relatively frequent also.

15. Experience Type and Talent.

The first thing which drew attention to the relation between experience type and talent was the observation that all painters gave relatively many M responses and that particularly talented subjects, talented in several fields, always fell in the area of the experience type scheme with the ambiequal showing little or no coartative trend. Different sorts of studies including experiments with artists as subjects and study of spontaneous and directed productions of all subjects have lead to certain conclusions. These require further study and differentiation, however.

A dilated experience type is fundamental for most talents. The influence of coartation on talent—what talents can occur in coartated subjects—remains a question to be examined. Other problems include the changes in talents, and the question of whether some talents may be made more effective by coartation. The talents which have been studied to some degree at least, fit into the experience type scheme as shown in Table XVII.

Table XVII.   **Talents.**

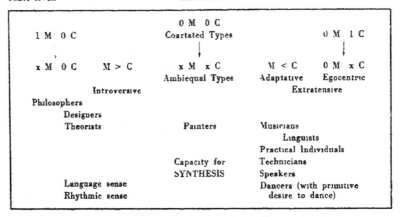

This rather rough summary is to be interpreted as indicating that only a person of the ambiequal type is capable of including all the talents in a single individual. In ambiequals the introversive talents are likely to be more effective, however. Introversives may have talents more characteristic of extratensives to some extent, probably to the extent indicated by the relation between M and C in the test. This mixture of introversive and extratensive talents becomes more common the nearer the M-C relationship approaches the ambiequal type, and it becomes less apparent the further from the ambiequal the case lies. Extratensives may have introversive talents if they approach the ambiequal in experience type, but apparently art becomes skill as one passes the middle of the chart. Music, language and technical skill are, apparently, the only talents which appear in highly developed state in the extratensives.

All this material is in a crude and undifferentiated state and does not allow complete understanding. There are, for instance, painters who fall into the extratensive type. But there is a great difference between the introversive painter and the extratensive one. The latter is predominantly reproductive in his work, while the introversive is creative in his. This difference probably holds for all the different talents, that is, the introversive is creative, the extratensive is primarily reproductive. I dare not judge music in this respect, but it is certainly true that talent in the field of languages and in technical skill represents reproductive functioning. The differentiation of talents according to their introversive and extratensive features is, in itself, a large task. The following Table (XVIII) attempts to demonstrate such a differentiation, using painters as the example [1].

Table XVIII   **Painters.**

			0 M 0 C			
I M 0 C			Schematists			0 M I C
			Empty formalists,			
			resulting in «logical» color sequences			
					Copyists	
				Commercial Artists, Decoration		
†						†
x M 0 C	M > C		x M x C	M < C		0 M x C
Abstract						Naive
Futurists	Symbolist					Enjoying Color
	Expressionist			Impressionists		
	(intrapersonal motives)			(extrapersonal motives)		
	Black and White			Colors		
		Synthesis of				
		Motion, Form, Color				
		Intra- and extra-personal motives				
		The timeless classic art.				

Obviously, such a differentiation could be extended to show much more delicate nuances. In actuality, each artist represents an individuality of his own.

Turning to other talents, the extraverts may have extraordinary ability to handle language and ability in repartee though there is little «sense» or «feeling» for language. In the introversive, however, poor ability to speak may be combined with a deep «sense» for language. Those who actually contribute to languages, and the really great speakers must comprise both faculties. An example of such is found in Luther. According to the theory outlined, such persons must fall in the ambiequal type.

Extratensives are agile, elegant dancers; it is, however, the introversives who really enjoy rhythmic dancing. In handwriting we find another specific

[1] I am greatly obliged to the artist, E. Lüthi, of Basle, for many suggestions in this field.

problem. Introversive people have more individualistic scripts, while extratensives write with greater skill in the traditional patterns. In the field of gesture, the introversives show individually specific gestures. while extratensives use the more traditional movements for expression.

The contrast may be expressed in still another way. namely, that introversives are cultured. extratensives are civilized.

Coartativity is necessary if there is to be talent in the field of systematic scientific endeavor. Introversive dogmatism or more extratensive reproductive labor follows upon minimal degrees of coartation; polypragmatism may also appear on the part of the minimally coartated individual. Maximum coartation leads to empty formalism and schematisation.

Talent in organizing demands a mixture of introversive and extratensive features, and there must be a capacity for coartation as well The extratensive features are the more important. In contrast, in the ability to make observations one finds the introversive features to be more important though there must be some features of extratension. Observers in whom the introversive features are too marked are biased in one direction and are dogmatic.

Knowing the experience type of an educated subject, it is a simple matter to guess his favorite philosopher. Introversive individuals swear by Schopenhauer, dilated ambiequals by Nietzsche, coartated individuals by Kant, and the extratensive group by some evanescent authority, Christian Science or something of that sort.

While these observations are quite superficial, nevertheless it is certainly true that talent and experience types are inseparably related. There are probably no unit talents, but rather experience types which present optimal situations for the development of potentialities aroused by some actuating stimulus. Unit or single talents are observed simply because others have not been developed. The fact that only one has been developed results from lack of stimulus, not from any constitutional incapacity. In no case does a talent represent a single possibility of development. It is, rather, the result of two factors. first, a constitutional capacity dependent on the experience type, and, second, a stimulus which activates the person so that the constitutional capacity is transformed into talent. It should be pointed out that there are many different capacities possible within the same experience type.

16. Variations and Comparison of Talents.

The fate of talents is dependent upon the variations of the experience type. This is the case because, as was pointed out in the last section, talents exist as potentialities of certain experience types which are optimal for them. Therefore, comparison of experience types and comparison of talents cannot be undertaken separately.

In general. variations in talents are the same as variations in experience type. Like the experience type, talents are dependent upon mood, fatigue, etc., and there is a state to which they return after a change which may be called «habitual». «Creative mood» comes with dilated experience types. «inspiration» is a part of rapid and forceful dilatation of the usual experience type. Depression prevents inspiration because it coartates the experience type.

The fluctuations of experience type in the course of a life time correspond to the fluctuations of the talents It will be possible to make a more definite statement about this problem only when the physiological changes of experience type, changes of varying degree, which occur in every life are more fully understood. «Exhaustion» and «dissipation» of talent. and the fact that an artist begins, in his later years, to imitate his own works, means that the experience type has been deflected from the optimum for the particular talent in question. The experience type has become more extratensive, there is less capacity for introversion. so that the talent approaches the less productive but more technical sort. When a talent shows marked development. this is an indication that the introversive features have become stronger as determinants. As a rule, there is an increase in capacity for introversion about the thirtieth year, though this may not hold for all races. The «late maturation» of many Swiss artists has its foundation in a late shift in the experience type.

The development of Ferdinand Hodler is of great interest in this respect. He showed tremendous expansions of the experience type in both the «intro» and «extra» directions in his career. At first he reveled in color, portrayed joyful folk-scenes full of action. Eventually he used almost no color in his paintings, but depicted powerful movements, impressive in the control they indicate In him there was a gradual growth of kinaesthetic features, and a shutting out of color. Finally, he employs the color blue almost exclusively: blue is the favorite color of all who control their passions. The predominance of introversive factors is unmistakable in the larger paintings. The content of the latter also show the trend toward introversion which culminates in the picture «A Glance into Eternity». It is remarkable that he could produce the portrait of General Wille in the same period. The contrast between these two pictures reveal a tremendous control over introversive and extratensive tendencies in his constitution as well as over his techniques of expression.

Alfred Kubin furnishes another example. One can follow the relationship between the variations in his experience type and the changes in his artistic activities in his autobiography[1]. When he was most profoundly introverted he could neither paint nor draw, but he was able to construct a philosophical system and to write his novel. «The Other Side», telling of a «journey into the unconscious». When extratensive factors increase, he goes back to draw-

---

[1] In Alfred Kubin, Die andere Seite Verlag St. Müller, Munich and Berlin.

ing, starting with black and white. turning, as these factors become more effective, to color eventually Many other examples such as this could be given.

Comparative studies of experience types must include comparison of talents. Differences in experience type in men and women should indicate differences in the talents the two sexes show. (The determining influence of instinct, discussed in the following section, must not be neglected in this connection.) Comparative studies of the experience types of different ethnic groups must include comparison of their talents.

Here, too, many examples are available. The only one to which the test has been applied is that furnished by the Bernese and the Appenzeller. Since introversive features are more apparent in the Bernese. talent in drawing, as an example, should be more common in them. This is found to be the case. The Bernese do show far more talent in drawing than do the Appenzeller. Bernese patients in institutions draw spontaneously far more frequently and their creations are often quite original in conception; when the Appenzeller does draw his work is likely to be a copy of something such as an embroidery design. On the other hand, the Appenzeller has a great deal of talent for eloquence and wit, something which certainly cannot be said of the Bernese. I do not know whether talent in music is more common among them than among the Bernese.

The reactions of various groups to color is noteworthy. Those who inhibit and suppress their emotions, especially coartated types, tend to avoid color, to be shy of it. This is probably most apparent in English art. Markedly introverted people prefer art in black and white. With increase in extratensive features in the experience type there is an increase in the enjoyment of color; an example is found in the Southern Europeans Ambiequal types of all peoples are the synthesists.

With appropriate means of analysis, these comparative studies may even include various cultural epochs. Quoting from Stern, page 374: «Baerwald has tried to illustrate the difference between two cultural epochs by using psychological categories, contrasting Goethe's period with our own times. Goethe's period may be expressed as one of drawing and rhythm, that is, formal in its imagery type, abstract in thinking, in affective responses controlled by a rather calm mixture of emotions. The present times are, in contrast, characterized by a «colorful-melodic» or material sort of imagination, concrete reasoning, and disquieting mixtures of emotions [1]. In terms of this experiment, these results may be expressed as follows: Goethe's times were predominantly introversive, that is, rhythmic and formal (using formal in this special sense), abstract and emotionally stabilized, while the present period

[1] Baerwald, Psych. Faktoren des modernen Zeitgeistes Schr d. Ges. f. psych Forschung, 15, p. 1—85, 1905. Annotation after Stern, Differentielle Psychologie, Leipzig, 1911.

is more extratensive, that is, more colorful, melodic, concrete and unstable emotionally.

There is at present an unmistakable trend toward introversion again. Old gnostic paths of introversion are being trod again and people are so tired of extratension that systems like anthroposophy are receiving support in academic circles. As is always the case in such a movement, the danger is that many will not only reject extratension but also disciplined reasoning. Materialism thus becomes mysticism and cultism. The fact that introversion was considered pathological for so long is the result of the materialistic-extratensive epoch which is now drawing to a close. The extratensive spirit of the period brought forth some dubious ideas, especially when introversion was lost to such an extent that culture and civilization were confused. Culture always grows out of introversion; civilization is an extratensive adaptation and usage, but is not, in itself, culture. To possess only introversive features in the experience type is to be completely introverted and this is not culture either, but represents, at best, a sort of private cultism.

17. Experience Type, Talent, and Instinct.

The experience type includes eo ipso certain constitutional possibilities for development of talents. There is an apparatus for talent development in the experience type, just as we have seen that the experience type represents a receptive apparatus generally. It is probably rare even in the most talented ambiequal types that any considerable portion of the possibilities contained in this apparatus is activated for productive, creative work.

This «disposition» for the formation of talents is not, then, talent itself; something more is required. What is necessary is a powerful emotional set which aspires to a goal and at the same time produces goal-images for itself. This we call instinct, or will, or libido; this transforms the «disposition» into talent. The instincts change the «Anlage» of the experience type into manifest talents and productive tendencies.

The activation of potential talents is a common phenomenon, so common that it is possible to determine the approximate optimal experience type for the various talents though the number of experiments is relatively small (about 150 talented individuals have been studied). The frequency of the activation of talents indicates that the «will» is not quite free in the choice of talents, but that the «disposition» plays a somewhat determining part as well. The «disposition» paves the way for the instinct and it has, thus, eo ipso, the tendency to become a talent.

Many talents remain undeveloped. Frequently the test indicates that a subject has a talent for drawing. On questioning, it is found that the subject was able to draw quite well while at school but that afterward he just never got around to doing it: his father and brother were good at drawing, however. An individual who is recruited early into an extratensive profession never has opportunity to attach any emotional drive to his talents because of situational circumstances, though he may have the «Anlage» of introversive apparatus which might lead to the development of talents. He may realize now and again that he has missed his proper profession The neglected talent does not always call attention to itself in this way, however: the constant stimulation of extratensive factors can cover up all such warnings. A person may retain a definitely introversive experience type despite the fact that he lives very extratensively or he may stress the extratensive features while at work and the introversive features during vacations. Such an individual who has become the victim of exclusive one-sidedness will, some day, break down because of the discrepancy between the experience type and the necessities of life. There is a great deal of truth behind the suggestion that such a man has over-worked. He has actually over-worked one part of the apparatus with which he approaches living, neglecting other parts. It is relatively certain that a marked gap between the possibilities of development indicated by the experience type and the demands of external circumstances leads to neurosis

As has been indicated already, it is possible to determine the presence or absence of imagination in an individual from the results of the test; it is, however, impossible to state whether this imagination is creative or receptive. For receptive imagination there is required only the fundamental apparatus plus occasional impulses of activating energy for stimulation. Productive imagination requires very different, more intensive and libidinous emotional currents. A novelist who writes his first two books on the basis of poetic introversion and then builds a house with the money received from royalties, employing his creative powers in its construction and wasting emotion still more on critics, may so impoverish his imaginative apparatus that he can afterward write only literature for the drawing-room. He produces stories which are extratensive, adaptable to everyone. Thenceforth, he confabulates rather than imagines.

Another example based on observations made with the test concerns a young man who chose painting as a profession because his father was an artist; he wished to be in the same profession because of admiration of his father. Both the father and the son «love the profession passionately»; it is libidinized in them. The father, having a strongly introversive experience type, is original and creative. The son, however, is predominantly extratensive and could develop a good technique in his art, but he lacks originality entirely. He is, primarily, a good copyist. His experience type does not extend far enough into the introversive sphere to produce that constellation of features which is necessary for creative work. No matter how much libido he devotes to his profession it cannot be sufficient.

Obviously, this correlation between instinct and experience type must be significant in pathology. Fixation of the libido within the realm of introversion by means of pathogenic suppressions results in what Jung originally called «introversion (see p 81).

18. Experience Type, Personality [1] and Talent.

In the discussion above it has been shown that personality and talents perceptive and, probably, imagery type. and significant elements of affect and intelligence, are all direct outgrowths of the experience type of an individual. These vast functional action patterns are intimately inter-connected and for this reason each must, to a greater or lesser degree, be subject to the same changes as the others Changes in these functional patterns can only be conditioned by intra-individual changes in experience type. The changes can be corrected and restrained somewhat by other means such as the instincts on the one hand and disciplined reasoning on the other, but not controlled. To say this in other words, changes in the functional patterns may be restrained to some degree by means of voluntary direction of that part of the ever-changing experience apparatus which has been selected for emphasis as a goal idea. «Principles» are actually instinctively fixed goal ideas which serve as protections against upheavals in the experience type, which keep these upheavals from spreading over the entire psychic life. Furthermore. disciplined reasoning itself is not completely free but is dependent on the experience type to a large degree. If disciplined thinking is to be liberated from changes in the experience type completely, it can only be done by the individual concerned sacrificing the ability to experience at all.

19. Experience Type and (Mental) Illness.

The relationship between experience type and the mental illnesses has been touched upon already; only a few remarks will be added here. The subject is so vast, and problems so numerous that our material is too small to settle the issues and many more experiments will be necessary to come to any definite conclusions.

Two possibilities must be considered· the presence of disease may cause a shift or change in the experience type, or the form of the illness may be determined *by* the experience type. As was the case before, we deal here not with the content of the thinking, but only with the manner of action of the psychic processes. These possibilities might'both be combined; this is probably very frequently the case.

In the schemes presented on page 74 manic-depressive insanity presents a striking picture, being found in the middle column only. Depression falls

[1] German = Charakter.

with the coartated types, elation with the dilated. It is conceivable that the disease has pushed the experience type toward the middle of the scheme the other possibility is that the ambiequal type is pre-existant and that there is in it the predisposition for illnesses of the nature of elation and depression. Factual grounds for either possibility may be advanced On the whole. however. the ambiequal type is quite rare. whereas elation and particularly depression are quite common. This supports the view that the disease drives the type toward the midline of the schemes. toward the ambiequal type.

On the other hand. it has long been recognized that there is a clinical relationship between manic-depressive insanity and compulsion neurosis which also falls in the midline of the scheme. Talented persons very frequently show a tendency toward elated or depressed moods for varying periods of time and to various degrees. (According to Moebius. Goethe showed this.) Definite relationship exists between genius and compulsion neurosis. (Seen in Napoleon I according to Dostojewski.) It seems likely that both of the possibilities listed above operate in manic-depressive insanity.

In schizophrenia. the results may be summarized as follows· dementia simplex belongs to the coartated type. catatonia to the ambiequal dilated type. paranoia to the introversive. and hebephrenia to the extratensive type. The various forms of the disease frequently overlap clinically, and they overlap here, too, depending upon the mixture of features in the experience type. On the whole. schizophrenics follow the pattern of experience types shown by normal subjects. More introversive races produce more typical catatonics and productive paranoid cases whose hallucinations are more kinaesthetic in type. The extratensive races produce more hebephrenoid catatonics and the paranoid cases which occur are less productive. These cases have, for the most part. auditory hallucinations.

Nothing definite can be said as yet concerning the possible influence of disease on experience type and vice versa so far as schizophrenia is concerned. It is probable that schizophrenic catastrophies, especially sudden catatonic attacks. cause sudden shifts in the experience type. Such shifts do not. however, change the experience type from its «habitual» composition sufficiently to make this change the essential determiner of the form of the psychosis. Individuals who were originally introversive become paranoid when the schizophrenic «factor . that unknown something which causes schizophrenia, gets into their psyche Those originally extratensive become hebephrenic. and those originally near the middle of the experience type scheme or definitely ambiequal become catatonics when they become schizophrenic.

Probably an acute exacerbation (in catatonia) is accompanied not only by a shift. but by a sudden dilatation of the experience type. During convalescence from an acute catatonic attack there is frequently marked coartation evidenced. often giving the impression of defect. The symptoms observed are mild depression lack of interest, resignation and automatic and apathetic mode of work. Sometimes there is a gradual dilatation of the type with the passage of time, in other cases there may be no change.

There could be greater certainty in the results of these studies if the changes in experience type in the course of normal lives were better known. Perhaps with this knowledge the problem of the age of onset of the different types of schizophrenic illnesses might be clarified. Why is it that hebephrenia occurs in puberty, catatonia between the ages of 18 and 30, paranoid states between 30 and 40, and paranoia and querulous delusional states even later?

The determination of the type of neurosis which occurs in an individual must be similar to what has been described for determination of the form of schizophrenic illnesses. On the one hand the neurosis will influence the experience type, and on the other, the experience type will be influential in determining the form of the neurosis. All individuals, whether introversive or extratensive, may develop anxiety neuroses, but nevertheless, there are differences between the conditions and these differences depend on the pre-existing experience type. The nearer the type approaches the ambiequal, the more certain it is that what has been simply fear will become compulsive anxiety. Individuals of ambiequal type have compulsion neuroses when they become neurotic at all. The following conclusions can be drawn on the basis of the study of some cases: ambiequal individuals with more introversive features suffer compulsive phantasies; those with more extratensive features show compulsive movements; those who would fall exactly in the middle column of the scheme are neurotic sceptics and pedants.

The findings in epileptic cases are of great interest. There may be some introversive features but extratensive tendencies are always more numerous in these cases. There is an increase in the absolute number of movement and of color responses and the rate of increase becomes more rapid the faster the patient deteriorates toward epileptic dementia. Color responses seem almost to constitute a measure of dementia. In epilepsy there is a constant widening of the experience type in both directions as the dementia progresses but the spread is always more to the extratensive side: this phenomenon still escapes efforts to understand it.

The organic psychoses, paresis and senile dementia, do certainly change the experience type. Introversive features decrease, extratensive features increase so that in a relatively short time the experience type arrives at ego-centric extratensivity. This is not only because the patients are in the older age groups where there is a tendency toward a shift in the extratensive direction in any case; I have two tabo-paretics between 25 and 30 who gave exactly the same results as did the older paretics.

The organic psychoses, therefore, definitely change the experience type. In all the other instances mentioned above the experience type exerts a determining influence on the form of the psychosis or neurosis. Only the form of the neurosis or psychosis is subject to this influence, not the kind of illness that will appear. The noxious etiological agent has, in itself, nothing whatever to do with the experience type.

20. The Development of the Experience-Type.

Kinaesthesias and color influences in perceiving have proved to be the representatives of essential psychic functional patterns. They are not to be considered as anything but representatives of those functions. Any other designation for them would allow too many unfounded implications Little is known of the deeper relationships of these factors to the patterns they represent, and we are not able to say which is primary and which secondary. If the origin or genesis of the experience type were known, it might be possible to give a more complete discussion of this topic, but as yet only a few connections in the extensive network of relationships have been recognized.

According to our findings, the optimal goal of development of the experience type would include:

1. Highest possible development of disciplined thinking or logical function short of coartation of introversive or extratensive features and sacrifice of the ability to experience. (Development of these functions beyond the optimal is seen in pedants and «purely intellectual» individuals.)

2. Highest possible development of capacity for introversion short of complete arrest of disciplined thinking (as seen in dreamers) and short of the destruction of the capacity for emotional adaptation (this extreme seen in abstract individuals who are «in the world but not of it»)

3. Highest possible development of capacity for extratension short of exclusion of disciplined thinking (as seen in careless, lighthearted persons) and short of suppression of the capacity for introversion (this last extreme is seen in men whose only interest is business).

In other words, the optimal goal of development is the harmonious relationship of three principles, rationality, capacity for «inner» life and emotional willingness to adapt. Various relationships are possible which, though different, may be called «harmonious».

It is fairly certain that the experience type of a small child of between two and a half to three years—though the limits of the period are not known—is ambiequal and dilated The child is markedly kinaesthetic and at the same time markedly egocentric-extratensive in experience type. Education and development of disciplined thinking coartate the type. Learning to read plays an important role in this coartation due to the fact that it teaches clear form perception.

The functioning of the three principles, disciplined thinking, introversion and extratension, already shows wide individual variations long before school age. With more or less success, disciplined thinking combats introversive day dreaming and extratensive flightiness The more marked the introversive and extratensive features in the individual are. the more they resist this coartating force; the less effective are these features, the easier it is for coartation to take place. There is a concentration of the child's energy on school work, which, when developed to the maximum, results in the ,model pupil, personality.

The easier it is for the child to learn and, even more important, the better memory he has. the more energy there will be left for introversive and extratensive features. (Memory is a function which has almost no influence on the test results.) The extreme of this case would be found in the child for whom learning is too easy, so easy that he does not attain the physiologically necessary—or at least socially necessary—degree of coartation. In such a case the child will not get the necessary practice in adaptive thinking until he is older or, perhaps, not at all.

The development of the experience type is. then, a process of coartation conditioned by the growth of disciplined thinking and taking place within certain optimal limits. The coartative and coartated types are a result of hyper-effectiveness of this process. The normal ambiequal type represents the ideal result of the development of the experience type.

The problem can be restated as follows: What causes this physiological process of coartation to vary so widely among individuals? It might be easier to answer this problem, if instead of the development of the experience type, one of the correlated patterns of function was studied. Suppose we take the imagery type. As has been pointed out earlier, the ambiequal dilated experience type as seen in the small child should be accompanied by a mixed imagery type. There should be no significant predominance of the kinaesthetic, or visual, or auditory spheres. In a two and a half year old child, one actually is quite unable to note predominance of any one sphere of imagery. Why does one child develop a visual type and another an auditory? It is possible that the determining factor is a sort of functional preparedness of certain pathways of the central nervous system. If this were found to be the case, there would remain the problem of the relationships of all the other characteristics as, for instance, in subjects who belong to the same experience type as do individuals with auditory imagery type.

V. THE USE OF THE FORM INTERPRETATION TEST IN DIAGNOSIS.

1. Practicability.

Originally this method was used exclusively as an approach to theoretical problems. The discovery that the results could be used in making diagnoses was an empirical finding which had not been looked for. The experiment became an examining test secondarily. In the first instance the diagnosis served as a control for the findings in the test. Following this, the attempt was made to make diagnosis from records obtained by colleagues from subjects quite unknown to me. I am especially indebted to Dr. E. Oberholzer for his cooperation in this work.

It was conceived that this constituted a test of the method, that is. the more correct the diagnoses, the better the method proved itself to be, even though no indication of age. sex, state of health, presence of neurosis or psychosis accompanied the protocol. Incorrect diagnoses were and still are made. This is due to the fact that clinical symptoms of primary importance may appear unimportant in the test results, and that the test indicates secondary clinical symptoms as of great importance, so that, while the individual symptoms may be correctly described, the putting together of these to form a diagnosis may be at fault.

The test is primarily a qualitative examination. The quality of symptoms can be determined from it, but the quantitative degree in which these appear remains uncertain. as does, therefore, also the relative importance of symptoms in a mixture of them Experience and practice with the test play a great role in the evaluation of quantitative importance of symptoms, but it should be possible to increase the conclusiveness of the computations in the test by means of control experiments taking up each symptom individually Other psychological methods might also be used in control research.

After a further period of development it should be possible in almost every case to come to a definite conclusion as to whether the subject is normal, neurotic, schizophrenic or has organic brain disease Even now it is possible to arrive at a clearly differentiated diagnosis in most patients, and at a specific personality diagnosis in neurotics and normals

It is important to note that the test often indicates the presence of latent schizophrenia. neuroses which are barely perceptible clinically. and constitutional mood trends. The inadequacy of the test in estimating the quantitative importance of findings can be so great that it cannot be said whether a symptom is manifest or latent. It is impossible to determine from the record of the test, in some cases, whether a schizophrenic reaction is manifest, latent, or dormant for the time being. Catatonics who have almost completely recovered may appear more obviously ill in their records than cases who are clinically obviously still quite active. Sometimes the test findings indicated as schizophrenic people who had never shown the slightest indication of the disease but who had schizophrenic parents or siblings. In contrast to these cases, there were those in whom the results of the test indicated normal or, more frequently, neurotic condition due to the subject fearing the development of psychosis because psychosis was already present in the family. These matters will be reported in later publications.

2. Possible Objections to the Test.

The use of the test for diagnostic purposes may arouse occasional objections. It might be said that the test would reduce the difficult art of diagnosis to a mechanical technic and that, eventually, every laboratory diener could produce psychograms by following certain instructions just as he stains tubercle bacilli. Such an objection would be untenable. To be able to draw conclusions from the scoring of so large a number of factors requires a great deal of practice in psychological reasoning and a great deal of experience with the test. To acquire this experience demands a great deal of clinical material for comparative study, and every person wishing to use the test has to get the experience for himself. Only studies on varied types of individuals can furnish the basis for the acquisition of experience. The test lends itself to psychiatric diagnosis only in the hands of workers capable of collecting psychologically comparable material. By collecting data from children of various ages, a teacher could make useful diagnoses concerning personality, talents and idiosyncrasies of his pupils, but would not dare to make psychiatric diagnoses on the basis of his experience.

It is to be understood that the test is primarily an aid to clinical diagnosis. The diagnosis of patients unknown to the person scoring the protocol is useful as a control as a matter of practice for the experimenter.

' The fact that the subject is taken unaware in the experiment is the basis for serious objection He settles himself for a harmless test of the imagination and what he is subjected to is far more than that. It would require a long discourse to explain the real nature of the test, and besides, such a procedure would completely disturb the «habitual» attitude and spoil the result. The management of this difficulty has to be accomplished in different ways by the individual examiner. I hope that the test will be able to discover more latent talents than poor vocational adjustments and frustrated illusions; that it will free more people of the fear of psychosis than it will load with such fears; that it will afford more relief than aggravation.

3. Computations for the Purpose of Diagnosis.

It is impossible to furnish instructions on how to reach a diagnosis from the protocol, nor is it possible to furnish any simple table for this purpose. Many factors have to be considered, such as the experience type, the evidences indicating the mood, the components of intelligence, the number of responses, the extent of the patient's cooperation, approximate reaction time, etc. In reaching a diagnosis one or the other of these factors will require more thorough study as the work goes on, until a complete diagnostic picture is developed.

There are many individual ways of going at the test which could not all be mentioned heretofore. Some of these will appear in the examples, others may be deduced from these fairly easily.

4. The Content of the Interpretations.

The content of the interpretations offers little indication as to the content of the psyche until it is considered in relation to the psychogram—granting that the results of this test for the discovery of patterns of thinking can be called psychograms. Occasionally, the content of the responses gives some information about the degree of energy the subject applies to his work and the amount of pleasure he gets from it, and indicates how adaptable he is under his working conditions. This is the case when an engineer repeatedly uses parts of machines in his responses, and when a housewife frequently mentions dress patterns. In drawing conclusions from such answers, however, one must consider all the interpretations in the protocol, and the behavior of the subject while interpreting.

Of greater importance than the above are the «complex responses». These correspond to the «complex (determined) associations» of the Jung-Riklin association experiments. Such interpretations, that is, responses which bring to light the content of the subconscious, suppressed or emotionally charged material, are extraordinarily rare. They occur most frequently in the neurotic subjects, even in them they appear frequently only when the subconscious is already in a state of upheaval, as when the subject is undergoing psychoanalysis. Schizophrenics occasionally give answers which may be considered as falling within this group, but they are rare, even more rare than in the neurotic subjects. If one is aware of the complexes of the schizophrenic subject, it is more often possible to detect such answers in their protocols. Profoundly catatonic patients, if they submit to the test at all, give more numerous complex determined responses.

The test cannot be considered as a means of delving into the unconscious. At best, it is far inferior to the other more profound psychological methods such as dream interpretation and association experiments. This is not difficult to understand. The test does not induce a free flow from the subconscious but requires adaption to external stimuli, participation of the «fonction du réel».

Certain tendencies in the subconscious are occasionally revealed by comparison of the content of the interpretations with the rest of the findings. Suppose we have two markedly introverted subjects. One of them responds with many answers indicating movement in extension (see p. 29). The other responds with movements of flexion. This difference is probably sufficient to indicate that the first subject actively struggles against his introversive tendencies in his responses, while the second surrenders himself to his imagination. If, furthermore, the first subject sees passionate struggles and the second Christ-like figures, halos, and martyrs in the blots, and if both subjects show color shock, there is justification for the conclusion that the first subject suffers from neurotic inhibitions and feelings of insufficiency against which he revolts, while the second subject considers himself quite holy and neglects his relations with the outside world. Frequently such deductions in various directions are possible, but only when the subject gives many responses, particularly many original answers. With the exception of hysterical subjects, extratensives attack the task in a practical way, and they rarely find in the plates the figures seen in dreams The psychic sphere from which the interpretations come is far removed from the sphere of their dreams.

5. The Test and Psychoanalysis.

The test cannot be used to probe into the content of the subconscious, as has been noted above. Nevertheless, it can be of some service to the psychoanalyst. In the first place, it often, and eventually will perhaps always, make possible a differential diagnosis between neurosis and latent or manifest schizophrenia. The test can clear up those unpleasant situations arising when one has an analytic patient in whom there is a suspicion of schizophrenia which cannot be dispelled. It is, furthermore, possible to relieve the minds of people plagued by a fear of insanity, and, if latent schizophrenia must be diagnosed, the analytical therapy can be modified accordingly.

Findings in the test such as detailed in the previous chapter occasionally make possible the prognosis of an analysis. The prognosis is probably more favorable in cases where kinaesthesias of extension predominate than in cases in which flexion movements are more numerous.

The existence of marked contrasts between the experience type and the usual mode of living may allow certain conclusions to be drawn concerning the genesis of the neurosis (p. 114) and concerning the indications for instituting possible activities of sublimation.

It is interesting to compare the findings of the test before and after analysis. From our material, the influence of the analysis may vary widely, probably for various reasons. Sometimes the shift in experience type is so slight that the test will continue to indicate a neurosis though it be almost entirely cured. On the other hand, many of my cases and cases of others show a considerable shift of the experience type as a result of the analysis. One of these cases is described in example 12 below, protocols being reproduced as they were obtained before and after analysis. In such cases there is an important change in the affectivity, a complete change in personality and an equalization of introversive and extratensive features.

One subject gave no color responses at all before the analysis: after a few months of treatment, he produced a number of color answers. This means that the suppressed affect became more free and the experience type more dilated. In other cases, CF responses were more numerous than FC's before analysis; after treatment there were more FC's than CF's, implying a transformation of egocentric into adaptive affectivity. The material at hand is insufficient for further conclusions but from the cases cited it can be demonstrated experimentally that analysis has a liberating, integrating, and equalizing influence.

Analysis can also change the intelligence type; this is especially apparent in the freeing of certain rigidities of apperceptive types. The rigid W type in neurotics who are constantly driven by high ambition due to feelings of insufficiency frequently disappears. Grumblers and persons given to brooding, though they may have deviations of conceptual type severe enough so that it includes Dd and Do responses, can show normal types after analysis.

Except as noted above, the importance of the test in psychoanalysis is probably more theoretical than practical. For example, certain relationships may exist between the experience type and the regression described by Freud in which patients revivify events connected with previous fixations. In such situations it may be that the whole experience type in its totality is the subject of the fixation. The question now becomes, how does this revivification of fixated experiences come about? In some cases, the experience type may have been arrested in its development at an early stage; other faculties which have nothing to do with the experience type have carried the individual in his development. Such factors would consist in intellectual training, social imitation and other factors which may be acquired independently of the experience type. In such cases, the regression is actually faulty progression. In other situations, the experience type changes because of emotional suppressions, and there is a concommitant narrowing of both introversive and extratensive features. Here there is regression in the more strict sense of the word, because the narrowed experience type corresponds to an earlier experience type in the individual. The return of the experience type to its former narrow state reactivates the entire mode of living of the earlier period. together with all its aspirations and memories. Thus the re-living of a fixated situation could take place, and the return of the libido to its former fixation would correspond to the narrowing of the experience type.

A return to an earlier experience type causing reappearance of memories of the earlier period may be seen in manics and catatonics. In exacerbations of these illnesses, even though they be years apart, one sees the same thoughts, plans and hallucinations reappear again and again, though these phenomena have apparently been entirely forgotten in the interval.

Examples.

The examples cited below give primary attention to the records of normal or healthy subjects and to border line cases. For this reason they are discussed briefly. The protocols of psychotics at the end of this section may serve as illustrations of the responses in the conditions and may be used for comparison with normal records [1].

1. Average Normal.

Female, age 26, employed.

I. Two Santa Clauses with brooms under their arms (the figures on the side)	DM+ H
Two figures, female, lifting their arms (middle)	DM+ H
II. A butterfly (frequently interpreted; must be considered F+)	WF+ A
Two marmots (red above)	DF+ A
III. Two marionette figures	WM+ H
IV. A butterfly (plate reversed, column-like middle part and neighboring wings) . .	DF— A
An ornament on a piece of furniture (Plate in normal position)	WF+ Orn. Orig.+
V. A bat	WF+ A
VI. A moth (flame-like parts at top of the figure)	DF+ A
A tree (plate reversed, whole picture) . .	WF+ Pl.
VII. Two human heads (upper third)	DF+ Hd
Two animal heads (middle third)	DF+ Ad
VIII. (No color-shock) Two bears (red)	DF+ A
Rocks (the middle figures)	DF— Obj.
IX. Two clowns or darting flames (brown above)	DM+ H
	DCF Fire

---

[1] For list of symbols and abbreviations see p. 14.

X. A rabbit's head (green medial) . . . . DF - Ad
Two caterpillars (green medial) . . . DFC - A
Two mice (gray lateral) . . . . . . DFC - A
Two pigs' heads (blue medial) . . . . DF - Ad
Two spiders (blue lateral) . . . . . DF - A

The computation shows:

Responses· 21.

W	: 5	M	: 4	H	: 4 (+)
D	: 16	F	: 14 (1—)	Hd	: 1 (+)
Dd etc.:	—	FC	: 2 (1—)	A	: 9 (8+, 1—)
		CF	: 1	Ad	: 3 (+)
		C	: 0	Pl	: 1 (+)
				Obj.	: 1 (—)
				Orn.	: 1 (+)
				Fire	: 1

F+ : 93 % (1300 ÷ 14 = 93)
A : 1200 ÷ 21 = 57 %
Orig. : 5 %+
Apperceptive : W—D
Sequence: optimally rigid.

Conclusions:

Experience type: 4 M: (2 FC + 1 CF + 0C), i. e. more introversive than extratensive features. Affective status: reactive. approachable (1 CF), not unstable to the point of moodiness or impulsiveness, stabilized by good emotional adaptability (2 FC) and by introversive features (4 M). Good capacity for empathy (4 M : 2 FC). Little ambition in intellectual make-up (21 responses, 5 W), concretely practical and adaptive (5 W, 16 D), without pettiness or pedantry (no Dd, Do, or S). The sequence is optimally rigid, the forms are very good, therefore, the conclusion that the thinking is adaptable. A marked tendency to stereotyped associative patterns (57 % A). Only one original answer, therefore little originality, constricted range of ideas, but easy adaptation to the mode of thinking of others. Neither intellectually nor emotionally egocentric. On the whole, little activation of the introversive elements, a predominance of the adaptive functions, despite introversive experience type. Not imaginative, but does not despise imagination in others.

The subject is an attendant in an insane asylum; quiet, steadfast, diligent, making no fuss about her responsible position, and very much devoted to her work

2. Sample Test of Subject of Above Average Attainments.

University graduate, age 29

I. A bat	WF+ A
Two large figures in waving coats standing near a basin	WM+ H
Plate reversed, upper lateral part: The ride on the Blocksberg[1]	Dd M+ H Orig.+
Middle above: The head of a bug	DF+ A
II. Butterfly	WF+ A
Red above: Two dwarfs moving towards each other	DM+ H
White intermediate figure: Lamp-shade . .	SF+ Obj.
III. Two waiters or men in tails holding vessels	WM+ H
Plate reversed: Enlarged head of a mosquito	WF+ A Orig.+
Plate reversed: An old woman, wash-woman, perhaps, who is holding up her hands (the feet of men usually seen are the arms of the woman, the body of the woman is formed by the male figures including all white parts which are lying in between) .	WM+ H Orig.+
Red above: The knight's head of a chess figure	DF+ A Orig.+
IV. An Indian well for elephants: above the basin, below the base	WF+ Obj. Orig.+
Middle part: The tail of an insect	DF+ Ad
Plate reversed (so that the column-like middle part is directed upwards). On both sides of the middle part: Two women with flying scarfs, dancing around a fountain (Fountain = middle part)	DM+ H Orig.+
Small black extension from middle part: Horse's feet	DdF+ Ad
Lateral extension of the whole figure: Dogs' heads	DF+ Ad
V. A bat	WF+ A
VI. The double-edged axe of Thor	WF+ Obj. Orig.+
Below, middle: Small insect pincers . . .	DdF+ Ad
Above, the flaming figures: Like flames on heraldic weapons	DF+ Obj.
Whole figure reversed: Two large profiles with large noses and Van Dyke beards .	WF+ Hd

---

[1] Witches ride on the Blocksberg

VII Upper third· Two children's heads . . . DF · Hd
Middle third. Two busts . . . . DF - Hd
Lower third: Lazy rabbits with ears drawn
backwards . . . . DF→ A Orig.—
Intermediate figure: Lamp . . . . . . SF · Obj. Orig.—
VIII. (No color-shock) red: Salamander . . . . DFC← A
Gray: Prepared skull of a deer . . . . . DF—· Ad Orig.—
Red-yellow: Butterflies . . . . DFC→ A
Yellow alone: Fool's cap . . . . DdFC← Obj. Orig.—
White between both blue parts: Segments
of a reptile . . . . SF→ Ad
IX. Intermediate figure· Beetle, the hind feet
are brown, the feelers are green . . . SF— A Orig.—
Red: Fallen rose leaves . . . . DCF+ Pl.
Green, middle: Jellyfish . . . . DdF— A Orig.—
Green, oblique: Two hares running away . DF⊥ A
X. An artistic design for dishes . . . . . . WCF+ Orn.
Gray, middle above: Larynx and trachea . DdF÷ Anat. Orig.+
Gray, above: Skeleton and part of skull,
of an animal . . . . DF+ Anat.
Intermediate figure between gray above
and red: A sea animal . . . . DSF+ A Orig.+
Gray, laterally: Two beetles . . . . . DF← A
The whole reversed: A flower. red, the
petals, inside the stamen and pistil, outside
the leaves; gray, middle: calyx . . . . WFC+ Pl. Orig.+
Blue, laterally: A figure like beetles make
under the bark of a tree . . . . . . DF+ Pl. Orig.+

Computation:

Responses: 41.

W	: 12	M : 6		H	: 6
D	: 19	F : 29 (1—)		Hd .	: 3
Dd	: 5	FC: 4		A	: 14 (1—)
S	: 5	CF: 2 (tendency to more)		Ad	: 6
		C : —			
F+	: 97 %			Pl.	: 3
A	: 49 %			Obj.	: 6
Orig.	: 41 %			Orn.	: 1
Apper-				Anat.:	2
ceptive	: W—D—Dd—S				
Sequence. loose					

The large number of F+, W, O, and M responses indicate an intelligent, and the great variability of original responses, an educated individual. Experience type: 6 M: (4 FC+ 2 CF+ 0 C) more introversive than extratensive features, relatively near the ambiequal type.

Affective Status: reactive, vigorous, obliging, good capacity for empathy, enthusiastic; allows himself to be carried away by his emotions (the forms become hazy in the colored plates). The emotional lability does not extend to impulsiveness but is quite egocentric.

Intelligence: More abstract than concrete. Has more need and greater ability for abstraction than for combination (predominantly primary W responses). More abstract than concrete thinking. The number of D responses is small in relation to the total responses and to the number of W's. The number of Dd and S answers rather too large. From this we conclude that he is able to understand quickly, but is less skillful in completing plans, more enthusiasm than endurance. The subject likes to make corrections but is not always rational in this performance. There is an unmistakable need for thoroughness and a tendency to opposition (S). Not pedantic, on the contrary he would be opposed to pedantry, though the S responses indicate stubborn opposition in his make-up sometimes leading to pedantry. Combining emotional and intellectual status we find enthusiasm for special tasks, not so much ability for continuous, patient, concrete work as for discovery of associated problems using a clear associative activity with ever-present thoroughness.

The original and animal answers reveal the broad education and the special training of the subject as well.

The subject is a naturalist, very talented, able to draw and paint. He is a keen observer and his conceptions are clear. He has a well rounded education. There is a tendency to become scattered; he is easily upset. Very thorough in everything which attracts his interest, but jumps from one subject to another easily. Emotionally he is very flexible, good rapport, both intensive and extensive. The forms indicate culture. Imagery type is visual.

3. Sample Test of Subject of Below Average Attainments.

Craftsman, age 26.

I.	A large bird (because of the wings) . . .	DWF+ A
II.	The human pelvis (black only)	DF+ Anat.
III.	Two human figures (certainly not seen as moving)	WF+ H
IV.	A degenerated heart	WF— Anat. Orig.—
V.	A butterfly	WF+ A
VI.	The head of a blindworm (upper medial end)	DF+ Ad
VII.	A butterfly (the confluent lower third) . .	DF+ A
VIII.	(No color-shock) Two bears or guinea pigs	DF+ A

IX. The body opened from neck to thighs . . WFC - Anat.
X. Cross-section of thighs (blue laterally) . . . DF - Anat. Orig.—

Computation:

Responses: 10

W	· 5 (1 definite DW, others probably DW)	M : 0	H : 1 (+)	
D	: 5	F : 9 (2—)	Hd : 0	
Dd etc.	· — (but tendency to Do)	FC: 1 (—)	A : 4 (+)	
		CF: 0	Ad : 1 (+)	
		C : 0	Anat.: 4 (—)	

F+ : 75 %
A : 50 %
Orig. : 20 % orig.—
Apper-
ceptive : DW—D
Sequence: ? (only one answer to each plate)

This subject interprets diligently and painstakingly, but has such a poverty of ideas that he gives but ten responses. The way some of the responses are given leaves the impression that he believes he has found the only possible interpretation. The forms, while not worse than those statistical methods have shown must be considered as good, are nevertheless as poor as they could be and still remain in the «good» classification. The DW responses, the 20 % original answers, the lack of M's and the tendency to confabulation indicate inferior intelligence on the borderline of feeblemindedness. The form visualization, the conceptive type (5 W, 5 D), the fact that complete human and animal figures are interpreted rather than parts of bodies, all these features indicate that the subject is not a moron.

Experience type: 0 M . 1 FC (which could as easily be CF), indicating more extratensive than introversive features. Type is strongly coartated, but the coartation is certainly not due to depression, but to diligence, that is, to a conscious effort to work accurately and to exercise disciplined reasoning. (There are no depressive features; the number of W's especially is too large for depression, and the tendency toward confabulation is too marked.)

50 % animal responses represents stereotypy which might be even greater than the animal percentage indicates. It must be considered that four of the answers were anatomical; in uneducated persons anatomical answers always indicate a more or less well developed complex concerned with the intelligence. a desire to do better.

Emotionally approachable, rather unstable, but not badly adapted to his situation. (Based on comparison between F and color responses.)

The subject is a good, practical workman. He is unintelligent but is able to adapt himself to various kinds of work. He has little initiative, is stereotyped, but is diligent, ambitious, and emotionally adaptable. He appears to be much more intelligent in his ordinary living than in the test: this is because of the ability he has to adapt himself to circumstances. He cannot do precision work, nor work of high quality.

4. Feebleminded Individual.

Imbecile, age 17.

I. Below medial: The mouth of a fish . . . DoF— Ad Orig.—
Above medial: Two horns . . . . DF+ Ad
II. A bat (the black parts) . . . . DF— A Orig.—
Red above: A foot . . . . DF— Hd
III. Two Negro heads . . . . DoF— Hd
The legs of the figures: Feet . . . . . DoF+ Hd
IV. An animal (the lateral extensions designated
as legs) . . . . DWF— A Orig.—
The most lateral extensions: Two wings . DoF+ Ad
V. A bat . . . . WF+ A
VI. The flaring figures above: Crow's wings . . DoF+ Ad
VII. The confluent part of the lower third: Just
like a river . . . . DdF— Map Orig.—
VIII. Red: Dogs . . . . DF+ A
Red-yellow: Wings . . . . DF— Ad
IX. Green: Russia (because Russia is usually
green on maps) . . . . DC— Map Orig.—
Brown above: Two horns from an animal . DoF+ Ad
X. Green medial: Fish . . . . DF— A
Yellow medial: Sun and moon . . . . . DCF— Sun
Blue middle: Two animal heads . . . . . DF+ Ad

Computation:

Responses: 18.

W	: 2 (DW)	M : 0		H : 0	
D	: 9	F : 16 (9+, 7—)		Hd : 3 (2+, 1—)	
Dd	: 1	FC: 0		A : 5 (2+, 3—)	
Do	: 6	CF: 1		Ad : 7 (5+, 2—)	
		C : 1		Map: 2 (—)	
F+	: 56 %			Sun : 1	
A	: 66 %				
Orig.	: 27 %—				
Apperceptive	: D—Do				
Sequence:	Relatively orderly.				

The subject was in a special class until one year before the test was done. Comparison of this with the previous test shows a smaller number of F and W responses, a larger number of Do, original answers of poor quality (O-), high animal percentage, the poor apperceptive type, predominance of Hd and Ad over H and A, and finally, an egocentric extratensive experience type. All of these individual factors are expressions of defects which in their summation make up the typical findings in feebleminded subjects. The relative rarity of color responses and the insignificance of the tendency to confabulate indicate that we deal in this case not with an excitable but with a torpid imbecile.

5. Hypomanic Mood.

Female, age 45.

I. A bat	WF+ A	
Two warriors in armor battling each other	DM+ H	
II. Two clowns dancing	WM+ H	
Two animal heads (black only)	DF+ Ad	
Two squirrels (red above)	DF— A	
III. Two clowns (red above)	DFC— H Orig.—	
Two writers advising each other (the black)	WM- H	
IV. Middle part: An Eskimo	DF— H Orig.—	
The whole plate is an animal from the bottom of the sea, a squid, perhaps	WF+ A	
The plate reversed: A fountain statue, someone sitting on a stick	WM+ H Orig.+	
V. A bat	WF+ A	
Or an airplane	WF— Obj.	
VI. A jungle animal	WF— A	
VII. The confluent lower third: An aeroplane	DF— Obj.	
Middle third: Animal heads	DF+ Ad	
VIII. Blue and gray together: A carrousel	DFC+ Obj. Orig.+	
An escutcheon	WCF— Obj. Orig.—	
Laterally: Two bears	DF+ A	
IX. Brown: Two clowns who want to play together	DM+ H	
Green: A large bear	DF+ A	
X. Green medial: A rabbit	DF+ A	
Yellow medial: The inside part of a narcissus	DCF+ Pl.	
Yellow medial: The mast of a ship	DF+ Obj.	
Blue: Sponges from the bottom of the sea	DFC+ Pl.	
Gray laterally: Crabs	DF— A	
Blue middle: Like an animal on a coat of arms	DFC— A Orig.—	

Computation:

Responses: 26.

W	: 9	M	: 5	H	: 7 (2—)
D	: 17	F	: 15 (5 --)	Hd	: 0
		FC:	4 (1—)	A	: 10 (3—)
F--	: 66 %	CF:	2	Ad	: 2
A	: 46 %	C	: indicated	Pl.	. 2
Orig.	: 20 % ±			Obj.:	5 (3—)

Apper-
ceptive : W—D
Sequence: orderly.

Experience type: 5 M (4 FC. 2 CF, C indicated). The subject showed a reaction the opposite of color shock, experiencing a real joy and freedom in interpreting color. The experience type is almost ambiequal. The M responses appear to be secondary; she demonstrated the movements vividly but frequently pointed out the human figure which moved only later. Furthermore, the movements are not as clearly conceived as those in examples 1 and 2 above.

The F+% is too low for the normal ambiequal and the animal percentage is too high. There is also some appearance of confabulation, especially in the responses for the colored plates.

Intelligence: An energetic, generous type, without pettiness. More whole than detail responses. The original answers are not good for the most part. Such a result could be combined with 5 M's only in case of manic mood.

Emotionally unstable, excited. There is indication of impulsiveness. Egocentric extratensive but at the same time full of a desire to participate, to talk, and to be active.

The extratensive features of the personality are more activated than the introversive. This may be seen from the fact that the introversive factors do not correspond to one another; normal subjects have a greater number of good original responses if they achieve 5 M's. The kind of original answers given reveals the subject to be uneducated.

The subject is mildly cyclothymic and is generally in a hypomanic state. Short depressive phases occur only rarely. She is usually full of energy with a considerable urge toward activity but flighty and inconsiderate as are the egocentrics. Because she is so flighty, and because of the lack of inhibitions she appears less intelligent than she really is.

6. Introversive Tendency in an Individual in Extratensive Occupation.

Male, age 29.

I. A vampire	WF + A	
A window display; skirt, corset, draperies .	WF + Obj. Orig. +	
Half a man (on the inner side of the lower half of the middle)	DF + Hd	
Erlking with the child under his coat (the side figures)	DM + H	
Reversed: middle above: An idol	DF + H	
Middle, black on black: A crocodile lying on its belly	DF + A Orig. +	
II. Two carnival clowns	WM + H	
Lamp (intermediate figure)	SF + Obj. +	
The upper half of the black part: Roosters	DdF + A	
III. Traveling salesmen	WM + H	
Red above: Pinscher (dog)	DF + A	
The black middle figures, reversed: Two Negro heads	DF + Hd	
Breast and arms of the figures with head: Stuffed birds	DF — A	
Red middle: Modernistic butterfly tie . .	DFC + Obj.	
IV. Used boots	DF + Obj.	
Laterally: Snakes	DF + A	
Above, small detail: Ivy leaf	DdF + Pl. Orig. +	
The whole figure: Moritz, from Busch's story of Max and Moritz, as he falls into the pond	WM + H Orig. +	
V. A bat	WF + A	
Head: A hare's head	DF + Ad	
Profile at lower edge of wing: Sleeping night watchman	DdF + Hd Orig. +	
Middle of bat: the head without the ears and legs: A Zurich policeman in civil clothes. I know him	DdF + H Orig. +	
VI. Uppermost part: Light buoy	DF + Obj.	
Large part: A stretched ox-hide	DF + Obj.	
Plate placed on narrow edge: Southern coast of U. S. A. including Florida	DF + Map	
VII. An exhibit of larvae	WF + Ad Orig. +	
Below: A carnival article with a buckle in the middle	DF — Obj.	
Reversed: Two danseuses whose head-dresses touch each other in the back	WM + H Orig. +	

VIII. A Japanese dignitary: gray hat: the inter-
　　　mediate space between gray and the two
　　　blue halves is the face: the blue and yel-
　　　low-red parts are the dress . . . . 　　DFC ± H Orig.+
　　Laterally: Mice . . . . 　　DF+ A
　　Yellow-red reversed: An old Swiss military
　　　tunic . . . . 　　DFC+ Obj. Orig.+
　　Or two lungs . . . . 　　DFC— Anat.
IX. Witches with long fingers dancing over hell　WCF+ Hell
　　　　　　　　　　　　　　　　　　　　　DM+ H

　　On the inside of the green figure, at the
　　　border of the brown: The head of an
　　　ostrich . . . . 　　DF+ Ad
　　Also the green: A torn bagpipe . . . . . 　　DF+ Obj. Orig.+
X. Red and medial gray together: Drunken
　　　firemen colliding with a post (above, gray)　DM+ H Orig.+
　　Blue laterally: Two cornflowers . . . . 　　DFC+ Pl.
　　Green, middle: Modern hair comb with
　　　ornament . . . . 　　DF+ Obj. Orig +
　　Gray laterally, conceived together with blue
　　　middle: Bowl of a pipe . . . . . . 　　DdF+ Obj. Orig.+
　　Blue middle: A chat between two foxes who
　　　are in a gorge (just the heads) . . . . 　　DF+ Ad

Computation:

Responses: 41.

W	: 9	M :	7	H	: 10
D	: 26	F :	28 (2—)	Hd	: 4
Dd	: 5	FC:	5 (1—)	A	: 8 (1—)
S	: 1	CF:	1 (tendency to more)	Ad	: 3

F+	: 93 %		Plant: 2
A	: 27 %		Obj. : 11 (1—)
Orig.	: 34 %+		Anat.: 1 (—)
Apper-			Map : 1
ceptive	: W—D		Hell : 1

Sequence: optimally rigid.

This full record is included here to illustrate the very adaptable intelligence as it shows in the test. The subject is a member of a talented family
who became a merchant more because of external circumstances than of his
own desires. Most typical finding is the sequence of F and M responses; frequently the M's appear only after a number of F's are given. It is character-

istic that all the answers are good forms: this is not so much the result of a
wealth of engrams as the distinctive availability of appropriate associations
and a marked facility in putting together abstract associative processes with
processes of combination. At the same time there is optimal rigidity of succession. There is no stubborn insistence in the attempt to make W responses, but the preference for D's which is typical in individuals of a concrete
frame of mind. This concrete mode of thinking is also expressed in the eleven
object responses. The original responses, like the other reactions, show a
peculiar mixing of concrete thinking and imagination. However, these answers never show any tendency toward confabulation. The O answers are
numerous and come from various fields of interest. As for the other responses, here and there a few banalities appear, answers which are «too
easy» for the subject in comparison to the quality of the total result; an
example of these is the «modernistic tie». On the whole, the subject has a
rich experience type with marked introversive traits which have not been
cultivated because of lack of time. Life imposes strong demands on him for
disciplined thinking. The subject has «orderly» emotional make-up with a
well developed capacity for rapport, both intensive and extensive, emotional
adaptability is particularly good. The good control of emotions is shown,
furthermore, by those answers in which the colored figures and the white
intermediate spaces are jointly interpreted almost as though they were perceived like placards. No evidence of pedantry or grumbling tendency. The
introversive trends, the availability of associations and the emotional adaptability taken together form the basis for a certain talent for humor in the
subject. He is a good observer and reports what he has seen and experienced
in an original manner.

7. Imaginative Individual.
Female, age 36.

I. Two men swearing something on an altar .	WM+ H Orig.+	
II Two young dogs juggling something on their noses	WF+ A Orig.+	
III. Two jilted suitors who are meeting each other: they hold bouquets in their hands	WM+ H	
IV. Reversed: middle part: A tiny king from a fairy tale. He is greeting two queens in waving veils who approach from the right and left	DM+ H Orig.+	
Placed on narrow edge: Swan swimming along the bank of a river	DF+ A Orig.+	
Likewise: The extensions usually considered as boots, dogs' heads, etc.: A bent over old woman standing in front of a tomb .	DM+ H Orig.+	

Laterally: Two profiles of vagabonds with
large, pendant lips . . . . DF— Hd
V. A flying rabbit . . . . WF— A
VI. A monument to a soldier . . . . DF+ Obj.
Laterally: Two small busts, just like in a
memorial street . . . . DdF+ Obj. Orig.+
VII. Two women's heads with rococo hairdress
pointing upwards . . . . DF+ Hd
Two animal heads (upper and middle thirds) DF+ Ad
VIII. A bear climbing a tree-stump . . . . . DF+ A
A fairy tale motif stylized . . . . WFC+ Style
A fire at the bottom . . . . DCF+ Fire
Blue: A buried treasure . . . . DF+ Obj. Orig.
Gray: The root of the tree under which the
treasure is buried . . . . DF+ Pl.
Red: The animals guarding the treasure . . DF+ A
Reversed: The whole is the head of a fly
magnified . . . . WFC— A Orig.—
IX. Brown: Fencing soldiers wearing pointed
helmets . . . . DM+ H
Plate on narrow edge, green: A child taking
a walk with a doll . . . . DM+ H
Red (plate in same position): Head of a man
(upper red part) . . . . DF+ Hd
The whole reversed: Eruption of Aetna . . WCF+ Aetna
X. Red and gray: Women with gray heads
walking toward each other . . . . . DM+ H
Gray, laterally: Beetle . . . . DF+ A
Blue: Crabs or sea-anemone . . . . . . DF+ A
Green, medial: Sea-horse . . . . DF+ A

Computation:

Responses: 27.

W	: 7	M : 7	H	: 7
D	: 19	F : 16	Hd	: 3
Dd	: 1	FC: 2 (1—)	A	: 9
		CF: 2	Ad	: 1
F+	: 100 %	C : indicated	Obj.	: 3
A	: 36 %		Plant	: 1
Orig.	: 30 %+		Fire, Aetna: 2
Apper-			Style	: 1
ceptive	: W—D partially combined			
Sequence: optimally rigid				

Experience type: 7 M · 12 FC + 2 CF · C indicated. There is great ability to make experiences, to experience. Definite introversive features with strong features of extratension at the same time. M and C responses are very well visualized. Original answers are quite variable and banal responses are completely lacking, leading to the conclusion that subject has marked individuality and has developed it by effort. Wealth of associations which are available. The relation of W and D responses and their sequence indicate presence of concrete, practiced logic, without grumbling or pedantry. Wholes and details are partially combined because of the wealth of associations. There are several typical combined W's. No confabulation. The forms are very clearly conceived. The interpretations are pleasant indicating enjoyment of form and color.

The sharply conceived forms are worked in with associative material having its origin in fairy tales and similar sources in the associative process so that the tendency to combine is stronger and more emotionally attractive than the tendency to make abstractions. This is typical of «imagination» and shows that this function is receiving active attention from the subject, and that there is present in the subject a capacity for productive imagination. The imagery type is distinctly visual and, at the same time, strongly kin-aesthetic. Auditory imagery is much less in evidence.

Affectivity: No color shock, therefore no suppression of extratensive features. Good emotional approach to people and capacity for empathy and the emotional life is strong and impulsive, disturbed by the egocentric qualities of the affect which are at least as strong as the introversive qualities mentioned above. This leads to affective lability and to moods in which the impulsiveness is more important. The emotional life is, however, powerfully stabilized by the introversive features of the subject. The rapport is more intensive than extensive.

The subject is from a talented family and is educated and intelligent with very good capacity for synthesis. Confabulation is absent, but the factors making for combination (synthesis) become so powerful in the moody spells which sometimes appear that they lead to the evolution of «forebodings» and like experiences. The visual imagery is vivid leading to 100 % F+. The subject does not draw but has a fine feeling for composition. Enjoys bright colors.

8. Pedant.

Female, age 30. Housework.

I. Two wings	. . . .	DoF+ Ad
II. Two bears' heads (black alone)	. . . . .	DF+ Ad
III. Two monkey heads	. . . .	DoF+ Ad
IV. Skin of an animal	. . . .	WF+ A
V. Bat	. . . .	WF+ A

VI Two heads (Plate reversed, the upper part of the figure): There are two clear profiles with Van Dyke beards. (The whole is often interpreted as two speakers turning their backs on each other) . . . . DoF+ Hd
VII. Confluent lower third: Butterfly . . . . DF+ A
VIII. Two guinea pigs . . . . DF— A
IX. Brown elevations medially: Two owls . . . DdF— A Orig.—
Red diagonal: Head of a cat . . . . . . DF+ Ad
X. Green middle: Head of a hare . . . . . DF+ Ad
Gray middle: Two Indian heads . . . . . DF+ Hd
Gray laterally: Cockroach . . . . DF+ A

Computation:

Responses: 13.

W	: 2	M :	0	H	:	0
D	: 7	F .	13 (1—)	Hd	:	2
Do	: 3 (tendency	FC:	0	A	:	6
	to more)	CF:	0	Ad	:	5
Dd	: 1	C .	0			

F— : 93 %
A : 85 %
Orig. : 8 %—
Apperceptive : D—Do
Sequence: Indication of reversal

The experience type is completely coartated by conscientiousness and diligence. Modest, quiet, emotionally stable. There is stereotypy, poverty of ideas and lack of originality. No grumbling. Very strict with herself. Little capacity for affective rapport, but not depressed. This is the test of a housewife and such findings are not infrequently seen in this group, namely, they are practical, intelligent except for the restrictions of pedantry and the fact that the intelligence has been stereotyped early and is quite unassuming.

9. Normal, Advanced Age.

Female, age 80. Well-preserved mentally.

I. Plate reversed: Flower vase . . . . . . DF+ Obj.
Plate upright: A ship with two people (upper part) . . . . DF— Obj. Orig.—

The whole plate. A butterfly . . . . . .   WF   A

The small black spots all around: Flies and
  mosquitoes . . . .   DdF   A Oriz

Two dark spots in the black: Eyes .   .   DdF   Hd Oriz.

The whole plate: A modern bomb . . . .   WF   Obj. Orig.

II. Red: Two birds (the nose of the faces =
  the beaks. The red extensions running in-
  to the black = the feet) . . . .   DF- - A Oriz. -

The black: Two animal heads . . . . .   DF - A

Red radiating figure: Butterflies . . .   DF - A

Plate reversed: Also animal heads (the black)   DF - A

III. Acrobats (not visualized as moving, the arms
  are taken for legs) . . . .   DF+ H

Red outer figures: Animals, dogs looking at
  their tails . . . .   DF+ A

Black (the legs of the figures): Fish . . .   DF+ A

Black middle figures: Rabbits . . . . .   DF+ A

IV. A monster, because everything is ‹together› .   WF - A

Middle part: An owl . . . .   DF+ A

Plate on narrow edge, the ends of the boots:
  A woman with a bag full of wood on her
  back. Not seen as moving . . . . . .   DF+ H Orig.+

V. A butterfly . . . .   WF+ A

VI. The body of a butterfly . . . . . .   WF— A Orig.—

VII. Again a butterfly (lower confluent third) .   DF+ A

Upper and middle third together: An animal,
  just like a leaping dog . . . . . .   DF— A

VIII. «It's pretty.» A wild boar (red) . . . .   DF+ A

Blue and gray: Butterfly . . . . . .   DF— A Orig.—

IX. Between the brown and green: Head of a
  horse . . . .   DF+ Ad

Red diagonal: Head with pipe in the mouth   DF+ Hd

X. Gray laterally: Beetle, mouth like that of
  a pig . . . .   DF+ A

Blue laterally: A beetle with all horns . .   DF— A

Gray middle: Toads . . . .   DF— A

Blue middle: The heads of two dogs . . .   DF+ Ad

Green laterally: A sheep lying down . . .   DF+ A

Yellow in middle: The head of a child, in
  a cloud . . . .   DF— Hd

Computation:

Responses: 31.

W	: 5 (3—)	M : 0		H	: 2
D	: 24	F : 31 (11—)		Hd	: 3 (2-)
Dd	: 2	FC: 0		A	: 21 (7—)
		CF: 0		Ad	: 2
F+	: 65 %	C : 0		Obj..	3
A	: 74 %				
Orig.	: 26 % -				
Apper-					
ceptive	: W—D				
Sequence:	mixed				

This case was diagnosed «blind» and the diagnosis proved to be wrong. The disparity between the experience type and the form visualization led me to assume latent schizophrenia or schizophrenia which had reached a level of good preservation as the most probable diagnosis. Later cases showed, however, that similar results may be obtained from aged subjects otherwise normal. I had no data as to the age of the subject when the diagnosis was made.

Coartation of experience type. Unclear forms. Marked stereotypy.

Neuroses.

10. Hysteria.

Female, age 30.

I. Butterfly	WF+ A
II. Two dogs doing tricks. «As for the red, I have no idea what it can be»	DF+ A
III. Two men with hats in their hands greeting each other	WM+ H
IV. A polyp	WF+ A
V. A sort of moth	WF+ A
VI. Just like a turtle	WF+ A
VII. Just like the pelvis of a woman	WF— Anat.
VIII. A sheep	DF+ A

«God, what colors! Funny! I don't know a thing!»

IX. A sort of head (between brown and green) DF – A
I really don't know what to say. A funny
concoction of colors and figures.»

X. Just like at the bottom of the sea. sea-plants DCF + Plant

Computation:

Responses: 10.

W	: 6	M : 1		H	: 1	
D	: 4	F : 9 .1—+		Hd	: 0	
		FC: 0		A	: 7	
F-+	: 86 %	CF· 1		Ad	: 0	
A	: 70 %	C . strongly indicated		Anat.: 1 (—)		
Orig.	. 0 %			Plant: 1		

Apper-
ceptive : W—D
Sequence: ? (only one answer each)

Color shock very significant. Marked avoidance of color. Type is markedly coartated. Slight tendency to perceive kinaesthesias, marked tendency toward color answers, that is, more extratensive than introversive features. The extratensive features are, however, markedly restricted by the affectively determined uncertainty in the patient. Labile, impulsive, emotional, unpredictable, little emotional understanding. Poor education and unoriginal (no original responses). Rather marked stereotypy.

11. Neurasthenia.

Male, age 37.

I. Pelvis	WF— Anat.
Two hands reaching for something	DoM+ Hd
Plate on narrow edge, the wing: A head in	
Pope's tiara	DdF+ Hd Orig.+
II. A human pelvis	WF— Anat.
Black: Two pairs of bloomers	DF+ Obj. Orig.+
Reversed: Two chopped, bleeding bodies . .	DCF+ Hd Orig.
Black diagonal: Two muffs	DF+ Obj. Orig.+
III. Two Homunculi	DF+ H
Two fish	DF+ A
Middle: Butterfly	DF+ A
Plate reversed, middle figures: Two ultra-	
degenerated heads	DF+ Hd
Red laterally: Little devil or dog	DF+ A

IV. The whole plate: A coat of arms . . .   W F— Escutcheon
    The point of the boot. Crocodile . . . .   DF — A
    Laterally· Snake . . . .   DF— A
    The point of the boot: Head of a dog . . .   DF— Ad
    Middle column: Chess figure, a castle . .   DF— Obj. Orig.+
    Black, inside the boot: Either a satyr or a
      monk . . . .   DdF+ Hd Orig.+
    Uppermost part: Griffin, seen from the front   DF+ A Orig.—
    Point of boot, held vertically: Woman bent
      over a book . . . .   DM+ H Orig.+
    The small neighboring edges· A pile of
      sheaves of grain . . . .   DdF— Obj. Orig.+
    A small contour: A human face . . . . .   DdF+ Hd Orig.+
    The heel of the boot: A poplar . . . . .   DdF— Pl. Orig.+
    Next to the upper part, held diagonally: A
      clown's face . . . .   DdF+ Hd Orig.+

V. A bat . . . .   WF+ A
   Reversed: Butterfly . . . .   WF— A
   Plate on narrow edge. An old woman carry-
     ing two umbrellas under her arm . . .   WM+ H Orig.+
   At upper edge of wing of bat: A human
     profile, with beginning cancer of nose .   DF+ Hd
   The ends of wings of the bat: Two gnawed
     calf bones . . . .   DdF+ Obj. Orig.+

VI. Church flags (the whole plate) . . . . .   WF+ Obj. Orig.+
    The two extensions, lateral and below the
      large blot: Two men kneeling . . . .   DdM+ H Orig.+
    Middle line: Curling iron . . . .   DdF+ Obj. Orig.+

VII. A butterfly (confluent lower third) . . .   DF+ A
     Middle third: Bears' heads chopped off . .   DF+ Ad
     Upper part: Degenerated human heads . .   DF+ Hd
     Upper and middle third together: Human
       pelvis . . . .   DF— Anat. Orig.—

VIII. Two small young bears . . . .   DF+ A
      «Each bear is stepping on the wing of a
        butterfly with one of its feet» . . . .   DFC+ A
      Two blue flags . . . .   DFC+ Obj.
      Gray above: A coat of arms . . . . . .   DF— Escutcheon
      «Something between a woman's bloomers   DF— Obj. Orig.—
        and a pelvis with skin removed . . . .   DCF— Anat. Orig.—
      (The red and yellow butterfly reversed.)

IX. A skeleton with spine . . . .   WCF— Anat.

On narrow edge, red: A head chopped off,
something is flowing from the nose . . . DF - Hd

Green: A head, cracked in the back and
opened The head is cut off at the neck . DF   Hd

The brown parts reversed: Two person-
greeting each other effusively the brown
medial humps are the heads, the horns
are the gesticulating hands) . . . . . DM + H Orig.—

Very small parts of the figure: Two tilted
pots . . . . DdF— Obj. Orig. —

And two candles . . . . DdF— Obj. Orig.—

In the middle line, in the region of the red:
A cross with a boy tied to it . . . . DdM - H Orig.+

X. Blue: Squids . . . . DF+ A

Gray laterally: Two beetles . . . . . DF + A

Green above: A magnet . . . . . . DF— Obj. Orig +

Blue middle: Two men holding to each other
over an abyss . . . . DM+ H Orig.+

Gray above middle: Two mice standing on
their hind legs . . . . DF— A

Between the «mice», using the gray parts,
too: The Dalai-Lama, just the head . . . DdF+ Hd Orig.+

Computation:

Responses: 55.

W	: 8 (4—)	M :	7	H	:	7
D	: 33	F ·	43 (10—)	Hd	:	12
Dd	: 13	FC:	2	A	:	14 (2--)
S	: 0	CF·	3	Ad	:	2
Do	· 1	C :	0	Anat.	:	5 (—)
				Obj.	:	12 (3—)
F+	: 77 %			Coat of		
A	: 29 %			arms	:	2 (—)
Orig.	: 50 % ±			Plant	:	1
Apper-						
ceptive	. W—D—Dd					
Sequence: mixed						

Intelligence: Capability for making abstractions and combinations is small. The number of whole responses is small compared with the number of M's and original answers. A person who grasps details. In spite of this, the subject cannot be said to be practical minded because 50 % original answers are present and because of the numerous Dd responses. The combination of the latter with the poorly interpreted W leads to the conclusion that there is a tendency toward indolence, sluggish opportunism, in reasoning. Experience type: 7 M: (2 FC · 3 CF · 0 C). i. e., rather marked introversive features with extratensive features less marked. The color answers are for the most part CF, therefore, the affectivity is labile and egocentric. No significant impulsiveness but subject is temperamental and moody, irritable and sensitive. There is emotional understanding present in this person, but it is submerged by the egocentricity.

The number and the kind of original answers is important: original responses make up practically 50 % of the interpretations. Nevertheless, the subject is not imaginative. He enjoys making interpretations, but his interpretations do not show the combinatory character typical of the really, imaginative person. The type of the original responses shows that the subject is not a specialist.

The man is not imaginative, but is certainly given to fantasy. The content of the original answers reveals to some extent the subject matter of these fantasies, to wit, women, female dress, questions of degeneration, sado-masochistic themes (the bodies hacked off and bloody, the boy crucified), and finally, religious questions

The M responses are based on flexion kinaesthesias for the most part — bent women and men. This reveals the passive individual who is simply resigned to his «fate».

His intelligence is passive and grasps only what crosses its path and pleases. He behaves passively in regard to his own introversive and extratensive features. He sinks into his own fantasies as easily as he is influenced by his companions or is controlled by his moods. He succumbs without resistance to hypochondriacal introspections, in fact to his whole illness. His activities consist in self-torture: his life is that of a dreamer apart from the world about him, interested in very few things.

The «neurasthenia» is, in reality, primarily arrest of development. The whole psychic life of the patient is very like that of a day-dreaming child. There are no signs of schizophrenia.

12. Compulsion Neurosis.

Professional Man, age 28.

I Two bears' heads	. . . .	DoF+ Ad
The body of a butterfly	. . . . . .	DF+ Ad
Lower point: Female sex organs	. . . .	DdF— Sex
The small figures above: Uvula	. . . .	DF— Anat. Orig.—
Laterally: individual spots: Splinters of shrapnel	. . . .	DdF+ Obj.

Intermediate figure: The wings of a butterfly   SF   Ad Org

The wings: Halves of open umbrella . . .   DF   Obj. Org

The lateral figure: Two reclining women   DM · H

Darker figure, inside the middle part: Dev-
ilish figure, with hands hanging down .   DM · H Orig.—

The whole middle figure: A woman's figure
with legs tightly pressed together . . .   DM   H

II. Two dancing figures holding up their hands
(without red) . . . .   DM · H

Red below: Half sun . . . .   DCF   Sun

Lateral contour: Head of a man . . . .   DdF · Hd

The stripes on the inner side of the black:
Wings . . . .   DdF÷ Ad

Black: Animal heads . . . .   DF — Ad

Intermediate figure: Oil lamp . . . . .   SF — Obj.

III. Waiters in frocks in a caricatured position.
taking off their hats. Their legs are also   WM — H

fish . . . .   DF · A

Above red: Small monkeys, sitting . . .   DF — A

Black middle figures: Mice . . . . . .   DF — A

IV. Part of an elephant (laterally) . . . . .   DF + Ad

The same: Two gnarled branches . .   DF — Pl.

Or measuring worms . . . .   DF — A

Middle column: Part of the body of a
butterfly . . . .   DF — Ad

The whole is an animal skin . . . . . .   WF · A

Laterally, below the lateral extensions together with outer contour of the boot: An
Eskimo in a sleeping-sack . . . . . .   DM — H Orig. +

The whole is also a figure on a chair . . .   WM+ H

Plate on narrow edge: A woman walking,
bent over . . . .   DM+ H Orig.—

Intermediate figure: Figures cut by a fret-
saw . . . .   SF — Obj. Orig.+

V. A bat . . . .   WF+ A

Below: Sexual organ opened up . . . .   DdF— Sex Orig.—

Lateral extensions: Legs in sport socks . .   DoF + Hd Orig.—

Under the bat's wings: Profile with bushy
eyebrows. . . . .   DdF+ Hd Orig.+

Thin lateral extensions: Strongly magnified
legs of insects . . . .   DdF+ Ad

End of the thick extensions: Bear's paw . .   DdF+ Ad

Head of bat: Head with derby hat . . . .   DdF+ Hd

VI. Cross, crucifix	DF∓ Obj.
The whole plate: Animal skin	WF± A
The flame above: Bird's wings	DF± Ad
At the base of the cross: Moss or snow	DFC± Moss
The small points, laterally: Eagles' heads in modern lapidary style	DdF+ Ad
VII. Upper third: Child's head	DF+ Hd
Middle below: Butterfly	DF+ A
Middle third: Bears' heads	DF± Ad
Plate reversed: Clouds on which God, the Father, is enthroned	WF+ Picture Orig.+
Lower third: Foetus	DF— Anat. Orig.—
Middle part: Cat ready to jump	DF— A Orig.+
VIII. Mice (red)	DF± A
Blue: A kind of crystal growing out of a rock	DCF+ Obj
Gray above: Dog's body stretched out	DF+ A Orig.+
Intermediate part between the two extensions: Thorax	SF± Anat.
Gray: Deer horns	DF+ Ad
Also the middle: Clothes, laundry, or something like that	DCF+ Obj.
IX. Claws of a stag beetle	DoF+ Ad
Figure with sabres	DM± H
Green transverse: A man with glasses, the hair is combed back, the head is seen moving	DM∓ Hd Obj.+
Reversed: The whole is like a flower	WCF∓ Pl.
Middle figure: Bust	DF+ Obj.
In the middle, between the green and red parts: Something smoking	DdCF Smoke
Red transverse: A child bundled up	DF± H
Middle of intermediate figure: A central light which radiates and forms figures	WFC+ Abst. Orig.+
X. Blue laterally: Sea animals, like crabs	DF± A
Blue middle: Two steers	DF— A
Green: Caterpillars	DFC+ A
Green middle, pale parts: Sexual organ of a woman	DdF— Sex
Gray above: Small animals with eyes and mouth	DF+ A
The gray stick above: Mast	DF+ Obj.
Gray laterally: Like a mouse	DF— A

The red. Meat . . . . DCF   Meat
An extension of the red. A squirrel turning
  around . . . . BF   A Orig
Green middle, reversed. The head of a beetle
  with two large eyes . . . . . . DF · Ad Orig

Computation:

Responses: 71

W	: 8	M · 10		H	: 10	
D	: 44	F : 52 (8--)		Hd	: 6	
Dd	: 12	FC: 3		A	: 17 (3-	
S	: 4	CF 6		Ad	: 15	
Do	: 3	C : indicated		Obj.	: 9	
				P'ant	: 2	
F--	: 85 %			Anat.	: 3 (2--)	
A	: 45 %			Sex	: 3 (--)	
Orig.	: 24 % ±			Picture:	1	
Apper-				Sun		
ceptive	: W—D—Dd			Moss		
Sequence· on the whole. rather loose				Meat		}
				Smoke		
				Abst.	: 1	

The experience type is broad: 10 M (3 FC + 6 CF + C indicated) The
type is nevertheless doubtlessly coartated. The M responses appear only after
a few forms have been given. The conscious searching for interpretations
causes the suppression of the tendency to indulge his impulsive responses.
This indicates suppression of the introversive features. Color. on the other
hand, when it is involved in interpretations, gives rise to poor form visualization; it becomes uneven and irregular. Red is avoided except for Plate VIII
where the distinct animal figure is the first thing the eye falls upon. Except
for the anatomical answers, the form visualization is clear. The anatomical
and original responses indicate strong and conscious intellectual ambitious-
ness. There is a wealth of associations loosely connected; associations are
available and clear. Considering these last features, stereotypy is too marked
and this is due to that the fact that the subject tries to interpret sharp forms
by conscious effort. The apperceptive type suffers on this account. there is too
rapid a shift from W to D and the succession loses itself in Dd responses
too rapidly. The conscious control of interpretations permits 3 Do responses
to creep into the results The case shows a clear lack of the proper distribution of the energy of logical function on important and unimportant matters,
an insufficiency of the ability to make abstractions, and there is the ambition to give a large quantitiy of answers thus allowing banal interpretations

to appear. On the whole, there is a certain scattering which. however, does not give the impression of being schizophrenic in character.

Affectivity is very active, egocentric features are far more active than adaptive ones. The capacity for emotional understanding is not very great and is liable to be overwhelmed by the egocentric affect. It is clear that the affective instability is severe enough to include impulsive reactions. rages, stubbornness, emotional outbursts and various moods.

Introversive features are. without doubt, subjugated to and suppressed by conscious functions. Extratensive features are under similar control, but every now and then escape control to give rise to sudden impulsive outbursts. Both introversive and extratensive tendencies should be subject to a controlling mechanism according to the outline of the pathology of neurosis given earlier and we find that this is the case here. The «active energy» is not directed toward either the introversive or the extratensive features of the personality, but acts primarily in accentuating the conscious functions. The diagnosis of compulsion neurosis can be made in this case quite definitely for the following reasons, there is suppression of affective response, a coartative process is certainly active. the experience type is almost ambiequal, and finally there is a tendency to give Do responses and toward exaggerated self-control. Furthermore, it can be concluded that the compulsions are more introversive than extratensive since the introversive features are more easily aroused (more M than C responses); in other words, compulsive fantasies are more in evidence than compulsive acts. Furthermore. since form visualization is good and the general attitude of ambition to produce quantity is apparent. it can be assumed that the compulsion symptoms are, like other functions. controlled by the conscious functions to the greatest extent, and the neurosis as well as the whole compulsive condition is recognised by the subject.

There are 4 S responses in the record These represent the factors of struggle: they are the «fighting factors». Their effect extends to the intelligence and shows an attitude of energetic oppositionalism so that the subject attempts to demonstrate viewpoints which are usually overlooked. They thwart the suggestibility evidenced by the CF responses and represent negative suggestibility which is in itself an evidence of conflict against being suggestible. Finally. the S responses represent opposition to everything. even the extratensive features so that there is mistrust regarding others. There is scepticism in regard to the introversive features. a deep sense of insufficiency even in regard to the libidinized function. reasoning. resulting in compulsive doubts. tormenting ambitions. pedantic thoroughness. a grumbling state of inability to finish anything and a desire to know everything.

The results in this case show the compulsion neurosis so clearly that they allow the following further conclusions. there is compulsive sensitivity and an irritability which. because of the over-emphasis of self-control, must continually turn against the subject himself. there are compulsive attempts to untangle everything without losing a single item, tremendous desire for activity and aspiration shown by the fact that the kinæsthetic responses are almost exclusively extension movements. All this is, however, combined with doubting, brooding and a sense of lack of warmth in the approach to living and a lack in capacity to make experiences.

After five months of psychoanalytic treatment, the subject gave the following findings:

I. Laterally. Bears turning around	DF · A
Also, men's heads	DoF · Hd
The wings of an aeroplane	DF · Obj
Middle part: Danseuse	DM → H
Plate reversed, lateral edge of figures at the side: Children's heads	DdF Hd
Plate reversed, middle part: Dalai Lama, sitting	DM H Orig.—
Part of the middle section: Arch of a bridge	DdF · Obj. Orig →
Intermediate figure: Bird	SF · A Orig.—
The plate upright· Head with hood . . .	DdF— Hd Orig. →
II. Oil lamp exploding	WCF – Obj.
Head of an antelope (red)	DF → Ad
Just like a pair of monks who are kindling a fire and dancing around it. Black reversed: The monks	DM → H Orig. →
Red: The fire	DCF Fire
Red above: Shoe and sock, well seen, reversed	DF → Obj.
Or a hand with a very much enlarged finger	DF— Hd Orig.—
Black: Dog's heads	DF → Ad
Also black: A man sticking his head in his collar, ready to scold	DM + H Orig. →
Transition into gray: Like a distant staircase	DdF → Ldscp. Orig. +
III. Red above. Small monkeys	DF ↓ A
Whole plate: A waiter in a frock coat . .	WM → H
Middle, red: Red cravat	DFC → Obj.
Middle black figures: Small bears	DF + A
The same reversed: A little man bending down	DM ↓ H Orig. +
Red laterally: Young bear, but it has a leg like a goat	DF + A
IV. An animal skin	WF ↓ A
Two figures with waving scarfs, running toward the middle column: Goddesses of Revenge	DM · H

Laterally: Weasel	DF÷ A
Below the two female figures: Two small figures, who are leaning with their hands on something	DdM+ H Orig.—
Intermediate figure: Swans	SF+ A Orig.+
On narrow edge: Woman with a sack over her back (the points of boot)	DM— H Orig.+
Whole plate: A monster in a sheepskin, with large boots	WM+ H
V. A bat	WF+ A
Upper edge of wings: Death mask	DF+ Hd
VI. Reversed: Two boys: upper part of the whole figure: Heads. Larger part: Body of boys, turning their backs to each other	WM+ H Orig.+
Upright: Tennis racquet	WF+ Obj. Orig.+
On narrow edge, the lateral extensions: A torso, raising the right arm, the left one is missing	DM+ H Orig.—
In the middle line: A turned object as formerly used on furniture	DF+ Obj.
The flaring figures: A waving coat . . .	DF÷ Obj.
Narrow edge, the upper small extension of the large blot: An arm raising itself from the chaos	DdM+ Hd Orig.+
The pliers between the heads, above middle: Nut cracker	DdF+ Obj. Orig.+
In between: Labia of the vulva	DdF+ Sex
VII. Upper part: Head of a supercilious woman	DF+ Hd
Horn of the middle third: The paws of a Pinscher	DdF+ Ad Orig.+
The whole: Heavy jewelry	WF+ Orn. Orig.+
Middle part: Bears' heads	DF+ Ad
On narrow edge, middle third: Head of a man. He is talking	DM+ Hd
Lower third: Figures in winter capes . . .	DM+ H Orig.+
At the joint of the two lower thirds: Naked man	DdF+ H Orig.+
The whole: A toy where one hammer must hit the other	WF— Obj. Orig.+
The connecting piece between the upper and middle third: Shoulder and arm . . .	DdF+ Hd Orig.+
VIII. Mice	DF+ A
Gray: Hands of a lady. She is allowing someone to kiss her hand	DM+ Hd

Intermediate figure between gray and blue.
Chest . . . . SF Anat.
Butterflies red-yellow, and blues . . { DFC- A
                                       DF+ A
Red-yellow: On cervix . . . . . . DF Sex
Blue: Two flags . . . . DFC - Obj.
The whole: A dance around these flags . WFC - Comb.
IX. Figures in pointy hats. They are fencing . DM- H
On narrow edge, green: A fat cook . . . DM + H Orig. —
Red. Child's head. The whole red: A bund-
led up baby . . . . DF- Hd
Intermediate figure, reversed: A bust for
fitting clothes . . . . SF+ Obj.
Or a cello . . . . SF- Obj.
X. Blue, laterally: Sea plants . . . . . DFC -- Pl
Green, middle: A measuring worm . . DFC- A
Gray: Ship's mast . . . . DF+ Obj.
Blue, laterally: Small figures, jumping
through one another . . . . . . DdM- H Orig.+
Gray, laterally, upright: Primitive walking
being . . . . DM- H
Blue: A single point. A gesticulating orator DdM - H Orig.+
Another point: A weasel looking backwards DdF+ A Orig.+
Blue, middle: Dogs' heads . . . . . DF- Ad
Or figures stretching their hands to each
other . . . . DM+ H Orig.+
Pale green, between the caterpillars: Little
figure with halo . . . . DF + H Orig.+
Yellow: Sunflowers, after Kreidolf . . . DCF- Pl.
Blue point: Woman running away in terror:
or looking at it this way, she has fallen
on her back . . . . DdM+ H Orig.+

Computation:

Responses: 76.

W	: 10	M : 24 (!)	H	. 23
D	: 44	F : 43 (5—)	Hd	: 11 (1—)
Dd	: 16	FC: 6	A	. 14 (1—)
S	: 5	CF: 3	Ad	: 5 (1—)
Do	· 1	C : indicated	Plant :	2
			Obj.	: 14 (2—)

F	88 %		Anat. :	1
A	: 25 %		Sex :	2 (1 -)
Orig	: 11 % v±		Orn. :	1
Apper-			Ldsep.	1
ceptive :	W D--Dd		Comb..	1
Sequence: rather rigid			Fire ·	1

Interpretations are the same as in the first test nine times, and in six responses the picture is the same although the meaning attributed is somewhat different than in the first experiment.

The second set of results, obtained after the analysis, are quite different from the first. The experience type has changed quite completely. The introversive features are more free and are more powerful than they were before. The affectivity is more adaptive and less egocentric (FC's predominate over CF's) The affective load is gone. There has been a gain in adaptability and emotional approach and rapport is steadier. Introversive and extratensive features are more free; the signs of coartation so significantly apparent in the first test in the suppression of introversive and extratensive features are now much more rare. The capacity for experiencing is again undistorted.

The factors correlated with the M responses have changed in accord with the increase in M's. The percent original answers is far larger and the percent animal responses is much less. Here and there a few free abstractions and combinations appear in the interpretations. The greater freedom is also indicated in the relationship between H and A responses on the one hand. and the Hd's and Ad's on the other; there has been quite a shift in both.

The intelligence type has been changed the least. There has been an increase in the number of W's and a decrease in D's: this is an expression of the greater freedom and energy of the associative activity. The shifts here are not nearly so great as in the case of the experience type, however. Reasoning is still concrete, tends to get lost in much detail, and is unaccustomed to grasp the whole of any situation.

These results are partly due to the marked diligence in producing a large quantity of responses. This is clearly apparent when the results of this diligence are neglected by considering only the first four answers to each plate. The findings are then as follows:

Computation of first set of data.

Responses: 40.

W : 5	M 4	H 3
D · 25	F . 31	Hd : 5
Dd . 6	FC· 2	A · 12

Do .	3	C.F. 3		Ad	3
S .	1	C . indicated		Obj.	2
				Sex -	3
F	84%			Anat -	2
A	: 50%				
Orig.:	12%				

Computation of the second set of data.

Responses: 38.

W	7	M : 11	H	: 10
D	25	F : 21	Hd	: 5
Dd	3	FC.: 4	A	: 9
Do .	1	CF· 2	Ad	: 3
S .	2	C : 0	Obj.	: 7
			Anat.:	1
F	. 95%		Sex.	: 0
A	: 32%			
Orig.:	21%			

The ambiequality of experience type is expressed in this set of data for the first test, as it is in the complete computation. All other characteristics mentioned in the discussion of the full data are also evidenced in this set. The features indicating improvement seen in the complete data of the second test are expressed equally well in the latter computation. Comparison of the two computations shows the influence of the searching for interpretations, that is, of the ambition to produce a large quantity of responses.

The subject has changed in the course of the analysis. That «reflex spasm of compulsive, conscious guard over every thought and experience from within or without, causing the strangulation of the capacity to experience, has disappeared. Freed of coartation, the introversive and extratensive features have dilated to reach a type again capable of experiencing fully. This dilatation is seen in many phenomena of affective and intellectual functioning

13. «Nervous Exhaustion».

Female, aged 45.

I Thinks for a long time, then: «All that recalls the past life. - I recognize the abdomen. (Middle, above, reversed.) . .	DF	Sex Orig.--
When I reverse the plate, I also see the male sex organ (Black below middle.) .	DdF-	Sex Orig.--
II. Again the same --there below, blood (red radiating figure)	DC	Blood

«Everything from the past.» «The male sex
organ» (small black point. middle above)   DF – Sex Orig.—

III. ,Two clowns who are fighting with each
other, but something blocks their path—
the middle picture (the red figure), they
can't get together . . . .   WM— H

IV. ‹Some sort of plant› .   . . .   WF + Pl.

V. Bat . . . .   WF— A

VI. The lower part reminds me of the female
sex organs» . . . .   DdF— Sex
«The upper part. too ›—only the middle part   DdF— Sex

VII. «I wonder whether that is again the female
sex organ ‹ (confluence of the lower thirds)   DF + Sex
Middle third. «Just like heads; like the devil
with horns» . . . .   DF + Hd
Upper third: ‹Real Negroes› . . . . . .   DF + Hd

VIII. Marten . . . .   DF + A
Intermediate figure. between blue and gray:
A human skeleton . . . .   SF— Anat.
Red-yellow: Animals, but I don't know what
kind . . . .   DF— A
Gray: Two hands . . . .   DdF + Hd
«If the upper part is a skeleton, then this
(the blue) could be a human soul and the
four animals are tearing and chewing it»   DFC Abstr. Orig.—
«I wonder whether these are feet.» (Two
very sharply drawn feet protrude on both
sides near the middle line from the gray
part below) . . . .   DdF + Hd Orig. +

IX. Two horses' heads (between green and
brown) . . . .   DF— Ad
Baby (doll) (red, plate on narrow edge) .   DF— Obj.
«Just like the human vertebral column» (Rod
in middle line) . . . .   SF— Anat. Orig.—
«The two snakes must give in› (the horses'
heads) . . . .   DF + Ad
«I wonder whether this isn't again the abdomen. the female sex organ» (middle of
red part) . . . .   DdF— Sex Orig.—

X. «A real carnival» . . . .   WCF Carnival Orig. +
«Just like two children's heads, or moon and
sun» (yellow middle) . . . .   DCF Sun

Isn't that the inner portion of the female
sex organ? (the large red blot) . . . . DCF Anat. Orig.- -
This could be the sperm from the male sex
organs (the brown spots between the red
blots) . . . . DdF-- Anat. Orig.---
A deer (gray laterally) . . . . DF - A
Bushes or woods (blue laterally) . . . . DF— P! Orig. --

Computation:

Responses: 29.

W	: 4	M :	1 (tendency to more)	H	: 1
D	· 16			Hd	: 4
Dd	: 7	F :	23 (10---)	A	: 4
S	: 2	FC:	1	Ad	: 2
		CF:	3	Anat.	: 4
F+	: 56 %	C :	1	Sex	: 7
A	: 21 %			Plant	: 2
Orig.	: 36 %			Obj.	: 1
Apper-				Blood	
ceptive	: D—Dd			Sun	3
Sequence: Scattered				Carnival	
				Abstr.	: 1

The findings in this patient were quite a surprise. She had held a responsible position for many years and finally saw a physician because she had
gradually become obnoxiously querulous and because she had begun to suffer from «nervous» complaints. The experience type is that of an egocentric
extratensive individual. The type of answers given, the numerous responses
involving self-reference, the repeated indication of belief in the reality of the
pictures interpreted, and the emotional coloring in the answers, all these
findings indicate a more introversive type. Such relationships are found in
epilepsy and in schizophrenia. Epileptics confabulate and perseverate more
than is the case here, however, and also have more kinaesthetic answers. We
can, therefore, be dealing only with a schizophrenic illness. The number of
Dd, the fixation on sexual matters, the scattered sequence. the wide variability (in quality) of responses, and the tendency toward absurd and abstract
replies, all these speak for such a diagnosis. From the results noted above.
one would have to say that the case is one where there is marked scattering.
and that the case is of many years duration so that there is now a definite
schizophrenic deterioration. But this is not actually the case. All one can
say is that the patient avoids correct rapport with her surroundings and goes
her own way entirely and that she falls into hypochondriacal and anxious

states and querulous periods. The father of the patient has been schizophrenic for years and has sunk into a schizophrenic state of deterioration.

This case is one in which the test is liable to confuse a latent psychosis with a manifest one. A comparison of this protocol with the examples of schizophrenic records given below will show that the results in many cases of manifest schizophrenia approach the normal result more closely than is the case in latent schizophrenics.

Psychoses.

1 Schizophrenia.

14. Dementia Simplex.

Female, aged 38

I. Lower half of the middle figure: A part of man, like legs	DoF - Hd
II. Small black spots near the black ears: An animal's head	DdF Ad Orig —
III. Human heads (the heads are usually seen) .	DdF Hd
IV. Two small heads (black spots within the black area)	DdF Hd Orig -
The whole: A mother's body. «because two small heads are in it»	DdWF Anat. Orig.—
V. A flying animal	WF ⊢ A
VI. Two spots within the black area. Small heads	DdF- - Hd
VII. Middle third. Wild animals [1]	DF · A
Lower third: Butterflies	DF ⊢ A
VIII. Pigs (red)	DF-⊢ A
Middle of the blue squares: Small heads . .	DdF Hd Orig.—
IX. On the border of green and brown: Animal heads	DF→ A
Red below, cannot be described· An elephant's head	DF- A Orig —
Near the large brown branch: Pictures of men (is frequently seen as such, occa- sionally seen as moving, but not in this case)	DdF— H

---

[1] The word is distorted in the German.

X. Red: Something like a woman (ads shows
    the heads in red) . . . . DF H
    Gray above: Dragonfly . . . . . DF A
    Gray laterally: Animals[1] . . . . . . DF A

Computation:

Responses. 17.

W	: 2 (1 DdW)	M :	0		H	: 2 (1 -)	
D	: 8	F :	17 (8 −)		Hd	: 5 (2)	
Dd	: 5	FC:	0		A	: 8 (3)	
Do	· 2	CF:	0		Ad	: 1 ( )	
		C :	0		Anat.:	1 (−−)	

F   : 53 %
A   · 53 %
Orig.   30 %
Apper-
ceptive : D Dd
Sequence Scattered

This patient is a housewife who has gradually become more and more dull, indolent and stereotyped over the course of many years, and there has been little variation in her illness. She was never very intelligent, but the results of the test are quite different from what they would be in simple feeblemindedness. There is no depression; when the patient was admitted to the institution she asked quite without emotion whether she would always stay there.

15. Hebephrenia.

Textile merchant, aged 50 Ill about 20 years.

I. On the inside of the head of the lateral
    figures: A lion's head . . . . DdF — Ad
    Middle: A female body without a head. the
    breasts stand out («the woman's skirt is
    made of silk muslin») . . . . DF + Hd
II. Black· Two bears . . . . DF + A
    Reversed· Sheep's heads . . . . . . DF + Ad
    Red below: Hind part of a butterfly . . . DFC + Ad
    Red above: Silk cocoon . . . . . . DF — Obj Orig.—
III. Negro's head with stiff collar . . . . DoF + Hd
    The middle black figures, reversed: Negroes'
    heads which have been chopped off . . DF + Hd
    Red, middle: Brassiere, corset . . . . . DF + Obj.

---

[1] The word is distorted in the German

IV. A kangaroo, because in the middle of the
black area a few heads are visible and
the kangaroo has an abdominal pouch . . . DdWF— A Orig.—
The whole: Just like a Gambrinus on a
tavern sign . . . . WF+ H
The ends of the boots: Seals . . . . . DF+ A
V. A bat . . . . WF+ A
A small contour at the wing of the bat:
Head of an animal ✓which has never
existed . . . . DdF— Ad
VI. Floating iceberg . . . . WF— Obj. Orig.—
Upper end: A fish . . . . DF— A Orig.—
The whole is also a crystal formation . . . DWF— Obj. Orig.—
VII. Middle third: Animal mouths . . . . . DF+ A
VIII. Salamander (red) . . . . DF+ A
Blue: A new fine type of butterfly . . . DF+ A
Red-yellow: A lung . . . . DFC— Anat.
IX. Small spots of mixed colors between green
and red: Feces like those made by dwarfs
which are sold at fairs . . . . DdCF— C
Plate on narrow edge: Upper end of red:
Human heads . . . . DF+ Hd
Between brown and green: A deer's head . DF+ Ad
X. Green, medial: Head of a hare . . . . . DF+ Ad
The thick end of the red spot: Head of a
walrus . . . . DdF— Ad
Blue, laterally: Scorpion . . . . DF— A
Blue, middle: Head of a very young elephant DF+ Ad
Gray, laterally: A young kangaroo . . . . DF— A
Black-yellow, laterally. A young canary . . DdCF— A

Computation:

Responses: 30.

W	: 5 (1 DW, 1 DdW)	M: 0		H	:	1
D	: 19	F : 26 (10—)		Hd	:	4
Dd	: 5	FC: 2 (1—)		A	:	11 (4—)
Do	: 1	CF: 2		Ad	:	8 (3—)
		C : indicated		Obj.	:	4 (3—)
F+	: 61 %			Anat.:		1 (—)
A	: 57 %			Stool:		1 (—)
Orig.	: 20 %—					

Apperceptive : D—Dd
Sequence: Definitely scattered

At the time this test was done the patient was at the beginning of a manic-like excitement. He showed motor excitement and flight of ideas, but at the same time he perseverated, always repeating the same things. Associative series were interrupted by typically schizophrenic leaps in his thinking. All this is apparent in the sequence of the interpretations as well. The scattering of sequence, clear in the previous record, is even more apparent here though the forms are about the same in quality. Confabulation is much more evident than in the previous example. The experience type is definitely extratensive. M responses are lacking. The patient in a manic excitement of schizophrenic origin gives very few kinaesthetic responses; the true manic gives many. Patients with uncomplicated depression give no kinaesthesias; depressions in a schizophrenic setting practically always produce a few M answers.

16. Abulic, Hebephrenoid Catatonia, Showing Few Symptoms.

Male, aged 25. Illness of relatively recent onset while subject was in a prison camp.

I. Butterfly	WF—	A
II. Fantastic butterfly	WF+	A
III. Two monkeys playing [1]	WM+	A
IV. Fantastic carpet	WF+	A
V. Animal carpet	WF—	A
VI. The same	WF—	A
VII. Wild carpets	WF—	A Orig.—
VIII. Likewise, animal carpets	WF—	A Orig.—
IX. Likewise, animal carpets	WF—	A Orig.—
X. Sea animals, coral	WCF+	A

Computation:

Responses: 10.

W	: 10	M : 1 (questionable)		A : 10	
		F : 8 (5—)			
F+	: 44 %	FC: 0			
A	: 100 %	CF: 1			
Orig.	: 30 %—	C : 0			
Apperceptive	: W—				
Sequence: Single responses only					

[1] German = Spielaffen. Many words in this protocol are unusual and tend in the direction of neologisms.

Perseverating stereotypy of poor quality. Coartated, but the coartation is rather empty. The W's, F's, and A's are all conditioned by the indifferent, abulic (lazy) mood. In spite of this mood, the subject is attentive to the experiment as shown by the escape from the chain of perseveration. In such cases as this it is impossible to judge the quality of the form responses except by statistical methods.

17. Catatonia; Motor Excitement and Scattering.

Male, aged 40.

Hebephrenic for 20 years, gradually changing to catatonic form with many poorly systematized delusions. At present, he is in an excited hebephrenoid state with widely fluctuating delusions and few hallucinations. Previously, there was a wealth of hallucinations.

I. Two women, sportswomen (sees two shapes
  in the middle figure) . . . . DM+ H
 Two angels, polar bear angels (some subjects see angels in these lateral figures;
  others, polar bears. He interprets both
  and contaminates them into «polar bear DM+ H
  angels») . . . . DF+ A
 Or, pyramid angels (indicates the points of
  the lateral figures, as the pyramids) . . DdF— Pyram. Orig.—
 Or, attack angels (they throw up their arms
  as though they were in an attack) . . . DM+ H
II. Reversed: The sunrise . . . . DCF Sun
 Black: Two polar bears . . . . DF+ A
III. Two waiters . . . . WM+ H
IV. A bear bending down . . . . WM+ A
 In the middle part (held reversed) beneath
  the crown form. two small, dark, ring-
  shaped areas: «Handcuffs, number 6» (the
  same small detail is seen twice; as a hand-
  cuff and as the number 6, and the two DdF+ Obj. Orig.+
  interpretations are mixed) . . . . . DdF+ Number Orig.+
 Above: A small crown . . . . DdF+ Obj. Orig.+
V. A bat, or two dead Chinese (both interpreta- WF+ A
  tions given after not quite 3 seconds exposure. The bat's ears are the stiffened
  arms of the Chinese, the legs are the trail-
  ing pigtails, the wings are the crushed
  legs of the Chinese). They fell and were
  killed . . . . WM+ H Orig.+

VI. A pheasant-host likewise interpreted im-
    mediately after uncovering the plate.
    This is also a contamination of two inter-
    pretations of the same detail: the phea-
    sant is the flaring figure, frequently de-
    signated as birds' wings. The host, the
    head of the figure, his large beard, is the
    flaring figure; two oblique lines on both
    sides are his mustache . . . . . .   DF— Hd

Also purses (the knotty structures at both
    lower ends) . . . .   DF — Obj. Orig.—

From purses the subject jumped to Russian
    leather, from that he goes to yachts and
    then suddenly finds small spots within
    the black area which he designates as sea[1]   DdF— Sea Orig.—

VII. «Remains of camphor from the war. He
    means the areas of gas from gas attacks.
    The subject considers camphor as poison   WCF Clouds

VIII. Quite enthusiastic: «The resurrection of the
    colossal, coloric, red, brownish and blue
    venous tumors of the head». A very com-
    plex contamination . . . .   DWCF— Abstr. Orig.—

Resurrection: Shows how the red animals
    are resurrected . . . .   DM + A

Names colors . . . .   DCC

Coloric: Schizophrenic pleonasm; venous
    tumor of head; veins shown at different
    places   . . . .   DdCF— Anat. Orig.—

Other determining factors of the interpreta-
    tion cannot be obtained . . . . .

Or a market for fuchsia (whether the form
    has had any influence cannot be deter-
    mined, but the colors are sharply con-
    ceived The association «market» may in-
    dicate inextricability of the forms) . .   WC Pl. Orig.—

«I must not tell who these animals are; they
    might become angry.» (Probably seen as
    moving) . . . .   DF+ A

---

[1] In German this represents a klang association and flight purses to leather (Juchten)
to yachts (Jachten) to sea

IX «Perfect cattle-bears which occur in large   SF─| A
     lakes.» Composed. as far as the deter-
     minants can be recognized -by
   Bears (the green. frequently interpreted as
     such) . . . .   DF─ A
   Cattle horns (the brown points) which were
     completed by confabulating cattle for them   DF— A
   Lakes (again the green areas) . . . .   DC Sea
X. Nothing but the eternal Jew in Judea (the
     gray heads, middle above. which are fre-
     quently interpreted as Jewish profiles) .   DF─ Hd

Computation:

Responses: 30.

W	: 9 (two are contamin- ated DW, resp. DdW)	M	: 7 (even more)	H	. 5		
D	: 15	F	. 16 (11─)	Hd	: 2		
Dd	: 6 (tendency to more)	FC:	0	A	: 9		
		CF.	4	Ad	: 0		
		C :	3	Plant	: 1		

Obj. : 3
Anat. : 1
Pyramid: 1
Sun
Sea } 4
Clouds
Number . 1

F+ : 69 %
A : 30 %
Orig. : ca. 40 %─
Apper-
ceptive : W—D—Dd
Sequence: Very scattered

Abstr. : 1
Color : 1
Numerous
conta-
minations

Introversive and affective egocentricity are combined in this case. Adaptability of form to color has ceased; the capacity for affective rapport is lacking. The associations are extremely mixed up, absurd and spotty. Fantastic
contaminations, combinations and confabulations are mixed together. There
is great variability in the interpretations; the number of original responses
is relatively small only because the component interpretations of the contaminations have been separated Judging the responses as individual units
results in original percent of 90. i. e., complete inability to get into intellectual rapport with others.

18. Catatonia Showing Blocking.

Male, aged 53.

Patient became ill about 25 years ago. At present he is stiff, rigid and mute. On one of the rare days when the patient spoke at all it was possible to do the test.

I. Anatomy (the plate is frequently interpreted as pelvis or chest. This is probably
the basis for the interpretation «Ana-
tomy») . . . .   WF — Abstr.
   Two duelling figures (laterally) . .   DM — H
II. Two women knitting . . . . . .   WM – H
III. «A new theatre, as one can lift oneself
freely in the air (catatonic manner of
speaking) . . . .   WM – H
IV. Two animal heads (small detail, but well
seen) . . . .   DdF — Ad Orig.⊥
   Again a knitting woman sitting on the F—.   WM — H
V. A doggy—a dog (the whole figure is not
meant, but just the head, the legs, and
what lies in between) . . . .   DdF— A Orig.—
VI. A knitting woman (perseverating, but
designates very small horn-like projections, below medial, as the «hands» of the
woman) . . . .   DdWF — H Orig.—
VII. These are «Manititter», something crazy:
«four heads» (what «Manititter» means,
he does not say: four heads, probably hu-   DF+ Hd
man, frequently interpreted) . . . . .   DF+ Hd
VIII. «Two pigs, yes, that's what I was» . .   DF+ A
IX. Points to the gray half moons in the middle
of the intermediate figure, and the place
between the contiguous green areas and
says: «She must yearn until she falls into
eternity.» (The intermediate figure, reversed, is frequently interpreted as a
female body. The funnel-shaped spot,
where the green areas are contiguous, is
the entrance to hell, or something similar.
From the scattered talk of the patient,
one can see that «eternity» is something
sexual for him. The same area of the fi-

gure, the green funnel, is sometimes interpreted as a female sex organ. We are obviously dealing here with a complex answer. The signum must, therefore, be incomplete . . . . DdF— Abstr Orig.—

X. Designates very rapidly, one after the other: The area between the gray heads:
«Eternity» . . . . DdF— Abstr. Orig.—
Blue: The sky . . . . DC Sky
Green laterally: «More lawn to turn over» (this detail is rarely interpreted) . . . DdC Lawn
Red areas: Love . . . . DC Abstr.
Two extremely small white gaps within the gray heads: Father and Mother (this interpretation must have been determined by the duality only) . . . . Dd— Number, Father and
(All interpretations belong to the same complex.)   Mother Orig.—

Computation:

Responses: 17.

W	: 5 (1 DdW)	M	: 4	H	: 5
D	: 6	F	: 9 (5—)	Hd	: 2
Dd	· 6	FC	: 0	A	: 2
S	: 1 (in IX.)	CF	: 0	Ad	: 1
		C	: 3	Sky	: 1
F+	: 45 %	Number: 1		Lawn	: 1
A	: 18 %			Abstr.	: 4
Orig.	: about 35 % (see below)			Father and	
Apper-				Mother: 1	
ceptive	: W—D—Dd				
Sequence: Scattered					

Kinaesthesias and colors are roughly balanced indicating the ambiequal type of the blocked catatonic. Original responses make up far more than 50 % if one does not search for particular form interpretations among the schizophrenic answers but simply considers them as original. As in the last case, the visualization of forms is sometimes good and sometimes poor. Such wide differences in clarity of form visualization are seen only in schizophrenia. There are no FC or CF responses—no fine shading of the affect, no emotional adaptability

19. Paranoid Schizophrenia.

Female, aged 30.

Systematized ideas of grandeur and of persecution. At one time patient had catatonic attacks but at present there are few catatonic symptoms. She appears entirely orderly in her thinking and rarely expresses her delusions.

I.	Two men standing opposite each other . .	DM·· H
	The whole thing is an animal skeleton; an X-ray picture	WF · Anat.
II.	Black: Two dancing bears	DM – A
	Red above: Two flames	DCF Fire
III.	Two mannequins complimenting each other.	WM→ H
	Reversed, the same men: Ghosts with disheveled hair	DM— H Orig.+
IV.	A flea	WF·· A Orig.—
	A small detail which cannot be described: A bone	DdF— Anat. Orig. —
V.	Bat	WF+ A
VI.	A fan	WF→ Obj Orig.→
	Upper part: Animal head	DF→ Ad
VII.	Two spinster's heads with high hairdress (upper third)	DF+ Hd
	Whole plate: Pieces of cake dough raising	WFC+ Dough Orig. +
VIII.	Polar Bears	DF+ A
	Intermediate figure between the blue areas: Skeleton	SF+ Anat.
	Gray above: Squid	DF+ A Orig.+
IX.	Middle figure: A violin	SF+ Obj.
	Brown: Two dwarfs with outstretched arms	DM+ H
	A small detail on the green lateral contour: A face	DdF+ Hd
X.	Gray middle: Fleas	DF— A
	Green middle: Caterpillars	DFC+ A
	Red: Two wandering figures, without heads	DM+ H

Computation:

Responses: 22.

W	: 6	M :	6	H	: 5
D	: 12	F :	13 (4—)	Hd	: 2
Dd	: 2	FC:	2	A	: 7
S	: 2	CF:	1	Ad	: 1
		C :	0	Obj.	: 2

F+   : 70 %   Anat. : 3

A   : 36 %   Dough· 1

Orig.   : 27 % ±   Fire   : 1

Apper-

ceptive   : W—D

Sequence: somewhat scattered

On the whole the results in this case approach the normal findings very closely, especially in experience type, affective status and in animal percentage. Complex responses are absent here. There are some findings indicative of schizophrenia, particularly the simultaneous occurence of very good and bad forms, the F+ percentage at the lower extreme of normal averages (70 %) when considered in relation to the 6 M responses, the variability of the quality of the original responses, and, finally, the two very absurd Dd answers. The subject draws fairly well but has neglected it for many years, taking it up again only as the paranoid state became stabilized. Moody, as changeable in mood as the weather, very stubborn (S), and negativistic. In her more calm periods, such as when this test was done, she appears affectively normal, very adaptable, and shows relatively good emotional approach.

2. Manic-depressive Insanity.

20. Depression.

Female, aged 54.

Patient has suffered from manic and depressive moods for many years. It is only in the last five years, however, that she has actually been ill with «cyclic insanity», having manic and depressive phases in alternation.

I. Bat	WF+ A
II. Two heads (red)	DoF+ Hd
or two animals because of the clear legs .	DF+ A
III. Two animal heads	DF+ Ad
IV. Two legs	DoF+ Hd
V. Bat	WF+ A
VI. Bat (the wing-like figures above)	DF— A
VII. Two heads (upper third)	DF+ Hd
VIII. Bears	DF+ A
Red-yellow: Fish heads	DF+ Ad
IX. Inner side of the brown branches, above:	
A man's head	DdF+ Hd
Face with stocking cap	DoF+ Hd
Next to it, a shoe (very small)	DdF+ Obj. Orig.+

X. The green middle figures. Worms or fish   DF · A
    Blue laterally: Spiders . . . .   DF · A
    Blue middle: Animal heads . . . . . .   DF · A

Computation:

Responses: 16.

W	: 2	M :	0	H	:	0
D	: 9	F :	16 (1—)	Hd	·	5
Dd	: 2	FC:	0	A	:	8
Do	: 3 (tendency	CF:	0	Ad	:	2
	to more)	C .	0	Obj.:		1

F +-   : 93 %
A   : 63 %
Orig.   : 7 %÷
Apper-
ceptive   : D—Do
Sequence: rather rigid

21. Elation.

The same patient in manic phase about three-quarters of a year later.

I. Bat . . . . WF÷ A
    Two angels flying . . . . DM÷ H
II. «Two carnival clowns, but they don't wear
        any top hats» . . . . WM÷ H
    Red, above: Two little animals. rabbits or
        squirrels . . . . DF÷ A
    Black: Bears . . . . DF ÷ A
III. «Animals. I don't know what kind» (upper
       half of the men) . . . . DF— A
    Middle: Tie . . . . DF+ Obj.
    Red, above: Clown or animal . . . . . DF— A
IV. Bat . . . . WF+ A
V. Bat . . . . WF+ A
VI. Animal, «I don't know what kind» .   . WF— A
VII. Upper third: Heads . . . . DF+ Hd
    Middle and lower third: Its body . . . . DF— Hd
VIII. Pigs or bears . . . . DF+ A
    Whole plate: Like a christmas tree . . . WCF Obj. Orig.—
    Blue: The flags of the first of August[1] . . DFC+ Obj.
    Red-yellow: Head of marine animals . . . DF+ Ad

---

[1] Translator's Note: A Swiss national holiday.

IX. Brown: Two carnival clowns squirting some-
thing on each other . . . . DM— H
Green: Animals or something . . . . . DF— A
X. Colored stuff . . . . WC Color
Blue laterally: Like a crab . . . . . . DF— A
Gray laterally: Mice . . . . DF— A
Green: Caterpillars . . . . DFC— A
Gray above: Also animals. «I don't know
which» . . . . DF— A

Computation:

Responses: 24.

W	: 7 (several DW)	M :	3 (tendency to	H	: 3
D	: 17		more)	Hd	: 2 (1—)
Dd, Do, etc.:	0	F :	17 (7—)	A	: 14 (5—)
		FC:	2	Ad	: 1
F—	: 59 %	CF:	1	Obj. .	3
A	: 64 %	C :	1	Color:	1
Orig.	: 5 %—				
Apper-ceptive	: W—D				
Sequence:	relatively rigid				

At the time the test was done the manic phase was no longer at its peak. Usually the number of original responses, M's, and color responses is higher in manics. Nevertheless, it is clear that the protocol is that of a manic, especially when contrasted with the depressive findings. In the depressive, there is the painstaking care to recognize (the figure) with certainty, resulting in good forms. In manics there are confabulatory responses which are vague and of indifferent quality, W responses confabulated from various parts, and poor forms. In both phases the animal percentage remains relatively high: it may be slightly reduced in elation.

3. Epilepsy.

22. Typical Epileptic Dementia, Rapid Course.

Male, aged 26.

Patient has had epileptic attacks since the age of 13.

I. On both sides the same pretty picture, just WC+ Color
like my drawings; black and white Makes
wing-like motions with his arms and

finally says: God with wings. God, the middle figure . . . .   DM · H Orig.–

II. «Something made with ink, two colors, darker and lighter. Two praying people (stands as though he were praying, corresponding to the picture). As though I were double on both sides. Do good to one another» . . . .   WM + H

III. «Three colors on the paper: white, black and red. The same colors but in a different form» . . . .   WC Color

«The same as the last picture, only a little smaller: Two figures, seated» (the arm considered legs) . . . .   DM– H

IV. «Two colors, now lighter, now darker. the same print on both sides. The form is like a person, but it doesn't represent it well: a seated figure» . . . .   WC Color
    WM + H
«Such borders are occasionally painted on the wall» . . . .   WF + Orn. Orig.+

V. «Two colors, again the same thing.» Sees the bat's head, stretches his arms into the air and says: «A human head and outstretched arms» . . . . . .   WC Color
    DM — Hd Orig.—

VI. «The colors are always the same.» The upper end: «A plant with leaves» . . . .   WC Color
    DF— Pl.
The large part (therefore) a «flower pot» .   DF— Obj. Orig. —

VII. «Black and gray. light black.» On both sides again the same imprint . . . .   WC Color
Reverses the plate. Middle part: «A human head. here the eye; but the neck and head are not just right.» (Tries his own movements, turns and twists.) «The body is shrunken and here are the legs.» (The projection in the erect picture frequently interpreted as a high hairdress) . . . .   DM— H Orig.—
«As though water were in a container» (plate erect, intermediate figure) . . . . .   SF— Obj. Orig.—
«And now I want to add that all these drawings are made on paper.»

VIII. «Four colors again: Light red and dark red; light blue and dark blue; shall I indicate

this, too? Thoroughness is important in
life" . . . .   WC Color

Red: "Like a climbing bear, but of course it
isn't the right color." (Enumerates all
bears he knows and finds that none are
red.) "And again on both sides"   . .   DF— A

"On both sides the same nice imprint" (gets
into a position again, maneuvers with his
arms and legs and says): "I wonder whether this isn't something bad, like a man
with an erect sex organ, but it would be
too large» . . . .   DM— H Orig.—

Blue: «This could be a sea» . . . . . . DC Sea

Gray: «And that is a mountain» . . . .   DFC+ Mountain

IX. «Here are only three colors» (enumerates   WC Colors
them). «It is not the same nice print, but
otherwise it is rather nice.»

Brown: «As though the boogyman was standing there» . . . .   DM+ H

Red, diagonal: «A human face; here is an
eye» . . . .   DF+ Hd

X. Counts the colors. «I must say, first, that   WC Colors
the paper is white. On both sides the
same even imprint. It isn't a human figure.»

Red: «A mountain, as though it were beautiful in the sunset» . . . .   DCF Mountain

«If this is a mountain, then that is a sea
with many indentations in the shore and
streams flowing in» . . . .   DCF Sea Orig.—

Plate reversed, green middle: «As though
a rabbit were standing there, but the eye
is too large and the color is not correct» DF+ A

Computation:

Responses: 29, of which 10 are color enumerations.

W	: 13 (—10 color-enumerations)	M :	8 (4—)	H	:	7 (3—)
		F :	7 (3—)	Hd	:	2 (1—)
D	: 15	FC:	1	A	:	2
S	: 1	CF:	2	Ad	:	0
		C :	11 (10 enumera-tions)	Plant	:	1 (—)
F+	: 57 %			Obj.	:	2 (—)

A : $7^0 o$ (H: $31^0 o$. C· $34^0/o$'
Orig. : $27^0 o$' (apart from the color-
          enumerations)
Apper-
ceptive : DW - D
Sequence: rigid

Ornament: 1
Sea : 2
Mountain . 2
Colors : 10

Fantasy and confabulation are combined in the answers. Symmetry in the plates is carefully emphasized, and the colors are counted—typically epileptic careful attention to fundamentals. The secondary kinaesthesias are significant. The tendency of the epileptic to attribute values and to refer things to himself is apparent. Animal percentage is very low. Kinaesthesias and colors become the associative pattern which is stereotyped in this case, rather than the animal pattern. Computation shows a dilated experience type, a rare finding, and even here it is combined with marked perseveration.

23. Epileptoid.

Male, aged 29.

Hospital attendant. As a child he had spasms. Rather dreamy and sluggish, but his condition had never aroused a suspicion of epilepsy as a diagnosis. He had an isolated epileptic attack when frightened by a frenzied patient.

I Bat . . . . WF + A
    Middle: Vertebra of a man . . . . . . DF— Anat.
II. Black: Lobes of lungs . . . . DF— Anat.
    «I don't like the red» . . . . DC Color
III. «The red must mean something, probably
    the heart» . . . . DFC—Anat.
    Two men (not seen as moving) . . . . . DF+ H
    «Yes, the red is located near where the
    heart should be.»
IV. Middle line: Vertebrae (especially the co-
    lumn-like part) . . . . DF— Anat.
    «A peculiar picture, black, gray» . . . . WC Color
V. A part of the hinder parts, bony structure WF— Anat.
    Bat . . . . WF+ A
VI. A snake-like animal, because of the head . DWF— A
VII. Lower confluent third: Again, the hinder
    parts of a human being . . . . DF— Anat.
VIII. Animal, ice animals . . . . DF+ A
    Blue: Ice . . . . DCF Ice
    Middle line in the gray: Vertebrae . . . . DF— Anat.

IX. Green: Lung or liver . . . . DF   Anat.
   The half-moons in the intermediate figure.
     Kidneys . . . . DdF— Anat.
 X. Brown spots in the middle: The heart . . D Position (?)— Anat.
   Yellow, laterally: Kidneys . . . . . DCF— Anat.
   Red: Human sides, the flesh . . . . . . DCF— Anat.

Computation:

Responses: 20.

W	: 5 (1 C, 1 DW)	M	: 0	H	.	1
D	: 14	F	: 13 (9—)	Hd	:	0
Dd	: 1	FC	: tendency present	A	:	4 (1—)
		CF	: 4	Ad	:	0
F+	: 31 % (!)	C	: 2	Anat.:		12 (—)
A	: 20 % Anat. 60 %	Position: ? ? 1		Ice	·	1
Orig.	: 45 %—			Color.		2
Apperceptive	: W—D					
Sequence: loose						

The findings in this case are probably sufficient to make the diagnosis of epilepsy. There are color responses, a tendency to confabulate, indication of the tendency to attribute values to the figures, and perseveration. The animal percentage is small because the stereotypy has found another object, namely, anatomical responses. The findings are not audacious enough to be those of a confabulating feebleminded subject, and are not scattered enough to be those of a schizophrenic subject, especially since there are so many color responses. Comparative material is as yet too small to allow definite conclusions but the same preference for anatomical responses was found in several epileptoid cases.

4. Organic Psychoses.

24. Arteriosclerotic Dementia with Depression.

Female, aged 69.

 I Middle below: A fish head . . . . . . DoF+ Ad
   Laterally above: Bears' heads . . . . . DF+ Ad
 II. «He wears old shoes.» Patient only sees the
   «shoes», and not the entire man.
   «The shoes»: red above . . . . DF— Obj.
 III. «Human beings, if the back were not
   separated» . . . . DF+ H

IV. The points of the boots usually seen: Fish .   DF   A Orig.
     The same reversed: Two dogs' heads   . .   DF   Ad

V. A bird . . . .   W F   A

VI. The uppermost part: A bird   . . . . .   DF · A
     The most lateral extension: Dogs' heads   .   DF : Ad

VII. Middle part. Dogs' heads   . . . . . .   DF ·· Ad
      Upper part: Swans .   . . . .   DF   A Orig. —

VIII. Two pigs . . . .   DF -· A
      Gray: Two hands with fingers . . . . .   DF — Hd
      Red-yellow: Sleeping heads . . . . . .   DF ·· Hd

IX. Green: Bears . . . .   DF + A
    Brown: Birds (because of the beak-like ex-
     tension) . . . .   DF -- A

X. Gray laterally: Birds with long necks (fre-
    quently interpreted as storks) . . . .   DF + A
    Green medial: Fish . . . .   DF + A

Computation:

Responses: 18.

W	: 1 (DW)	M : 0		H : 1		
D	: 16 (numerous Do)	F : 18 (6—)		Hd : 2 (—)		
Do	: 1	FC: 0		A : 9 (3—)		
		CF: 0		Ad : 5		
F+	: 66 %	C : 0		Obj.: 1 (—)		
A	: 77 %					
Orig.	: 10 %—					

Apper-
ceptive : D—Do
Sequence: indication of reversal

25. Korsakoff Psychosis.

Male, aged 60.

Patient was formerly a very intelligent person, a teacher. Alcoholism became
worse and worse, culminating in alcoholic delirium in 1909, since which
time he has been in a Korsakoff psychosis.

I. Middle: «A frightened woman» . . . . .   DM+ H
  Plate reversed, the mushroom-like figure,
    laterally: «A queen watching from a dis-
    tance what her husband is doing in war»   DdM+ H Orig.+

II. Black: Two pigs . . . . DF— A Orig.—
    Reversed, black: Two dogs' heads . . . DF⊤ Ad
    Whole plate: Two marionettes dancing . . WM+ H
III. Two clowns . . . . WM⊥ H
    Medial round figures: Hedgehog . . . . DF— A
    Legs of the men: A flying fish . . . . . DF⊤ A
    Red above: Two parrots . . . . DF⊥ A Orig.+
IV. A giant with enormous feet is sitting there WM⊤ H
    Plate on narrow edge: Bears with open
      mouths . . . . DF⊤ Ad
    Head of the giant: A bat opens its mouth DdF⊥ Ad Orig.+
    Lateral extension: Smoke . . . . DF— A
    Plate reversed, lowest intermediate figure,
      between the leg of the giant and column-
      like middle part: A polar bear . . . . SF+ A Orig.⊥
    The intermediate figure above that: A pray-
      ing maiden . . . . SM+ H Orig.+
    The medial contour of this praying maiden:
      A man studying his interest (money) . . DdM+ H Orig.+
    «The whole plate is a giant. Have I said
      that already?»

V. Doesn't see the bat and otherwise does not
    pay any attention or use the symmetry of
    the plates. Places plate on narrow edge:
    One-half of the bat: «An arrogant woman»
    (extension kinaesthesia) . . . . . DM⊥ H Orig.+
    Places it on other narrow edge and points
    at the other half of the bat without
    noticing the symmetry: «A cautious bent-
    over woman» . . . . DM+ H Orig.⊥
VI. The most lateral extension, plate on narrow
    edge: A funny bear, struggling to rise . DM⊥ A Orig.+
    Upper part: Bismarck's profile with the
    three hairs on the head (the two horn-
    like structures) . . . . DF— Hd Orig.—
    Plate upright, the small figures on the left
    and right, above lateral: A quiet observer
    with folded arms . . . . DdM+ H Orig.+
VII. Middle part: A sleeping knight . . . . DF+ Hd
    The same face on the other side: A laughing
    old man . . . . DF+ Hd
    Plate reversed, upper parts: A tiger's mouth DF⊤ Ad

VIII. Blue diagonal (plate on narrow edge: A
    man with a tremendous mouth . .   DF   Hd Oriz -
    Red: Two wolves . . . . DF A
    Red-yellow: Monkeys . . . . . DF A Orig.
    The white intermediate figures, above me-
    dial: Two rabbits sitting up . . . SF A Orig. -
    Plate reversed: intermediate figure between
    blue and middle line: Two wrestling
    punchinellos . . . . SM   H Orig. -
    Gray: Two starved lions. Head at middle,
    legs and tail on side . . . . DF + A Orig. —

IX. Two tourists, sitting on a cliff and holding
    a telescope in their hands . . . . . DM + H
    Green, diagonal (plate on narrow edge): A
    woman waving farewell . . . . DM + H Orig. +
    Red: Plate on narrow edge: Bismarck with
    a pipe in his mouth . . . . DF + Hd
    Brown (narrow edge): A clown hanging . DdF — H Orig. -
    Brown diagonal, next to the most medial
    brown extension: A small woman sitting
    there looking at the sea. (A very clearly
    visualized picture. The woman leans on
    the tree and the middle line forms the
    horizon) . . . . DdF + Picture Orig.

X. Gray, laterally: Two storks . . . DF + A
    Gray, above: Rabbits . . . . DF — A
    Green, middle: Two weasels . . . . . DF — A

Computation:

Responses: 38.

W	: 3	M : 14 (almost all good)		H	: 14 (2—)
D	· 25	F : 24 (8—)		Hd	: 5 (2—)
Dd	. 6	FC: 0		A	: 14 (5—)
S	: 4	CF: 0		Ad	: 4
		C : 0		Picture:	1

F— : 66 %
A : 47 %
Orig : 53 % ±
Apper-
ceptive . D— (Dd)
Sequence: loose

Several times the patient interpreted the same detail twice in the course of the experiment. Sometimes the interpretation was the same in both cases. sometimes different. He immediately forgets his interpretations because of the great memory defect characteristic of the Korsakoff psychosis. Because of this, the flow of interpretations is not arrested as it is in normals who, after a while, are unable to find anything other than what has already been seen in the figure. Freedom of association, due in schizophrenics to dissolution of associative processes. is present in this subject because of the memory defect.

Color has almost no influence in the interpretations. The findings in this case greatly resemble those in paranoid cases, but differ in that there is less of the tendency to make associative «leaps», in that there are no absurd interpretations, and in that the affective attitude toward interpreting is more monotonous Interpreting is pleasant for the subject just as it is for the normal imaginative person.

There is one peculiarity that the subject shares with many paranoid patients, namely, the kinaesthetic vivification of very small parts of the figures.

26. Progressive Paralysis.

Male, aged 45.

Exalted form. Prodromal symptoms for two years and paretic exaltation for the last six months.

I. An angel and two Santa Clauses	WM+ H
II. Two drunkards	WM+ H
III. That's you and Captain Moser	WM+ H
IV. A flying falcon	WF— A
V. Also winged animals	WF— A
VI. A mountain butterfly	WF— A Orig.—
VII. Snow and clouds	WCF Clouds
VIII. Red-yellow, below: Hell	DC Hell Orig.—
Gray above: A crown	DF— Obj. Orig.—
IX. Intermediate figure: Entrance to a pit . .	SCF— Pit Orig.—
Brown above: The sun	DC Sun Orig.—
Green: Forest	DC Forest Orig.—
X. The entrance to heaven, clouds	WCF— Sky Orig.—

Computation:

Responses: 13.

W	: 8 (numerous DW)	M : 3		H	: 3
D	: 4	F : 4 (all—)		Hd	: 0

S	1		H	0	A	3
F	(The M's good:		CF	3	Ad	9
	the F's all bad)		C	3	Obj	3
A	23 %				Others	6
Orig	53 %					

Apper-
ceptive · W D
Sequence. (?)

It is striking in this case that the M's are clearly visualized while the F's. in contrast, show very poor visualization. The grasp of forms becomes worse with each succeeding plate, while confabulation becomes more unrestrained. W's become DW's, but the apperceptive type retains normal form in other respects. This man was very intelligent.

27. Senile Dementia.

Male, aged 78.

Patient has shown definite senile dementia for the last three years.

I. Two horses' heads (the wings) . . .	DF	Ad Orig.--
II. A plant figure	DWF	Pl. Orig.—
III. Something like a flower	WF—	Pl. Orig.-
IV The ends of the boots. Birds	DF—	A Orig.—
Reversed: Also animals	DWF--A	
V. A bird (however, he demonstrates something quite impossible)	DWF—A	
VI. A leaf	WF-	Pl.
VII. Flowers	DWF—	Pl. Orig.--
VIII. A sunshade (parasol), indicating the red animals, held diagonally	DFC—	Obj. Orig.—
Gray above: Also a sunshade	DF—	Obj. Orig—
Blue: Another sunshade	DF—	Obj. Orig.—
IX. Flowers, roses	DWCF+	Pl.
X. A rose (the whole?)	DWCF—	Pl. Orig. —

Computation.

Responses: 13.

W	: 8 (probably all DW)	M :	0	H	. 0	
D	: 5	F ·	10 (9—)	Hd	: 0	
		FC:	1	A	: 3 (—)	
F+	: 10 %	CF:	2	Ad	: 1 (· ·)	
A	· 31 % (see below)	C :	0	Plant· 6 (· ·)		

Orig.   · 70 %—

Appcr

ceptive : DW– D

Sequence. apparently loose

                                                                        Obj . 3 (—,

In this case the test was given in parts over a period of several days in order to interfere with perseveration which would extend through the whole series of plates. For this reason, the A% does not have the same significance in this case as in the previous ones. If the whole test had been given in one day the patient would, probably, have seen nothing but «horses' heads» or «sunshades», or perhaps nothing but plants and flowers. He always returned to plants in his responses; another patient with senile dementia in my material shows the same reaction. It is perhaps interesting to note in this connection that children of six to eight years also appear to prefer plants in their interpretations. Confabulation is very clear. The intelligence type remains more like that which prevailed when the patient was normal for a longer period in patients with senile dementia than in patients with paresis.

28. Encephalitis Lethargica.

Female. aged 32.

These results were obtained in the first weeks of the illness during one of the short periods in which patient was awake. The test was done with a parallel series of plates so that the computations only can be recorded here.

Responses: 19.

W	: 11 (part confabulatory. part combinatory, some primary W's)	M :	3	H	: 2
		F :	14 (3—)	Hd	: 1
		FC:	2 (—)	A	: 9
D	· 8	CF:	indicated	Ad	: 1
		C :	0	Plant	: 3
F+	: 73 % (with inclusion of FC— 68 %)			Obj.	: 2
				Picture:	1
A	: 53 %				
Orig.	: 10 %±				
Apperceptive	: W—D				
Sequence:	loosened				

The experience type is apparently normal.

The intelligence type, showing several confabulatory W responses, gives a strong impression of fatigue in the subject; the forms also suggest this. The forms are probably much clearer when the patient is well.

VI. SUMMARY.

I. The «Form Interpretation Test» consists in the interpretation of indeterminate figures by the subject. The results of this procedure allow computation because the same series of ten plates is used in every case.

Interpretation of the figures differs from actual perception only in some, not all, of the subjects. In these cases, the difference is due to that fact that the perception is carried out with more or less awareness of the process of assimilation of recent impressions and engrams. This is not a general but an individual difference: it is not an absolute difference, but one which shows gradual differentiation.

II. The problems of the experiment deal primarily with the formal principles (pattern) of the perceptive process. The actual content of the interpretations comes into consideration only secondarily. The clarity of form visualization, the relationships between kinaesthetic and color factors, the manner in which the plates are apperceived, whether as wholes or as parts, and also a number of other factors which may be computed from the protocol of the experiment; all these show typical relationships which are characteristic of the various categories of normal individuals and of the psychoses.

III. The experiment leaves room for completion by further work with standardized parallel series of plates and appropriate control experiments.

IV. Results of the experiment:

Certain optimal relationships of the factors of the test express certain components of «intelligence» of subjects In particular, the establishment of the mode of apperception of the plates allows the setting up of «apperceptive types» and intelligence types (abstract, theoretical, imaginative, grumbling, pedantic, etc.).

The relationship between movement and color factors represents the relation between introversion, the faculty of doing «inner work», and extratension, the faculty of turning to the outer world, in the subject. This relationship expresses a condition in the subject, or the form of a psychosis when one is present. This relationship may be formulated in terms of the «experience type». The following types may be distinguished:

1. Introversive Experience Type: Predominance of kinaesthetic responses. (Example: Imaginative subjects.)
2. Extratensive Experience Type: Predominance of color responses. (Example Practical subjects.)
3. Coartated (narrowed) Experience Type: Marked submergence of movement and color factors to the extent that the subject reacts with form responses exclusively. (Examples: Pedants. subjects in depressive mood or actually psychotically depressed. subjects with dementia simplex.)
4. Ambiequal Experience Type. Many kinaesthetic and equally many color responses (Examples: Talented individuals, compulsion neurotics, manics, catatonics.)

The results frequently show suppression of either introversive or extratensive factors, or both.

Color responses represent lability of affect. The more color responses predominate over kinaesthetic responses the more unstable the affectivity of the subject; the more predominant the kinaesthetic responses. the more stable the affectivity. Neurotic subjects suffer «color shock on encountering the colored plates. (This is evidence of emotional suppression.)

There is a correlation between the experience type and certain groups of functions and phenomena; certain definite experience types are correlated with certain definite components of intelligence, with definite situations of affective dynamics, also with definite types of character, with definite perceptive and, apparently, imagery types, with certain potentialities for the development of talents, with the sense hallucinated, and finally, with the form of neurosis or psychosis present in the subject. (Problem of the determinants of neuroses and psychoses)

The experience type has an habitual status. It is narrowed by depressive moods. dilated by the lighter moods. Fatigue and similar factors influence the experience type. In the course of the life of an individual it undergoes a number of shifts which are probably characteristic of all subjects. Variations in the experience type affect all the groups of functions and phenomena mentioned above: this is simply an expression of the correlations noted between experience type and the functions. Studies of the variations of the experience type include researches into variation at different times and under various conditions. Comparative studies of experience type include researches into the types in men and women and the development of the type in these groups, into comparisons of types in the same and different families, and finally comparison of types in different peoples and races. Such studies must include the study of variations and similarities of certain components of intelligence, personality, talents and imagery types as a part of the research.

The experience type indicates form or pattern, not content; it represents apparatus with which to act, not action itself. Content and action are determined by instinct and by disciplined thinking.

Disciplined thinking narrows the experience type. The capacity to experience is in some general way opposed by disciplined thinking.

V. The test has proved to be of diagnostic value. In normals it makes possible differential diagnosis of personality; in patients, the diagnosis of the illness. Furthermore, it presents an intelligence test almost completely independent of previous knowledge, memory, practice, and degree of education. It is possible by means of the test to draw conclusions concerning many affective relationships. The test has the advantage of almost unlimited applicability making possible without further data comparison of the results in the most heterogeneous subjects.

The Application of the Form Interpretation Test.

By

H. Rorschach, M. D.,
formerly Assistant at Herisau Cantonal Asylum

Published posthumously

by

Emil Oberholzer, M. D. (Zurich).

Reprinted by permission of the publisher, Julius Springer, from the
«Zeitschrift fur die gesamte Neurologie und Psychiatrie», Vol. 82, 1923

Introduction.

In 1921, in Volume II of the ‹Arbeiten zur angewandten Psychiatrie
(Publisher: E. Bircher, now Hans Huber, Bern). Hermann Rorschach published
the methods and results of diagnostic experiment based on perception, consisting in the interpretation of accidental forms   The work was published
under the title «Psychodiagnostics». He continued his work in the development of the experiment with untiring diligence following the publication,
and rapidly acquired a great deal of experience with the test. This experience,
combined with the acute psychological insight and scientific talent with
which Rorschach was endowed, made it possible for him to bring the interpretation of the results to a remarkably, almost dizzily, high state of refinement. This fruitful work was interrupted by Rorschach's sudden death on
April 2nd, 1922. He was in the midst of his promising elaboration of the
numerous problems raised by the experiment His work approached that of
a genius, and heralded a new phase in the study of psychology. The bulk of
his experience and conclusions went with him to his unfortunately early
grave.

The manuscript presented here is based on one prepared by Rorschach a
few weeks before his death for presentation to the Swiss Psychoanalytical
Society. He had discussed the relationship between psychoanalysis and the
test briefly in the Psychodiagnostics, but in this paper he demonstrated the

deeper relationships which exist between the two procedures. These relation ships are equally important to psychoanalysis as to the form interpretation test. and are important in the theoretical basis for Rorschach's conclusions

The publication of this manuscript is in accord with my friend's wishes as expressed in a letter written at the beginning of March, 1922 He had it in mind to include certain modifications and complementary information, the nature of which is unknown to me and consequently lost But I do not consider that the necessary omission of this material is sufficient reason for withholding publication of what we have The fact that Rorschach used this opportunity to demonstrate the construction of the psychogram in great detail and on a single case, an opportunity he did not have in writing the Psychodiagnostics where he was obliged to confine himself to a comparatively small number of summary examples, makes the publication of the manuscript a duty. The example presented herewith will surely offer added stimulus to others to pursue research along the lines Rorschach indicated. Furthermore. two new concepts not discussed in the Psychodiagnostics are included in this paper, namely, «vulgar responses . and «chiaroscuro interpretations. The case serves to illustrate many essentials concerning these categories of responses.

I have made only such changes as were absolutely necessary. I have not attempted to smooth out the style of the language for fear of interfering with the vividness of it. and have limited myself to clarifying those passages which were obscure or difficult to understand. Dr. Rorschach wrote out the manuscript at a time when he was extremely taxed with demands from all sides and when questions were raining on him from all quarters.

On the other hand, I have. in the first part of the work. added a number of explanatory sections, in order to make certain concepts in some measure accessible to any who have not read the Psychodiagnostics. These are generally in footnotes. In the third part, where the relationships between the analysis and the test results are dealt with, I have added a number of supplementary remarks on the analysis and the case history. These have been incorporated in the text in order to avoid footnotes which would disturb easy reading. I was unable to do more than this without adding the whole of the analytic notes and the history of the illness. Nor was it possible to overcome the difficulty imposed in that the manuscript presupposes both a knowledge of the results of the experiment and the basic principles of psychoanalysis. As has been noted above. it was also impossible to give enough data on the case to prove the correctness of the psychogram in its entirety. I must. therefore. content myself with the statement that I have nothing to add to the «blind» diagnosis made by Rorschach, and that I could not have given a better characterization of the patient than is supplied by the psychogram, though I had him under analysis for months. This psychogram is a testimony of the intricate and complicated trains of thought Rorschach was pursuing in more recent times. and proves the masterful application of interpretation of test results which he had worked out after the publication of the Psycho-diagnostics.   *Oberholzer.*

Ladies and Gentlemen:—

Two years ago I made my first report to you on the form-interpretation test. The experiment has developed a great deal in that time. The Plates and the methods of making records have remained the same but there has been further development in the application of results. in the evaluation of the symptomatic indications of the factors, and in the manner of interpretation. There has, however, been little progress in the development of the theory of the experiment.

Today I should like to present one case in order to illustrate the computation of the factors, the interpretation of the results and the method of making a diagnosis. I should also like to acquaint you with a new angle of the test which may come to have great importance in psychoanalysis.

1. The Protocol of the Experiment.
(Formulation of the Interpretations and Computation)

The following record was sent to me by my friend. E Oberholzer, for «blind» diagnosis Only the age and sex of the patient was indicated on the record The subject was a man of forty. He gave the following interpretations for the ten plates.

PLATE I.

1 «A bat». Formula for this interpretation is WF + AV W indicates that the plate was apperceived as a whole This apperceptive mode stands in contrast to D, Dd, S, and Do, all of which, with the exception of Do will be encountered below

D (detail) indicates that only a part of the plate was used in the interpretation, particularly one of those parts which, because of the configuration of the picture, attracts the eye most easily, or, because of its position on the plate, is most easily apperceived. These parts are, at the same time, the most common detail responses statistically.

Dd (small detail) indicates that the part interpreted is not one of those usually interpreted, i. e., is unusual and uncommon

S (space figure) is the symbol for interpretations in which the black parts of the figures are neglected in favor of the white spaces they outline [1].

F indicates that the form of the blot alone determined the response and that neither kinaesthetic nor color factors are influential The plus sign indicates that the form was clearly visualized, even though this conclusion does not agree with my subjective estimation The quality of form perception does not depend on subjective estimation, but on statistical frequency of responses Plate I is frequently interpreted as «bat» by intelligent normals as well as unintelligent subjects In fact, «bat» is one of the «vulgar responses», i e , it belongs to a group of interpretations which are given by one in every three normal subjects I have designated such responses by the symbol V.

---

[1] Do (oligophrenic small detail) indicates, according to Rorschach. those interpretations in which only parts of human figures are given where other subjects give complete figures which are clearly visualized (See p 39)

Finally, A «animal» indicates that the response was an animal figure

2 The second interpretation was, «bony structure [1]» The subject referred to the upper half of the middle part of the plate. This is an apperception of a detail and a form response, but the form is poorly visualized The formula : DF— Anatomy.

3 «A skeleton in a tight wrapping» DF— Anatomy This response may be designated as a clearly visualized form because the middle part which is here taken as a complete figure is frequently interpreted as a human figure It is quite possible that kinaesthetic factors influence this response but we cannot be sure Equally uncertain is the influence of shading in the «wrapping» response In such cases, where it remains a question whether we deal with a simple form interpretation or with a combination of factors we are forced to give the response the symbol F temporarily, correcting it later if necessary after comparing it with all the other responses.

4 The plate is again interpreted as a whole A flying creature». The bat and the draped skeleton are combined to form a new interpretation. If there were kinaesthetic factors in play at all they were certainly of secondary importance. The formula is WF + H H indicates that a human figure was interpreted

PLATE II

1 «Two Clowns» WM + HV This ist a movement response whether the subject says anything about the clowns being in motion or not. Comparative studies on a large material have shown that a kinaesthetic factor is necessary in this interpretation [2]

2. «And yet it may also be a wide parkway (Space form) lined by beautiful dark trees (black), and it loses itself in the distance in a fence (middle black); it is all quite in perspective » This interpretation is determined not only by form but by shading as well. Black and white are given value as colors Such color responses are not equivalent to genuine color interpretations and must be evaluated differently, as chiaroscuro responses. This will be discussed below These responses have one general characteristic peculiar to the group. namely, that they emphasize space and perspective, though this emphasis may not be actually stated I designate such responses by putting the color symbol, C, in brackets. This answer also approaches the original interpretations, those which appear but once in about a hundred normal tests The formula for the response is, then, SF(C) + Landscape

3. «And here it is red; it is a well of fire which gives off smoke. The smoke billows up to the top where the flames break out again » This, too, is a W response, determined in the first instance by the color and secondarily by the form. The formula is, therefore. WCF fire and smoke O (O = Original Response)

PLATE III

1. «Two dandies who bow and greet each other according to the prescribed forms of etiquette They are in dress clothes and carry their top hats in their hands.» I designate

---

[1] German· Knochengerust.

[2] Rorschach defines kinaesthetic responses in the Psychodiagnostics as follows: «Kinaesthetic responses are those interpretations which are determined by form perceptions plus kinaesthetic factors The subject imagines the object interpreted to be in motion The following may be taken as a rule. Responses may be considered as movement determined only when human figures are seen » But even then the answers are not always M's. The question always is does the movement indicated play a primary role in the determination of the response? Is it really a feeling of movement and not merely the apperception of a form which is only secondarily interpreted as being in motion? Kinaesthetic responses may be. as in the case of the forms, subdivided into well and poorly visualized M's. Those which do not correspond well to the form of the figures are considered M— (See pages 25, 26)

this as a whole response even though the red parts are not taken into consideration. The black figures are the essential parts of the plate. The formula is $WM + HV$ [1].

2. «It is as though that red thing in the middle were a power separating the two sides, preventing them from meeting.» This interpretation can hardly be designated other than D? Abstraction.

PLATE IV

1 «A column of smoke which shoots up through the middle, divides, and is diffused at the top · WF(C) + smoke O. This formula is given because color or rather white-black (chiaroscuro) and form together determine the interpretation.

2 «It might also be two human bodies in a bent-over position with their legs hanging down (the snake-like lateral extensions); there is the head (the black area just above the hump which marks the insertion of the lateral extension), the face is turned up (the hump just described), and the arms (the thin line at the side which, with the lateral extensions, encloses a white space)» This is a D interpretation, nearly a Dd. It is a genuine kinaesthetic response and, in addition, an original answer. The formula is $DM + HO$

3. «On the whole it gives me the impression of something powerful in the middle to which everything else clings.» This interpretation, again, cannot be put into a formula.

At the end the patient repeated his first impression. «A typical smoke formation, I don't see anything else»

PLATE V

1. «It is a symmetrical body in a position as though it were flying It has two feelers.» It appears that he means a flying animal so that the formula becomes $WF + A$

2 «At the side here there is the lower part of a human body, there are legs one is a wooden leg» (lateral extensions) $DF + Hd$.

PLATE VI

1. «It is a symmetrical figure with a mid-line axis which is accentuated. Everything is remarkably arranged around the axis.» This is, again, an interpretation which cannot be formulated It belongs in the category of descriptive responses.

2 «The pelt of a wild animal The tracing of the backbone is particularly marked.» A vulgar response: $WF + AV$.

3. «I don't see anything else Yet this white line in the middle is interesting; it is a line of force around which everything else is arranged.» This, again, is a half descriptive, half abstract response, one of those interpretations which does not allow classification Such are rather uncommon. In the interpretation of the findings they will be discussed in detail.

4 «The whole thing is an insect spread out, quite flattened out.» Formula: $WF + A$.

PLATE VII.

1 «This is a typical pelvis again» (the confluent parts): $DF -$ Anatomy.

2. «The center part (confluent part as before) from which rises thick clouds of smoke. The smoke takes on forms»: $WF(C) +$ smoke.

3. «These are distorted faces; they are like rodents.» Formula $DF + AdV$.

---

[1] This is not only a common or «vulgar» response but is, at the same time, a kinaesthetic one. I refer to Rorschach who says in the Psychodiagnostic on page 25 «Plate III is important for this consideration. It is usually interpreted as «two waiters carrying a champagne bucket» or some similar answer is given. In this interpretation the black fish-shaped forms below and laterally are thought of as the legs of the waiters, and the legs are, as may be seen, separated from the body Primary kinaesthetic factors are very probably necessary to make the abstraction represented by overlooking this separation Such answers are, then, to be considered as kinaesthetically determined»

ł .And here are two more of them› (upper third). Formula. DF ÷ Hd. ‹H› is used here because these parts are usually interpreted as human faces or distorted faces.

PLATE VIII.

There was no response for quite a while. There is a lack of associations which appears when the colored plates are presented I designate this reaction as color-shock. The subject then proceeded

1. «It is again in the category of animals (lateral figures). a sort of bear or dog, with a well developed body and short legs; the tail hangs down into the lower part of the figure.› Formula DF + AV.

2. «Another typical vertebra, like a spinal column›. DF + anatomy

He studies the plate a while, then says he sees nothing more.

PLATE IX

There was a long pause as before; it was even longer on this plate. The subject shook his head and said

1 «At best all one can say is two animal heads with turned up snouts» (In the green where it is confluent with the brown.) Formula. DF + Ad.

2. «The rest ist just a figure›you can't do much with›

3. «This is just like the Norwegian coast (Abdomen of the dwarf-like brown figure). It lies just like that and is heavily shaded: that would be the mountains. Here (outer part of the brown) is Sweden which is less mountainous.» Formula: DdF(C) + geography O This is a small detail apperception—the brown figure is usually interpreted as a whole

4. «There is that projection in the middle part, like a fountain.› DF + fountain.

The subject again explains, «I don't know, nothing much comes to me», expressing the associative inhibition due to color-shock.

PLATE X.

Here again some hesitation.

1 «From a distance it looks like a collection of tinted beetles › Formula: WFC + A. This is one of those interpretations where it is difficult to decide whether it was primarily the form, particularly the distribution of forms, which was the primary determinant of the response, or whether the color was primary and the form secondary In such cases it is wise to remember that rigid classification is not possible, and that even with great experience and careful consideration subjective conclusions based on analogy cannot be entirely avoided. It is quite possible that color has no influence at all in this interpretation and that it would have been the same had the plate been black instead of colored.

2. «These are polyps but they are blue» (blue lateral). Formula. DF + A.

3. «Here we have something like newts» (gray lateral). Formula: DF + A.

4. «These things standing up are two little animals with their feelers. They are standing on their hind legs» (gray above). Formula DF + A.

5. «The whole thing is like a path in a park and the dark parts are the trees (dark gray above). There is a path in the middle; it runs off a long, long way.› Formula: SF(C) + landscape O.

6 «It is like a bay of an ocean» (white between the red, the lower half). Interpretation of intermediate figure Like the previous responses of this kind, it takes into consideration the borders Formula. SF— geography

7. «.. the waves break on this steep coast» (red). Formula: DF(C)+ geography.

8. «The dark part in this blue star-shaped figure is a little man who holds onto the red here. He is taking a step.» Formula: DdM + HO. Clearly a movement response and also a small detail interpretation using only a part of the blue radial figure. This figure is usually interpreted as a whole (see the second response this subject gave for this plate).

9. . . and behind him there is a squirrel trying to follow it is sitting upright on these branches (squirrel—lighter part of the blue figure, branches—horizontal extensions below Formula: DdF + AO.

10. And this is like a distorted face (green below) two long plaits hang down from it. Formula: DF—Hd.

11. These two yellow parts are like barking dogs, two terriers standing guard as if someone wished to come into a house —they would come through this passage (white between the lower green)—and the dogs will bark at them. Formula DF + A

The following is a summary of the formulae without further comment

I. WF + AV	DF— anat.	DF + Anat	WF + H
II. WM + HV	SF(C) + land-scape	WCF fire and smoke O	
III. WM + HV			
IV WF(C) + smoke		DM + HO	
V. WF + A	DF + Hd		
VI WF + AV	WF + A		
VII. DF— anat.	WF(C) + smoke	DF + AdV	DF + HdV
VIII. DF + AV	DF + anat.		
IX DF + Ad	DdF(C) + geography	DF + fountain	
X WFC(?) + A	DF + A	DF— A	DF + A
SF(C) + landscape O		SF— geography	DF(C) + geography
DdM + HO	DdF + AO	DF— Hd	DF + A

The computation of the interpretations that could be expressed in formulae is given below. By computation is meant the adding up of the responses of the same apperceptive mode, or which are the same in other qualities.

1. Apperceptive Mode.

W 11 i.e., responses interpreting the plate as a whole were given 11 times.

D 17 i e, responses using normal details were given 17 times

Dd 3 i e., small and uncommon details were picked out by the subject three times. It should be noted that a number of the 17 D's were nearly Dd's No absurd small details were used, however; it is characteristic of most schizophrenics that they do choose absurd tiny details There is, nevertheless, a definite tendency to choose unusual though not absurd parts

S 3 None of these three is a pure intermediate or space interpretation since all use neighboring parts of the figures.

—————
34

2. Quality of the Responses.

F 22 i. e., 22 of the 34 responses given for the ten plates were form interpretations Of this number, 5 are minus in sign, that is, are poorly visualized, making F+% = 77 The number of F+ is rather higher than usual

M 4 i e, 4 interpretations were determined by kinaesthesias. The fact that several interpretations might possibly have been kinaesthetically determined must not be neglected, however, so that 4 may be considered too small rather than too large a count in this case Furthermore, there is a tendency to give «small M» responses and secondary M's. The symptomatic value of these movement responses remains rather vague[1]

FC 1 i.e., there is but one such interpretation and that is rather doubtful—the beetle collection in Plate X—in which form is the primary determinant though color also has influence

CF 1 i.e. a single interpretation—«Well of fire which gives off smoke» (Plate II)— which is determined primarily by the color of the blot though form is not entirely neglected.

C 0 There is, however, a tendency toward such «primary» color responses as seen in the interpretation last mentioned above. In C responses, the form of the figure has no part whatever.

F(C) 6 i.e., 6 responses in which light and shade were the primary determinants rather than actual color

—— ——
34

3. Content of the Responses.

H	5
Hd	3
A	11
Ad	2
Anatomy	4
Fountain	1
Geography	3
Landscape	2
Smoke	2
Fire	1
	34

H and A indicate interpretations involving the entire human or animal figure, Hd and Ad interpretations dealing with parts of such figures.

Relative Numbers.

Besides the F+ percentage already computed, experience has shown several other relationships of this sort to be of value in the interpretation of the results of the test They will be discussed in detail below.

1. Percent animal responses—in this case 38 % of all interpretations deal with animals or part of animals.

2 Vulgar responses, i.e., those interpretations which occur once in every three records. In this case they form 21 % of the total

3 Original responses are the rare interpretations which occur once in a hundred tests. Here, these too amount to 21 % This number might be judged actually higher rather than lower, the same is true for the Vulgar responses.

——————————————————————

[1] Since the publication of the Psychodiagnostics, Rorschach has designated kinaesthetic interpretations of small and unusual parts of the figures as «small M», differentiating them from the other M responses which are W's or D's. In this he was probably guided by the experience that, as a rule, only interpretations involving the whole or the normal details of the figures involve kinaesthetic influences «Small M's» are, for the most part, not experienced as kinaesthesias in the primary interpretation, but are added and felt secondarily. Sometimes they are purely confabulatory ornamentations of the interpretation and appear to indicate pleasure in confabulating and vivid affective life in the subject. Cf. H. Behn-Eschenburg, Psychische Schüleruntersuchungen mit dem Formdeutversuch. Inaug.-Diss., Zürich, 1921.

There are, furthermore, a few individual responses, i e., responses which have been given only by this patient. These are the fire and smoke interpretations of Plate II and the bowed figure of Plate IV. as well as the unformulated abstract responses, the line of force in the middle, etc.

4. The Apperceptive type which in this case is: $\underline{W}$ - D — (Dd — S)

This formula is intended to express the approximate proportion of the modes of apperception to each other. The normal formula is W D, if the number of responses were the same as in this case the distribution would be about as follows: 8 W, 23 D, 2 Dd, and 1 S. In our case the number of W's is relatively too large, the number of D's too small, and there are too many Dd's and S's. Consequently, we must underline the W and add Dd and S in parenthesis.

Sequence is orderly, or, at most, only slightly loose. This means that, in general, the subject tends to interpret first W, then D, and then Dd. so that there is a certain logical sequence of the mode of apperception

The figures obtained by calculations based on the record are by no means to be considered as absolute. A general view of the total findings must be retained so as to avoid being tripped up by the figure for a particular factor On the other hand, these figures form the basis of the interpretation, of what I have called the «psychogram» I consider it quite impossible to obtain a definite and reliable interpretation from the records. even after a great deal of experience and practice, unless the calculations are made

2. The Interpretation.

In view of the extraordinary variability of the findings, no definite directions can be given as to which factor would be the easiest and most convenient to use in starting the interpretation. It is, however, generally safest to begin with the color responses: these responses have been found empirically to be the representatives of the affectivity, the total affective responsiveness. Another reliable point of departure might be the unusual status of any one factor of the experiment, or any unusual correlation between the factors. This method offers many opportunities to arrive at definite conclusions quickly For instance, if well visualized forms constitute 100 % of the responses, that is, if all the forms have been chosen carefully, and, in addition, there is a definite tendency to interpret Do, pedantic, small details, then it is fairly obvious that we deal with a compulsion neurosis or a depression. If there are many whole interpretations, especially wholes made up by combining normal details (D). and at the same time many M's, then the subject is certainly imaginative. If the experience type is extratensive. i. e., if the color responses predominate over the M interpretations, and if there is a high percentage of well visualized forms and a high percent animal response, then the subject is a skillful and alert worker with good capacity for making adaptions. though somewhat stereotyped. If the sequence of W, D, etc., is rigid to the maximum, i. e., if the subject interprets a W, then a D and then a few Dd regularly for each plate, then the subject certainly is a skillful logician but an unaccommodating systematist, etc. Thus it is seen that there are a large number of correlations which can be grasped very quickly and thereby permit the establishment of the main lines of the psychogram without great difficulty. When no such correlations are present it is not so easy to attack the records When the factors tend toward average values and the findings approach the normal it is more difficult to analyse the record Too many «averages» make the records rather colorless.

The findings in the present case deviate from mere medium values in more than one particular and. in addition. exhibit a phenomenon which clarifies the problem to a degree at once. This is the sudden lack of ideas and the long pauses which occur when the subject encounters the colored plates. whereas previously, on the black blots. he had interpreted very freely. This is «color-shock».

The symptom value of color interpretations lies in the field of affectivity. The FC responses represent adaptable affectivity: CF and C. on the other hand, represent non-adaptable, egocentric affectivity. The proportions of the various types of color responses to each other make it possible to draw conclusions concerning the emotional dynamics of the subject. Color shock also contributes to such conclusions. It invariably indicates neurotic repression of affect. Suppression of color responses as expressed in color shock is a pathognomonic sign of neurotic repression of affect

There are other means of demonstrating this process of suppression. When the color responses are suppressed, kinaesthetic factors are usually, probably always, suppressed as well. My previous researches have shown that kinaesthesias represent the capacity for «inner» life, i. e., introversion. Plate I has been selected so that it allows interpretation as an M if the subject is at all kinaesthetically inclined. In fact, normal subjects tend to give kinaesthetically determined responses for Plate I beginning with the second or third response if, indeed, not with the very first. If it is found that the total record indicates some kinaesthetic tendencies and that, in spite of this, no M responses have been given for Plate I, then it is certain that kinaesthetic factors are being suppressed. The present subject gave kinaesthetic responses only after the first plate and in accordance with this fact we find that true color responses for the colored plates also appear late (in Plate X). It follows, therefore, that both color and kinaesthetic factors are in a state of partial suppression in this case and that the kinaesthetic (introversive) as well as the affective (extratensive) side of the experience type is narrowed and coartated by processes of neurotic repression[1].

---

[1] With reference to the concepts «introversion» and «extratension», note pages 72 to 87 in the Psychodiagnostics. I add a statement for superficial orientation. Rorschach reserved the usual expression «introverted» or «introvertivity» for the state in which the subject is turned in upon himself, and he calls the person showing a marked preponderance of M, introversive, M responses being representative of «inner» life or of living within ones self Persons with a large predominance of CF and C responses tend more to «outward» life and show more motor excitability and affective lability. These Rorschach designates as extratensive. In this he wishes to express the fact that these are not fixed traits but mobile potentialities, not contrasting but different psychisms the first being re-

There is a third sign of repression. In the absence of repression the subject interprets movement and color in the plates in a more or less haphazard
fashion. This free mixing of movement, form and color responses appears to
be characteristic of persons who are free of «complexes». This undoubtedly
means that the normal dynamics of human experience cannot be settled simply
by the terms introverted and extraverted. Evidently there is a to and fro swing
between introversivity and extratensivity. This free oscillation between introversion and extratension is restricted in the presence of repressive processes.
In the experiment, this restriction is shown by the fact that a normal subject
with kinaesthetic tendencies gives color responses when confronted with the
colored plates, but soon returns to kinaesthetic interpretations, perhaps after
giving four or five responses. (Color responses usually begin with Plate VIII.
the first that is fully colored). The repressed subject is virtually chained to
color. In the present case the first M interpretation is the eleventh response,
an evidence of the fact that the fluid relationship between the factors of
«inner» life and those of outwardly directed affect is disturbed by neurotic
repressive processes, an evidence that the normal, free and unobstructed flow
between introversion and extratension is disturbed in this subject.

At this stage it can be concluded definitely that we are dealing with a
neurosis, and that further investigation is possible. There is obviously no
psychosis—at least no manifest psychosis—for in psychoses color shock never
appears. The subject shows 4 M : $1^1/_2$ CF [1]. This would be the formula for
his experience type. The M's outweigh the colors even though factors other
than rigid adherence to the figures are considered. As was noted above, more
of the F responses could be considered as influenced by kinaesthetic determinants than were influenced by color. In other words, the tendency to give
kinaesthetic interpretations is stronger than the urge to interpret color; the
experience type of the individual is, therefore, more introversive than extratensive. Recalling the processes of suppression we have already shown to be
present in the patient, this conclusion might be expressed more correctly by
saying that the introversive features of the experience type were more resis-

---

presented by kinaesthesias and the second by color responses The adjective «introverted»
would, then, indicate the *rigid* preponderance of introversive tendencies over the non-
introversive or extratensive tendencies The terms «introversivity» and «extratensivity»
would denote the *capacity for,* and «introversion» and «extratension» the *process of,* becoming introverted or extratended, or turning toward one self or toward the outside world
In any given case, the range between introversivity and extratensivity is the experience
type. Rorschach calls the experience type coartated if the values for M and C responses
approach zero; when both introversive and extratensive capacities are present to a marked
degree, the experience type is designated as broadened or dilated

[1] Rorschach found it practical to balance the unit M against the unit CF He felt
theoretically justified in this practice since form enters into consideration in both M and
CF responses in addition to the primary determinants of movement and color FC responses
were evaluated as one-half and primary C's as one and one-half units (Psychodiagnostics,
p 35)

tant to repression than the extratensive features. The narrowing—coartation—has affected the extratensive features more profoundly than it has the introversive.

In my experience the general findings with regard to the neuroses indicate that in the more extratensive experience types hysterical symptoms predominate while in introversive types neurasthenic and psychasthenic symptoms are dominant. The nearer the experience type approaches ambiequality. i. e., the more nearly equal the number of movement and color answers become, the more compulsion phenomena appear in the neurotic picture. The clearcut compulsive neurosis lies between the hysterical and psychasthenic pictures in the experience type schemes. Therefore, it may be expected that our patient will show neurasthenic and psychasthenic symptoms, and it may be assumed that there will be some compulsion phenomena since the experience type is not too far from ambiequality. To review, then, we have concluded from the existence of color shock that there is a neurosis, and from the experience type that the neurosis is of a particular form, namely, psychasthenia with compulsive (obsessive) features.

Returning to the computations, it will be seen that the relationships referring to the affect are at first rather vague. FC, with the C in parenthesis (F[C]), predominate. These are interpretations in which color values do not have determining influence, but are replaced by values of light and shadow. The symptomatic indications inherent in such interpretations are not yet entirely clear; the interpretations appear to have something to do with the capacity for affective adaptability, but also indicate a timid, cautious and hampered sort of adaptability. Further, they indicate self-control before others and a tendency toward a fundamentally depressive disposition which the subject tries to control when others are present. On the other hand, there is at least one interpretation which reveals markedly egocentric affectivity, namely, the first color response, «fire and smoke» (Plate II). When the first color response is egocentric and is then followed by equivocal responses, as is the case in our patient, a violent and impulsive affectivity is generally indicated; nevertheless, this violent affectivity is subject to control. In this case, then, we see conscious rather than unconscious repression of affect, and less actual repression than conscious struggle against the subject's own affective reactions. Hence, for the time being, we can only conclude that there are two affective tendencies opposed to each other in our patient: 1. a depressive one outwardly controlled and rather timidly adapted, and 2. an egocentric-impulsive trend which is controlled to the utmost degree both outwardly before others and inwardly as well.

The color responses do not allow any further conclusions at this time, and we now turn to other factors of the experiment. The problem of intellectual rapport and adaptability furnishes a starting point, the solution of which may be sought in a number of factors.

Apperceptive type and sequence will be discussed first The apperceptive type is that of an individual who neither loses himself in small details (Dd) nor rigidly sticks to giving whole conceptions (W). The entire test shows, rather, that he first tries to give a whole response to each plate before turning to the D's and that the sequence is quite orderly without being maximally rigid. This means that there is no scattering nor any programmatic rigidity in his method of thinking, but that in general the reasoning displays common sense, that is, is capable of adapting itself to the task at hand discriminating important from side issues. On further examination, however, the sequence does show an individual peculiarity aside from the fact mentioned above, that the number of D's is rather small for the large number of W's and Dd's. This will be discussed later.

In Plate I the subject interprets a whole response first, then turns to the middle of the plate and interprets a bony structure, then the skeleton, and finally reverts to a whole response in interpreting the flying creature with the body lying in the middle of the Plate. With the second plate the first response is again a whole; then he turns to the middle as before and interprets a landscape and, after that, starting again with the middle part of the figure, the subject constructs a W, the well of fire with the columns of smoke above from which the flames burst out. Again in the third plate a W is given first, then the subject turns again to the middle, giving the interpretation. «It is as though that red thing in the middle were a power separating the two sides, preventing them from meeting». The sequence, first W, then a detail from the middle, then an inclusive interpretation starting from the middle, a W or a response composed of several D's (DW). This sequence reveals quite definitely a sort of programmatism in the thinking processes.

Several points are to be observed in this connection. First, this sequence furnishes an insight into the manner in which the subject first takes a general reconnoitering view, then fastens on the central detail, and finally develops the whole from this central detail, a sort of construction. The first W's, the reconnoitering ones, are usually rather abstract; they are ideas which the subject himself does not trust very much. Actually, the first interpretation for each plate is neither very original nor very clearly perceived. The later interpretations for each plate, however, all show a constructive tendency. The first abstract whole interpretations are as indefinite, hazy and uneven as these later constructive ones are definite, even and convincing. We can thus conclude that the subject reasons better inductively than deductively, better synthetically than analytically, and better concretely than abstractly. The fact that the first interpretation is abstract in spite of all this, allows the conclusion that while the subject certainly attempts to make a survey of the whole problem in every case by making a rapid reconnoitering review of it, he is nevertheless not satisfied with this and does not feel at ease until he can turn to the details and to a constructive production arising out of them.

The sequence permits one further deduction. The subject gives great attention to details, but not those details which draw attention by virtue of their prominent position in the plate. He disregards a number of normal details which are easy to interpret, especially avoiding those which are placed laterally, and usually turns to the middle of the plate for his details. Even when he has nothing concrete to interpret his attention still hovers around the center of the figure. Looking over these interpretations again, we see that they fall into the group that cannot be classified: the power separating the two sides, preventing them from meeting », «the line of force on which everything depends », «the power around which everything is grouped », «the well of fire and smoke». All these have been constructed from a medial detail. Here again we see a certain programmatism in the thinking. Despite the predominance of concrete reasoning he has a tendency toward the abstract. This tendency must be psychogenetically determined since we cannot be deceived into believing that abstractive reasoning is easier for this subject than constructive thinking. Furthermore, it has been demonstrated that abstract interpretations generally are conditioned by «complexes». This would be particularly true in this case where they always arise from things in the middle line. The individual peculiarity of the sequence in our subject is, then, «complex determined». It would appear that a more or less compulsive over-emphasis of abstract reasoning is present here, and that this stands in opposition to the actual and natural disposition to be more concrete than abstract, more constructive than abstract.

Consideration of the apperceptive type leads a step further. As was mentioned in connection with the computation of the factors, the number of W's and Dd's is somewhat too large, and the number of D's rather too low. Neglecting the sequence for the moment, this apperceptive type would indicate that the subject shows a certain tendency to overlook the most tangible and essential things in the plates, the D's. These details are always the expression of the sense for grasping the immediate, essential considerations in any problem. The tendency to give W's, representing a tendency toward making generalizations, is somewhat over-emphasized. The tendency to get lost in details—to choose Dd's in the test—is also over-emphasized. There is, then, a contradiction here, in that the subject, on the one hand, tends to seek out far-fetched connections but, at the other extreme, also tends to brood over incidental niceties. This same contradiction which is found here in the field of intellectual processes has already been noted in the emotional processes. There the subject was found to have a strong though somewhat restrained egocentric-impulsive trend but, at the same time, a depressive trend and timid adaption which he covers up. We might at this time continue on this line of investigation to find further relations between this pair of contradictions and the responses from which these parts of the psychogram are derived. The method would be practicable but circuitous; it is, further-

more, very important in making interpretations not to get too far away from
the only basis of any interpretations, namely, the protocol and the computations made from it. If this precaution is not observed there is danger of
deriving too much from a single factor and to build one structure of interpretation on another.

For this reason it is necessary to search for another factor which will
furnish further indications concerning the intellectual adaptability of the
subject. Such a factor is number of vulgar responses—21 % in our case—and
their distribution. The vulgar responses represent the share in the collective
or common way of sensing or perceiving things. The number of vulgar
responses is low even when responses which approach the vulgar are included.
On this basis, we conclude that the subject does not share in the common
mode of perceiving to any great extent. We will now relate this small percentage of vulgar responses with the already established fact that the subject
gives too few D interpretations, which indicates that his sense of what is
tangible and essential is somewhat reduced by a need, perhaps on an obsessional basis, for indulging in abstract processes of reasoning. Indeed, among
the vulgar responses which are present, there are none which make use of
D's. The number of detail responses, and these are the ones which are also
frequently vulgar, is small in this case. Here, again, is a contradiction: even
though the subject interprets concretely and constructively he lacks, nevertheless, a certain simple skill and readiness in making adaptions. What this
is, is the quick wit of the practical man who, because of his freedom to grasp
any opportunity, can see through and master any situation. It is the genuine
opportunism of the practical adjustment to the matter at hand and self-as-
sured efficiency in conceiving and handling a situation.

The original interpretations are the opposite of the vulgar responses, and
in this case the two are equal in amount—21 %. It must be emphasized that
this is a genuine originality. It is not the originality of the shop-talker, nor
does it consist in hair-splitting differentiations, but is rather representative of
well-developed individuality with an independent way of looking at things.
This is apparent in the primary conception as well as in the elaboration of
the responses, and is especially in evidence in the constructive elaboration
of the original impression. Many of these responses are not only original, but
individual, that is, are responses given by this patient alone. These will be
discussed below.

The percentage of form and form-color interpretations are the last factors
to be mentioned in this connection. This subject gave 77 % clearly visualized
forms. If the FC responses in which C is placed in parenthesis—the black-
white interpretations—are considered, and these are closely allied with forms
and are all sharply conceived, then the F+ percent rises to 80 or 85. Furthermore, two of the poorly visualized forms which depress the F+ percentage
are anatomical interpretations. In subjects who are not physicians such res-

ponses indicate either a complex impelling the subject to try to give an impression of intelligence or a tendency to hypochondriacal rumination, or to both. An F+ percent of 80 to 85 is a good average finding. Higher figures approaching or reaching 100 % of well-chosen forms are seen only in outspoken pedants and grumblers in the «normal» group, those subjects who try to be most rigidly objective in their interpretations. This leads to the production of but 2 or 3 whole responses, to giving D and Dd responses exclusively; they do not dare to venture on constructive or combinatory trains of thinking. Our patient, in spite of the anxious and cautious predilection seen in the study of his method of adapting himself, is actually quite unrelated to this type.

The FC responses represent the capacity for affective rapport and adaptability, a kind of combination of affective and intellectual adaptability. They are, in general, characteristic of the normal individual who is well-adapted and is capable of making new adaptations. Our subject gave but one form-color response and this is a questionable one; it could have been a color-form or a form interpretation as well. Just this demonstrates the gap in the patient's emotional life; he is, on the one hand, expansively egocentric in his affectivity, but on the other, shows the consciously cautious adaption represented in the test by the chiaroscuro interpretations. His wish to apply himself to the task and his capacity to do so are beyond all question; Dr. Oberholzer states that he showed this trait to a marked degree in the performance of the test.

Before going further with the investigation, it would be well to summarize briefly what we have been able to learn thus far in the interpretation of the record. This is a neurosis in an introversive experience type; hence predominance of psychasthenic features. There are probably compulsive (obsessive) phenomena. There is deficiency of freedom in affective adaptions. Two contradictory tendencies exist. First, the depressively colored, all-too-conscious and highly intellectualized manner of adaptation; and second, the expansively egocentric trend in affective life. The intelligence is, on the whole, good, keen, original, more concrete than abstract, more inductive than deductive, although there is a contradiction in that the subject exhibits a rather weak «sense» for dealing with the obvious and the practical. This, too, represents a gap; on the one hand, there is obsessive compulsion in the direction of abstract, generalizing patterns of thought: on the other, a compulsion to begin his constructive pattern, not with what is practical and essential, but with a central point chosen on the basis of a «complex». He thus gets «stuck» on trifling and subordinate details, embroiling himself in them. There is, however, no scattering; affective and intellectual self-discipline and mastery are apparent.

Of the remaining factors, we have yet to discuss the three space figures. Space responses always indicate some sort of oppositional trend. When the experience type is extratensive, this takes the form of some «outward» opposition, defiance, a tendency to indulge in polemics, to make contradictions and to be aggressively stubborn. In an ambiequal experience type, this oppositional tendency is directed against the subjects own consciousness and gives rise to skepticism, doubt, hesitancy, vacillation, and indecision as well as emotional ambivalence and ambi-tendencies. Obsessional thoroughness, a desire to collect things, and a compulsion in the direction of completeness in all things are also not infrequently present. When the experience type is introversive, the space interpretations appear to indicate opposition to the subject's own «inner» life, resulting in constant self-distrust, feelings of insufficiency of every sort, self-criticism and circumstantiahty; frequently there is an admixture of phlegmatism and asceticism.

Our patient shows an experience type definitely introversive, but close to the ambiequal. Hence there will be a predominance of ideas of insufficiency, referring particularly to the innermost self, the productive sphere of the personality, a distrust of himself, his ability to produce. We shall also have to expect the phenomena of the ambiequal type, for in our subject both introversive and extratensive features are repressed, and the resulting coartation tends in the direction of ambiequality. Skepticism, doubt and ambivalence will, therefore, be present with the characteristics mentioned above. We may assume that both the tendency toward opposition to the «inner» self and opposition to the more conscious life combine to result in the following picture: grumblings and doubts about his own intelligence, indecision, phantasies of insufficiency, compulsive meticulousness, obsessive throughness, a drive to view things from all angles, the need to hear the other side of the story every time, having exacerbations of rigid objectivity and pedantic self-correction almost to the extent of becoming an ascetic. The neurotic element in the case is much more clearly demonstrated now than it has been before. It is striking to note how the study of the space responses defines the neurotic aspects of the record. This is frequently the case, though I am, as yet, unable to say why it should be. The space responses frequently furnish such clues, and it is probable that other factors would also contain clues for the investigation; this will be known only through further experience.

There is another characteristic of the space responses in this case which makes them specific for this subject, makes them individual. At least two of them are made use of in the elaboration of chiaroscuro interpretations, and both in a quite similar manner. I refer to the roads in perspective seen in Plates II and X. Two quite different situations are revealed in these interpretations. If we begin the analysis with the space responses we arrive at the conclusion that there are ideas of insufficiency in the subject; if we start with the other half of the formula, DSF(C), namely the chiaroscuro interpretation, we come to the conclusion mentioned above, that the affective adaptions are made carefully and are cautiously guarded. Thus it cannot be denied

that there is a very close relationship between the ideas of insufficiency and
the patient's methods for correcting them on the one hand. and this trend
toward measured affective adaptions on the other. It may also be assumed
that each of these two factors (S and F[C]. also has a relation to the content
of the interpretation: according to the findings in previous similar cases I
have seen. this proves to be the case Those subjects who gave striking
chiaroscuro interpretations also showed definite signs that the content was
influenced by «complex» material and this appeared in the form of correction of this influence. that is to say. as wish-fulfillments. Such interpretations
in this case deal with landscapes, one might say architectonic landscapes
Other individuals see castles and towers. temples and arches, etc. When such
answers occur in a test it is safe to conclude that the subject considers himself disrupted in his «inner» (mental) life. weak, out of joint. inwardly in-
harmonious: he projects these feelings in the form of wish-fulfillments into
the test. responding with constructions. streets, temples and arches. The feelings of insufficiency. the feeling of having builded badly in his own life, betrayed in introversive subjects by the space responses. and the trend toward
depression and caution in the affectivity shown in the chiaruscuro responses.
appear together to be the unconscious basis for the interpreting of things
constructed, such interpretations existing as compensations (corrections).

There is one final noteworthy characteristic of these interpretations. These
chiaroscuro responses emphasize the depth of the picture as a dimension
more than any of the other interpretations. Our subject also stresses perspective and in his other interpretations of this kind notes a three dimensional
quality. According to my experience, this indicates that a peculiar type of
psychological correlation is functioning here. There is a special talent for
the appreciation of spatial relationships, of depth and distance which appears to be correlated with the cautious and measured affectivity with depressive nuances. This talent frequently, perhaps always, is correlated with
feeling of insufficiency, the content of which is feelings of loss of solidity,
of instability, of being «out of joint with the times» Black and white interpretations which deal with architectural structures and which are original or
approach originality permit the conclusion that the subject possesses a marked
ability to visualize objects in space and has a talent for construction. I drew
this conclusion in this case and it proved to be correct though I had no ink-
ling of the patient's profession and he did not reveal it in the manifest content of his interpretations. Dr Oberholzer gave me the record of the analysis
later. It contains a number of remarks about the pattern [1] of his psychological
personality and these affirm the presence of constructive talents. He has
demonstrated this talent more than once in his work as a mechanical engineer

---

[1] German = Formale

by creative inspirations. In the same way, the notes of the analysis confirm the presence of the ability to visualize in space which is so well developed in this subject. He can tell, before any drawings are made and by mental visualization alone, whether or not a proposed construction can actually be reduced to drawings. Building plans become alive for him and give him a formative image of the finished and completed structure. On the other hand, it is impossible for him to conceive a new and original form.

With this matter of constructive thinking we are brought to consider the W responses which prove, in many instances, to be made up of details. These constructive whole responses alone do not allow the conclusion to be drawn that the subject has technical talents and capabilities for construction, but only indicate the ways and means used in reaching intellectual ends. A subject who shows constructive W responses will build up his conclusion from one or another unit and will have a tendency to adjust his whole according to the unit he first apperceived. He will create surprising conceptions but at times will fall into the production of works burdened by too much ideation. If certain intuitive powers are available to the subject he will be able to survey large groups of material and organize them with a remarkable certainty. On the other hand, should this intuition fail him, he will be blindly one-sided in his constructions and will tend to treat all things in the same way. But if it can be established that constructive talents as described above are present and if there are also a number of well-balanced constructive whole apperceptions, then it can be stated that these two groups of psychisms —constructive thinking and an actual talent for technical construction—may be combined to produce outstanding achievements.

I mentioned intuition above. If a subject interprets clever W's which arise particularly rapidly into his grasp, and if abstract and constructive as well as combinatory associative processes are intermingled in their production, we can conclude with certainty that he has intuitive capacities. In this record the fire and smoke interpretation of Plate II most closely approaches the signs of the presence of intuition. To be sure construction is preponderant, but the conception of this interpretation appears to have been the result of a *single* glance. It can be demonstrated that such intuitive interpretations are rich in «complex» material. On the other hand, it is almost exclusively persons with dilated experience type, those who furnish many movement and color responses, who give intuitive interpretations. The fewer M's and the fewer C's, the more rare are these intuitive interpretations, because neurotic repressions eventually stifle the intuitive powers. Not every intuition, however, has the full value of an intuition. To have this value, there must be capacity for coartation as well as for dilatation, for the forms first arise as the result of the conscious use of that psychic sphere the function of which is the production of clear, self-limited forms. There must, then, be capacity

for dilatation and coartation in the organ which serves to connect introversion and extratension functionally Intuitions can be of value only when
the subject has the ability to grasp and hold the intuition achieved in the
dilated experience as a whole form: that is to say, he must be able to shift
from dilated to coartated type quickly, and only if this is possible will the
intuitions be of value. The value is liable to be reduced under two conditions,
first, when there is too little capacity for coartation, and second, when the
habitual coartation is too marked If there is too little ability to coartate,
the intuition will remain sketchy and have the character of an aphorism, of
a castle of dreams, of unadaptable Utopias. On the other hand, when the
habitual experience type is one of too great coartation, that is when logic
alone is dominant, or when coartation is too great because of neurotic repressions, intuition becomes paralysed. This last is the situation in our case
where the neurosis cripples the freedom of «inner» productivity, as is frequently the case. Obviously this is no new contribution. What is new, however, is the fact that we are able by means of the test to follow the conflict
between the repressing conscious and the repressed unconscious, and observe
how the neurotic repressions narrow the productive sphere and see how
freedom of «inner life» is completely stifled by conscious restraints (corrections) and by compulsive super-criticism. On this basis we are able to understand why it is that our patient always throws himself into abstract thinking
first and does it in so inadequate a manner, and to understand why he allows
himself to be led by «complex» determined conceptions rather than his own
adequate constructive anlage. The reason lies in a compulsive state arising
out of depressive feelings of insufficiency.

And finally, a correction. Hitherto we have paid too much attention to
the introversive features in our patient and have neglected the extratensive
side. The fact that the patient produced an almost intuitive color-form interpretation with the first plate containing any color (Plate II) indicates that
the simple computation of the color responses undervalues the extratensive
features. Introversive features are certainly preponderant, but extratensive
features are not as weak as at first appeared, and it may be safely assumed
that at least occasionally it is possible for this experience type to swing toward the extratensive side. When subjects have had or still have extratensive
periods of some duration, 'he psychogram and, with it, the diagnosis must
be changed. In the extratensive periods the patient must necessarily be capable of showing spite and revolt tendencies and impulsive actions and aggres-
sive adjustments, and at such times the quality of the neurosis must change
so that hysterical-conversion symptoms replace psychasthenic symptoms, and
the compulsive phenomena take on a different character. Compulsive acts
and feelings and possibly compulsive movements may appear.

Nevertheless, the whole personality receives a certain stabilization in that
the introversive and rather autistic attitude toward the external world will

not be broken through easily. in spite of a strong desire in the patient to apply himself in this sphere For the most part the patient is a psychasthenic, always at odds with himself. dissatisfied with his accomplishments. easily upset but recovering again because of his need for application. He finds little full. free affective rapport with the world about him. and shows a rather marked tendency to go his own way. The dominant mood. the habitual. underlying affective tone is rather anxious and depressed and passively resigned. Thanks to the adequate intellectual capacity and capacity for intellectual adaption. all these conditions can be and are controlled to the greatest possible extent.

3. The Findings and Psychoanalysis.

The relationship between the findings of this experiment and psychoanalysis, the real topic of this paper. will be discussed in the following pages. This relationship may be demonstrated best by means of a scheme in which the interpretations given by our subject are arranged in the following order.

The middle column of the scheme lists those interpretations which are pure form responses (F) The column to the extreme left contains the interpretations which were kinaesthetically determined (M). The column between these two lists those interpretations which may have a kinaesthetic determinant (F tending to M). The right outside column lists the pure color interpretations at the bottom (C), above these come the color-form responses (CF), and at the top of the column, the form-color interpretations (FC) The fourth column, between the last mentioned and the form column, contains those FC interpretations in which the C is placed in parentheses, that is, the chiaroscuro responses, those in which a form interpretation tends in the direction of color. V indicates the vulgar responses, O the original responses, and the individual responses are printed in italics.

This grouping conforms closely to one which I have been using for a long time and which recurs constantly in the Psychodiagnostics. The middle column represents the conscious functions; the F percentage is an indicator of the clarity of the associative processes and, at the same time, of the length of the span of attention and the capacity for concentration in the subject [1]. The left half of the scheme represents the introversive, and the right half the extratensive features in the person tested. From the relations of the two halves of the scheme, that is, between M and (CF — C) certain obvious inferences concerning the extent and activity of autistic thinking may be drawn. The clarity of the forms and the orderliness of the sequence indicate the balancing factor, namely, the extent and effectiveness of disciplined reasoning. In correlating the concepts of the conscious and unconscious as used in psychoanalysis to the experimental factors, it is obvious that, in

---

[1] Compare the chapter on intelligence, p. 56

M

Two Clowns—V

Two dandies greeting and bowing formally—V

Two human bodies in bent over position with their legs hanging down—O

A little man who holds onto the red.—O

F tending toward M

A skeleton in a light wrapping

A flying creature

Bears or dogs with well developed body and short legs; their tails hang down—V

Two little animals with feelers standing on their hind legs.

A squirrel following, it is sitting on a branch—O

Two barking dogs standing guard as if someone wished to come into a house.

F

Bat—V

Bony structure

Symmetrical figure with accentuated midline axis

Pelt of a wild animal The tracing of the backbone is particularly marked —V

An insect spread out

Distorted face like a rodent's.

Distorted human faces

Typical vertebra, like a spinal column.

Animal heads.

Polyps

Newts

Bay in the ocean.

Distorted face with two plaits hanging down.

Abstracta

As though that red thing in the middle were a power separating the two sides, preventing them from meeting.

Something powerful in the middle to which everything else clings The white line in the middle as a line of force around which everything is arranged.

F tending toward C

A wide parkway lined by beautiful dark trees, it is lost in the distance All in perspective

A column of smoke which divides and is diffused at the top.—O

A typical smoke formation.

Norwegian coast and Sweden.—O

Path in park, dark parts are trees

Path in middle runs off a long way.—O

Steep coast.

FC

Collection of tinted beetle-

F(

A well of fire giving off smoke which billows up to top where flames break out again

C

Fire

regard to the symptom-values. the M and C and FC responses are more closely related to the unconscious than the form interpretations and that individual and original responses—in so far as we deal with genuine originality and not with «shop talk»—reveal more about the individual strivings of the subject and thus have more psychoanalytic meaning than the vulgar answers

In our case, it can hardly be mere chance that the most original M response should designate two men stooping, and that the most original color interpretation should be such a peculiarly constructed. almost intuitive. picture of fire with thick smoke and flickering flames. There must be a definite relationship between the interpretation of the stooping men and the introversive content. and between the fire picture and the affective tone of the subject. The subject cannot be conscious of this for he gives no attention to whether he gives M, F or C interpretations. The most striking and therefore the most individual interpretations, as I have pointed out in the section on interpretation, the abstract ones which could not be expressed in a formula. must have a background in the unconscious, however rationalized they appear to be. (These responses are gathered together in the scheme in the middle column just under the form responses.) If any of the interpretations reveal «complex» material it should surely be in these original and individual responses which include M and C factors, for in these there are definite relations between the formal and content spheres.

This assumption first proved to be true in the M interpretations. The actual object interpreted is not important— any more than the manifest content of a dream is of importance in dream interpretation—but the particular kind of kinaesthesia. Subjects who see predominantly movements in extension. figures stretching or rising, are significantly different from those who interpret bent and bowed, burdened and twisted figures, or figures in kneeling or recumbent positions. Subjects who interpret extension kinaesthesias are active individuals with strong drives toward importance and activity although they frequently show neurotic inhibitions. Those who see flexion kinaesthesias have passive and resigned natures [1]. Thus in Plate V, holding the plate with the narrow edge as the base, a representative of the first group saw a danseuse leaping upwards and making passionate movements. In the same plate one of the second group saw a stooped old woman carrying two umbrellas under her arm In the protocol of a politician which I received recently, the only kinaesthetic interpretation in the test concerned itself with two gigantic gods clinging to something. This man also gave several original color responses which constantly repeated the same theme, namely, the inside of the earth, the center of a volcano. the core of the earth, etc. He also, like our present subject, gave several abstract interpretations in which the center line and middle parts of the plate formed the stimulus for responses

---

[1] Compare p 29

which are variations of the same theme. These concerned themselves mostly with the germ out of which all things shall develop. Hence on the one hand we have gigantic gods and on the other the inside of the earth and the germ from which all grows. These interpretations arouse the suspicion that there are present ideas of re-making the world and show how he became a politician, particularly how he became a constructive organizer. Such experiences have taught me that the content of interpretations can have a meaning of its own, a meaning which is determined primarily by relationships which exist between «form» and content, between the pattern and the content of the interpretations.

We return now to our patient whom Dr Oberholzer has analysed to see what was demonstrated by the help of the psychoanalytical-historical material and the results of the analysis.

a) The M Interpretations.

The M responses represent introversion, the «inner life», in the pattern of reaction in the test. The greater the predominance of kinaesthetic interpretations over color interpretations, the more introversive is the subject and the greater the role of introversive mechanisms in his psychic life, with a tendency to regression and to react against the world.

In our case there is a clear predominance of flexion kinaesthesias. Indeed, the most original M interpretation of the whole test is the peculiar twisted figure of Plate IV. The conclusions drawn from the consideration of the whole test are borne out by this special type of M response; the subject is not only introversive, but flexion kinaesthesias play an important role in his introversion. There must, then, exist an unconscious passive attitude. The experiment allows approach to the unconscious to this extent.

If the process of interpretation of the record is reversed so that the record is approached after knowing the results of the analysis the result is the following, written by Dr. Oberholzer who followed this method:

«The flexion kinaesthesias reveal the deepest experience-reaction adjustment in the patient. They are the expression of his passivity and of the feminine part of his sexuality. This passivity is the result of a turning against his own person [1] which took place early in his life and which was due to an originally sadistic urge. Later the passivity was combined with the sex instincts to produce the feminine attitude. The original sadism is found not only in traits of cruelty in his dreams but also made itself felt early, and later as well, in his life in occasional outbursts during which the patient would strike out blindly, afterward being unable to understand the flaring up of his temper. The sadistic tendency was also expressed in occasional lack of consideration bordering on brutality in the pursuit of his business aims and interests, or in sudden outbursts of anger against his subordinates in which his «master-nature» comes to the fore, this in contrast to his habitually strong self control and his conscious dislike of all uncouth instincts. A part of his personality was not mastered during the transition into passivity and masochistic sufferance, and this part gave

---

[1] Freud, Triebe und Triebschicksale. Internat. Zeitschr. f. Psychoanalyse, 1915

rise, in the prepubertal period to an initial compulsion neurosis which took the form of obsessional thinking, in earlier childhood this part of the personality had given rise to phantasies of being a ruler. The initial neurosis dictated the later obsessional character of the patient who tried to regulate his elementary instinctive functions.

The M series is, therefore, what is «lived». I purposely avoid saying «experienced» in order not to imply that the patient knows the nature of this experience. M is the compulsion determining what is lived, and how it is lived. The patient sacrificed eight years of his life in what he knew was a futile battle to save his father's business. It was a struggle against most unfavorable circumstances which included the brutal selfishness of his own brothers. One of these brothers, distinguished because of beautiful, strong teeth, constantly appeared in the patient's dreams as a father substitute In the face of constant disappointments and bitternesses the patient «carried the burden» in memory of his father and because it was his father's wish — «for the sake of my father» After the inevitable liquidation of the business which put an end to the eight years of suffering, the neurosis broke out, continuing the «hammer-blows» of the earlier years.

The flexion kinaesthesias, therefore, belong to the deepest unconscious, and the content of them can hardly be called content in the usual sense of the word The proof of this which may be disclosed in this case, when considered in view of and in connection with the symptom values of other factors, becomes most remarkable, the relation of the kinaesthesias to the unconscious should occupy the first place in any theoretical foundation attempted in dealing with the findings of the experiment »

The kinaesthesias, when they become the determinants of the interpretation of the record as they have in this case, do actually bring unconscious things to the light of day, the analysis establishes the fact that they must stand in the closest relation to what is generally spoken of as the unconscious. The passive nature of the patient demonstrated by the analysis explains, on the basis of information from «within» the patient himself, other traits which appeared in the psychogram in the course of the interpretation. These are the ascetic tendencies in the patient's living, the ideas of insufficiency, and his distrust of himself, particularly with regard to his own productivity. We are able to understand to some extent the source of the contradictions in his make-up.

b) The C Interpretations.

In the Psychodiagnostic I was able to defend the view that the color interpretations, especially the C's and CF's, are in some way related to egocentric affectivity, to unmodified, almost instinctive affectivity. On the other hand, the content and the relation of the content to the general pattern remained obscure for a long time, although it was obvious that the content could not be independent of the accompanying affective tone. If a subject produces a series of genuine C interpretations (representative of impulsive affect) and the content of these interpretations turns ever again to the topic of fire and blood, it must be assumed that the strong affects of his psyche must have something to do with fire and blood, and that fire and blood have some relation to his powerful emotions. It will also make a difference whether a patient interprets the red section of a plate as an open wound, whether he sees rose petals. or syrup. or a slice of ham The question of how much the content of such interpretations belongs to the conscious and how much to the unconscious cannot be decided except in some appropriate cases. One such case was that of the politician. the world builder, mentioned above. He interpreted the center of the earth. chaos, the inside of the earth, as C responses; on the kinaesthetic side there are the gigantic gods. From these we can deduce that he himself wants to construct the earth anew. But this is only the manifest content; the latent content indicates something else. These gigantic gods are in an extraordinary position—the kinaesthetic interpretation gives the picture of the foetal position. The core and interior of the earth may, then signify something quite different, perhaps the mother's womb. This would mean that the color responses extend much more deeply into the «complexes» than at first appeared and that the egocentric affectivity actually has its source in the most highly emotionally toned psychisms. Evidently the content of the color interpretations is to be evaluated like the manifest content in dream interpretation where the latent content is brought to light only in dream analysis.

How does this problem appear when approached in the light of the analysis? I quote Dr. Oberholzer again:

«Smoke and fire form a part of the childhood experiences of the patient. The forge. which at that time was still a part of his father's workshop, is linked into his most important childhood memories of his father He, the father, was a master at the art of tempering. a special process to which he owed his reputation; these facts were known to the patient early in life. Even when he was hardly able to climb the steps he would slip into the shop again and again, or, if he were put out, would look in longingly for hours at a time regardless of wind or weather This workshop, as well as the large factory with machines and parts of machines which grew out of it later on, are the most frequently occurring elements in the manifest content of the patient's dreams. These furnished important sexual symbols from which, in the course of the analysis, it was possible to draw conclusions regarding his early sexual curiosity directed toward his parents and the feminine adjustment to his father. In one such dream he was watching a big boiler being brought into its foundation under a scaffold; in another, he saw cast iron standards being lowered into round concreted holes.

The content of the color interpretations is, then a part of the conscious symbolic material which the analysis worked with as it proceeded. the true significance and the relationships of these symbols being unknown to the patient It is to be expected that with a larger number of C responses a correspondingly larger part of the symbolic material could be elicited »

Here again we have proof furnished by the analysis. If during dream analyses motifs appear which are reminiscent of the content of color interpretations we shall be able to ascribe special significance to them, and give them a central position in the analysis.

c) The Abstract Interpretations.

The abstract responses are not actually form interpretations but originate in the fact that the picture has a central part, a middle area or a line in the middle. There is no perception of form associated with a visual engram as in other interpretations, but rather a description of an impression produced by the midline in relation to what surrounds it. The most definitely descriptive interpretation given by this patient and that most closely related to the abstract responses we are now discussing, is the first one in the column of the outline where the abstract responses are listed. Such descriptions are always the expression of phenomena of repression, a demonstration of negation. The purely abstract interpretations carry similar implications, although they also reveal a strongly affectively toned application to the task.

Let us take up all the interpretations built up on the theme of the central line.

First in Plate I, the «bony structure», then the «skeleton in a wrapping». Interpretations of bones and skeletons, etc., are found chiefly in neurotics who complain of inner emptiness, of loneliness, of (emotional) coldness. Shroudings, coverings and masquerades not infrequently reveal a tendency to conceal something. We have already seen this tendency to depressive feelings of emptiness and want of internal harmony occurring in conjunction with a tendency to conceal this depressive feature in the chiaroscuro interpretations The skeleton in the wrapping already mentioned is such a chiaroscuro interpretation. Thus in Plate I the mid-line is somewhat associated with affective poverty and depression with concomitant wish to conceal and dissimulate the affective situation in question.

In the second plate, the mid-line interpretation is a landscape seen in perspective; this is a chiaroscuro response also, but it is, as it were, a positive, constructive one. With some justification we can say that the affect described above is sublimated in this interpretation. However, there follows the interpretation «a well of fire» in this same plate; this is a C response which is flung out with what is almost the force of an intuition.

Abstract responses first appear in the third plate: «the power which separates the two figures and won't allow them to come together». In it the mention of two movement-motifs, a centripetal and a centrifugal, illustrates the ambivalence associated with the mid-line.

In the fourth plate there is again a cloud of smoke, and then the impression of the power in the middle to which everything clings. In the fifth plate there is the half-descriptive interpretation, the symmetrical body. In the sixth, a purely descriptive response, the symmetrical figure with the marked central axis around which everything is arranged. This is followed by another abstract interpretation, that concerned with the white line in the middle, «the line of force about which everything revolves». In the seventh plate there is first the section of the skeleton; there follows another response of fire and smoke with emphasis on the center. The eighth plate yields the response, «a part of a skeleton». The response to the ninth plate is a geographic interpretation belonging to the chiaroscuro type, and, secondly, the half-descriptive response. the fountain-like figure rising from the center. To the tenth plate he responds. «a path in a park», again a chiaroscuro interpretation. There follow a few unimportant interpretations at the end but finally he stresses the mid-line again in interpreting the passageway guarded by the barking dogs.

We see also that the interpretations associated with the mid-line are conditioned by the widest variation of factors. There are descriptive and abstract responses. color responses of the most intense as well as the most dilute type (C and FC), and. most important, chiaroscuro answers. These interpretations demonstrate the two fundamental affective sets in the patient, the depressive adaption and the egocentricity. Both are bound to the mid-line in content as well as position, the former in the interpretations of parts of the skeleton and the «path in the park». the latter in those dealing with the swell of fire . The ambivalence associated with the mid-line is also demonstrated in the opposing directions of the movement in Plate III In these interpretations associated with the mid-line, there is a tendency to give space and Dd (unusual small detail) responses. The W's, especially those which are constructive, also belong to the mid-line group of responses. The normal D response. the «inbetween» factor in the experience type, is crowded out by the W's, the S's and the Dd's. This finding is in agreement with the absence of the moderating values in affectivity, the FC responses which represent the free play of affective intercourse with the environment. All the «complex» reactions, are summarized in the mid-line interpretations; it is here that all the contradictions (of personality) are knotted together. The most powerful affect, finding its expression in the CF responses, and the most severe coartation and affective repression, expressed in the purely descriptive responses, are both associated with the mid-line of the plates. All this presents a mass of alternatives and contrasts which appears quite incapable of analysis: the solution of the problem probably lies in the abstract interpretations for these are the most extraordinary and individual responses.

In connection with these abstract interpretations the question of the relation of the mid-line to the surrounding parts is always cropping up; it is always the mid-line which holds everything to it, etc. The mid-line appears to attract the patient's attention with a sort of magical power. Suppose we visualize this relationship kinaesthetically; does the mid-line hold onto the other parts, or do the surrounding parts of the figure actively grasp the mid-line? It is possible to answer this question by considering the genuine kinaesthesias; none of these deal with the mid-line but always with lateral parts —witness the clowns, the dandies, the little men taking hold of the red parts of the figure—all exhibit movement toward the center. This implies that the subject considered the lateral parts those which were actively clinging. The wording of the abstract interpretations bears this out: the «powerful» in the middle to which everything is attached, the line of force about which everything is arranged, the middle axis around which it all revolves. If any movement is sensed in this connection, it is obviously not the mid-line which holds actively to the surrounding parts, but the surrounding parts which hold on to the mid-line, reach for the mid-line, strive to strengthen their grip on the mid-line. The mid-line is the abstract, magical power which supplies a secure place to hold to These deductions reiterate statements already found in the psychogram, namely, that the subject shows a relative incapacity to maintain a grip on a central thought and that he is passively orientated and lacks an active central force or power.

This is as much as can be gathered from the test. The analysis should clarify matters considerably, and it actually does so with startling success. I quote Dr. Oberholzer's statements regarding the abstract interpretations:

«In these interpretations, everything is concerned with power—a central line of power, a middle point of power, a center of power. The same situation exists in the analysis The central point was the father and the father was the power; this was true also in the symbolism of his dreams. In one of these dreams the father was symbolized as the queen ant who maintains the integrity of the ant state. In the dream the queen ant stings the patient on the finger. It will be recalled that after the father's death this son tried vainly to prevent the collapse of the estate In another dream he thought that he awoke during the night and saw the stars following their courses and he drew their courses which were curves passing through a central point. This dream recalled to him the first period of insomnia which preceded the development of the obsessional phenomena mentioned above and which had its onset after he had seen the performance of two tight-rope walkers. Later the associations led to a period as a boy of three to five years when there was the active desire to see the father's «spitzli» (a child's term for the genitalia) and when he would frequently awake in terror during the night. In the analysis he described the «power» as stocky in form so that I was able to say quite definitely that his father had been a stocky, thick-set man.»

In this connection I must return to the first interpretation for the first colored plate, Plate VIII. The subject interpreted the red figures at the sides as a sort of animal, bears or dogs, described as having a «thick-set body and short legs». From what has been said above, it can be assumed that this is not merely a coincidence, more especially since we deal with a red detail of the plate.

Having no knowledge of my deductions, Oberholzer continued:

«The M and C factors are seen concurrently in the abstract responses The content of these—it is always the same, this «power»—reveals the nature of the symbolic relationships of the color response; these relationships are unknown to the patient. We discover what he wants to experience. Ultimately it is the desire to experience the power of his father's genitalia; this appeared as a wish-fulfillment in many dreams both before and during the analysis.

The introversive and the most strongly affective content are amalgamated in the abstract responses, and the flexion kinaesthesias and the abstract responses fit each other like a lock and key. The striving of the kinaesthesias to «live» the content of the abstract interpretations is the most profound source of the yearning with which this patient is possessed, of his basic depressive and anxious mood, of the habitual pattern of his affect. From this source all that is found in the psychogram originates, the ideas of insufficiency, the sense of internal disunion, the inability to control himself and bring harmony into his being, it is the source of the yearning for peace, for a something strong to hold to, for unity within himself.»

The experiment has shown, then, that the power which is repeatedly mentioned in the abstract interpretations is something which the patient longs to possess for himself and that it carries the deepest affect with it; it is, so to speak, the object and goal of the kinaesthesias. Furthermore, it has been discovered that the adaption to this power is a passive one and that the unconscious seeks support from this power. Further, this power actually exercises a sort of magical influence by means of the unconscious affective control and signifies a kind of center in the patient's life; at the same time, however, in his deepest unconscious he does not wish to control this power actively, but wants to suffer passively under it. The analysis has only to substitute the real object, and it can be stated definitely that this power is the father. This key opens a number of paths at once. The most unconscious attitudes are now apparent. With the discovery of a fundamental attitude so pregnant with possibilities one can probably offer a prognosis for the analysis: if this power can also signify the analyst, then a transference must work miracles in the case.

This was actually the situation here. The patient had certain hysterical symptoms consisting in periodic violent attacks of dizziness leading to falls, which, at their zenith, were accompanied by vomitting, diarrhoea, and complete deafness in the left ear. The presence of hysterical symptoms can be read from the record of the test. Dr. Oberholzer reports that these paroxysms stopped after the first analytic period and recurred only once again and in a much later phase of the analysis in a serious attack. At this time the growth of the transference out of the deep, unconscious fundamental adjustment was under consideration. The patient had been paying his tribute to this fundamental attitude by these attacks of dizziness and left ear deafness ever since the liquidation of his father's business. The left side, as is so often the case, proves to be feminine and the fact that his mother was hard of hearing in the left ear for as long as he could remember explained the identification of the mother in the symptom complex. The fact of the mother's deafness was blocked out of the patient's associations for a long time.

d) The Form Interpretations.

There remain only the form interpretations, and these, so far as Dr. Oberholzer could gather from the analytic material, exhibit no important or distinct «complex» relationships. This is theoretically plausible for the form interpretations are the work of conciousness; the purer the form, the more certain that the response is determined by conscious thinking. The share of the unconscious in these interpretations is infinitely less than it is in the kinaesthetic and color responses. In practice, however, this is not always true

for there are neurotics whose ‹complexes› are related to the form interpretations. In any case, however, these complexes do not appear unmodified
but are changed: an example is found in the towers which were included in
the form responses of the politician discussed above which probably project
narcissistic desires.   But there are subjects in whom unmistakable signs of
‹complexes› can be demonstrated on the basis of the F series. These are ir-
rational types in whom unconscious material is constantly seeping into the
conscious, and subjects who are in especially good humor at the time of the
test; the good humor dilates the experience type and permits material, otherwise repressed, to get smuggled into consciousness. The stronger the repressions,
the less capable is the subject of getting into a lighter mood, and the more
definitely are all complexes excluded from the sphere of form interpretation:
but then it is more certain that these complexes will be represented in the
kinaesthetic and color interpretations.

Thus we see that the kinaesthetic interpretations furnish a deep insight
into the unconscious. They reveal the unconscious tendencies of the subject,
the basic attitude, whether it be active or passive. The color interpretations
are symbols corresponding to the symbols in dreams. In the unconscious they
represent something else, namely, the latent content, revealing the tremendous
affective relationships of the latent content. The form responses are usually
free of «complex» material; the stronger the repressions in the subject, the
less complex material in the form responses; the less subjective, the more
objective they are. The abstract responses furnish relationships between the
kinaesthesias and the color responses, between the unconscious attitudes and
the affect-colored goals of the unconscious. The practical value of this discussion can be determined only from a larger material; on the other hand,
the facts obtained by purely empirical methods should offer significant contributions to the theory of the relationships between the conscious and the
unconscious.

Summary

The Formal Psychogram: I designate as the formal psychogram all those conclusions drawn from the formal qualities of the protocol alone, excluding consideration of the content of the interpretations, and obtainable irrespective of whether the subject is known to the examiner or not. In our subject the formal psychogram reveals that we deal with a neurosis in which psychaesthenic symptoms must be predominant since the experience type is more introversive than extratensive, though approaching ambiequality. Because of this latter fact the neurosis must also show compulsion (obsessional) phenomena and at least periodic symptoms of hysteria. The main features of the neurotic character are ideas of insufficiency, feeling of inner disharmony, of inability to integrate himself, brooding about himself, distrust of his ability to produce, ambivalence, vacillation between broad-mindedness and pedantry, impulsiveness and passion which alternate with scrupulousness and timid, depressive attitudes, a tendency to autistic fantasies and inferences, especially autistic systematizations, and finally, a tendency to asceticism and inability to make decisions The form of the special body symptoms cannot be determined from the record.

Aside from the neurosis other traits were found, namely, good intelligence, original thinking, particularly concrete thinking, and a weakness in the field of abstract thinking. There was a significant anlage for constructive thought processes and—and the two are not the same thing—a talent for construction though there was little combinatory imagination. The psychogram also revealed a marked ability to apply himself and a tendency to neglect the essential and practical in order to construct large systems or, in contrast, to get hung up on small details. On the whole, the capacity for sharing common mode of perceiving is reduced; there are individual peculiarities, and a tendency to be seclusive. There is a reduction in the freedom of affective adaptions; there are fluctions of affect between egocentric moods and feelings of oppression, depression and anxiety. It might be said that the basic principles of his adaptability are expressed in the chiaroscuro responses. The whole record, because of the compulsive tone throughout, indicates a rather obsessional fundamentality in thinking existing at the same time with a sort of mild fanaticism, or at least a certain zeal in the defense of basic principles. This conception has been expressed in the discussion of the programmatic nature of his thinking already referred to.

The Comparison of the Formal Psychogram and the Content: The experiment alone allows the conclusion that the patient's unconscious expectancy is that he will be passive in the experiences that come to him. From the color responses we conclude that there are powerful, affect-charged complexes which must be repressed. From the abstract interpretations and their relation to the kinaesthesias, it can be concluded that the unconscious is seeking a

power to cling to. From the relationship of this last fact to the color responses, it can be stated that this power must be expressed symbolically in
the content of the color responses. These conclusions are fundamentally
«formal», and arise out of a comparison of the factors and content of the
interpretations. The psychoanalytical conclusions serve to complete the
formal psychogram with a few words. The abstract interpretations represent
the desires of the patient, desires he wishes to «live». The power referred to
in these responses is the goal of the passive attitude, the power of the father
which he unconsciously longs to experience. This is indicated in the color
responses where the power is symbolic of the father and his force. The
neurosis results from the conflict of this unconscious longing and the conscious
repression of it. We do not know what earlier and more primitive attitudes
and tendencies may have played a role in the production of the neurosis.

Publications

of Hermann Rorschach.

1) «Über Reflexhalluzinationen und verwandte Erscheinungen» (Ztschr f. Neurol. 1912)
2) «Pferdediebstahl im Dämmerzustand» (Arch f. Kriminalanthropologie und Kriminalistik, Bd 49, 1912)
3) «Reflexhalluzinationen und Symbolik» (Zentralblatt f Psychoanalyse, 1912)
4) «Ein Beispiel von misslungener Sublimierung und ein Fall von Namenvergessen» (Zentralblatt f. Psychoanalyse, 1912)
5) «Zur Pathologie und Operabilität der Tumoren der Zirbeldrüse» (Beiträge zur klinischen Chirurgie, 1913)
6) «Über die Wahl des Freundes beim Neurotiker» (Zentralbl f. Psychoanalyse 1913).
7) «Analyse einer schizophrenen Zeichnung» (Zentralbl f Psychoanalyse, 1913).
8) «Analytische Bemerkungen über das Gemälde eines Schizophrenen» (Zentralblatt f. Psychoanalyse, 1913)
9) «Assoziationsexperiment, freies Assoziieren und Hypnose im Dienst der Hebung einer Amnesie» (Corr.-Bl f. Schweizer Ärzte, 1917).
10) «Einiges über schweizerische Sekten und Sektengründer» (Schweiz. Arch f Neur u. Psychiatrie, 1917)
11) «Weiteres über schweizerische Sektenbildungen» (Schweiz. Arch f. Neur u Psychiatrie, 1919)
12) «Mord aus Aberglauben» (Schweiz. Volkskunde, 1920).
13) «Psychodiagnostik», Bern 1921.
14) «Zur Auswertung des Formdeutversuchs für die Psychoanalyse» (Zschr f. Neurol 1923). Posthum herausgegeben von Dr E Oberholzer
15) «Zwei schweizerische Sektenstifter (Binggeli und Unternährer), Imago XIII. Sonderheft. Internat Psychoanalyt Verlag 1927 Posthum herausgegeben.

Bibliography of the Important Contributions

on the Rorschach Method.

(To January, 1949)

1. *Abbott, W. D, Due F. O., and Nosik, W A:* Subdural Hematoma and Effusion as a Result of Blast Injuries. J Amer Med. Assn , 1943, 121, 739—741

2. *Abel, T. M* The Rorschach test and school success among mental defectives Rorsch. Res Exch. IX, 3, 1945, 105—110

3 — Group Rorschach testing in a vocational high school. Rorsch. Res. Exch. IX, 4, 1945, 178—188.

4. — *Piotrowski, Z A., and Stone, G.:* Responses of Negro and White Morons to the Rorschach Test. Amer. J. Ment Def., 1944, 48, 253—257.

5. *Aguiar, W. E. de·* (Possibilities of the clinical application of the psychological Rorschach method). Rev. Neurol. Sao Paulo, 1935, 1, 447—54 (Portuguese).

6 — (Application of the Rorschach psychological test in forensic psychopathology). Med.-Leg. e Criminol., Sao Paulo, 1935, 6, 62—63.

7. *Alliez, J., et Jaur, J.-M ·* Test de Rorschach et orientation professionnelle. Ann. méd.-psychol., 1945, Bd. 1, S 416.

8. *Andresen, H.:* Über die Auffassung diffus optischer Eindrücke; ein Beitrag zur Bedingungserforschung der Leistungsvollzüge beim Rorschach Test. Z. Psychol., 1941, 150, 6—91.

9. (Anon.) A review of Rorschach scoring samples. Rorschach Res. Exch. 1936—1937, 1, 94—102.

10. — Clinical validation of a Rorschach interpretation: The case of Lillian K: IV. Comparison between Rorschach interpretation and clinical findings. Rorsch. Res. Exch. II, 4, 1938, 162—163.

11. — Foreword to Volume I Rorsch. Res. Exch I, 1, 1936.

12. — Hilfstabellen zum Rorschachschen Formdeutversuch. Psychotechnique Institute of Zurich

13. — Liste d'interprétations-type (en français). . de Rorschach et de ses disciples. En vente au Secrétariat de l'Institut J. J. Rousseau, Palais Wilson, Genève

14. — List of fellows and members as of April 30, 1943 Rorsch. Res. Exch VII, 3, 1943, 124—129.

15. — List of members and fellows of the Rorschach Institute, Inc as of June 1946 Rorsch Res Exch. X, 2, 1946, 78—85.

16. *Apfeldorf, M.* Rorschach theory and psychoanalytic theory. Rorsch. Res. Exch. VIII, 4, 1944, 189—191.

17. *Apolczyn, L:* Metoda Rorschacha: technika exsperymentow (Rorschach's method; experimental technique) Psychol. wychow., 1938—39, 11, 27—37, 53—66 Psychol Abstr., 1939, 3745

18 *Arluck, E. W* A study of some personality differences between epileptics and normals Rorschach Res Exch.. 1940, 4, 154—156.

19 *Aubrun, W* L'etat mental des parkinsoniens. The mental state in Parkinson's disease.) Paris: Bailliere 1937, Pp. 136.

20. *Bänziger.* Die Frage der Schizophrenie bei einem Mitglied der Sekte Anton Unternährers Z. Neur. 110 1927

21 *Bailey, Pearce.* Etude des types psychologiques au moyen des testes. Librairie Lipschutz, Paris. 1933, Pp. 204

23 *Baker, E* Personality Changes in Adolescence as Revealed by the Rorschach Method. Psychol. Bull, 1941, 38, 705 (Abstr).

24 *Bohnsky, B.* A note on the use of the Rorschach in the selection of supervisory personnel. Rorsch. Res. Exch. VIII, 4, 1944, 184—188

25. — The Multiple Choice Group Rorschach Test as a Means of Screening Applicants for Jobs. J. Psychol, 1945, 19, 203—208.

26 *Barison, Ferdinando* Il fattore tempo nel reattivo di Rorschach Riv di psicol., 1940, Bd. 36, S. 24

27. — Il reattivo di Rorschach in 74 fanciulli ferraresi di 9—12 anni Arch Psicol. Neurol. Psychiat., 1940, 2, 1—77.

28. *Barrera, S. E* Introductory remarks to the panel discussion on personality studies in the convulsive states. Rorsch. Res. Exch. IV, 4, 1940, 152—153

29. *Barry, H.* (Ed) The significance of the Rorschach method for consulting psychology: A. Author's abstracts of the contributions to the round-table conference at the Eighth Annual Meeting of the Association of Consulting Psychologists. Rorsch. Res Exch I, 5, 1937, 157—164.

30. — *and Sender, S* The significance of the Rorschach method for consulting psychology. Rorschach Res. Exch.. 1936—37, 1. 157—167.

31. *Baumgartener-Tramer, F* Der Rorschach-Test im Lichte der experimentellen Psychologie (italienisch). Arch. di psicol., neurol. e psichiat, 1946, Bd. 7, S 135.

32. — Zur Geschichte des Rorschachtestes. Schweiz Arch. f. Neurol. u Psychiat, 1942, Bd. 50, S 1.

33 *Bayer, K P* Bedeutung des Rorschachversuches fur die Psychiatrie. Allg. Zeitschr. f Psychiat, 1943, Bd 122, S. 1.

34. *Beck, S. J.* Autism in Rorschach scoring a feeling comment. Character & Pers., 1936, 5, 83—85

35. *Beck, S J* Configurational Tendencies in Rorschach Responses Psychol. Bull. 1932, XXX p 632

36. — Effects of Shock Therapy on Personality. as Shown by the Rorschach Test Arch. Neurol. Psychiat., 1943 50, 483—484 (Abstr.).

37. - - Introduction to the Rorschach Method. A manual of personality study. With a Preface by F. L. Wells. Monograph No. I of the American Orthopsychiatric Association, 1937. Set up and printed by the George Banta Publishing Company Menasha, Wisconsin.

38 — Personality diagnosis by means of the Rorschach test Amer. J. Orthopsychiatry 1930.

39 — Personality structure in schizophrenia a Rorschach investigation in 81 patients and 64 controls. Nerv. ment Dis Monogr, 1938, No. 63. Pp. IX & 88.

40. — Problems of further research in the Rorschach test. Amer. J Orthopsychiatry 5. 1935

41. — Psychological processes in Rorschach findings. J abnorm. a. soc. Psychol 31. 1937

42. — Rorschach's Test Vol I: Basic Processes. New York, Grune & Stratton, Inc., 1944. Pp. 223.

43. — Rorschach's Test. Vol. II· A Variety of Personality Pictures New York: Grune & Stratton, Inc. 1945, Pp. 402.

44. — Some present research problems. Rorschach Res. Exch., 1937, 2, 15—22.

45. — Some recent Rorschach problems Rorsch. Res Exch. II, 1 Sept. 1937, 15—22.

46. — Sources of error in Rorschach test procedures Psychol Bull. 1940. 37, 516—517.

47. — Stability of the Personality Structure Psychol. Bull., 1942, 39, 512 (abstr.).

48. — The Rorschach Experiment: Progress and Problems. Amer. J Orthopsv., 1945, 15, 520—524.

49. — The Rorschach method and the organisation of personality. I. Basic processes. Amer J. Orthopsychiatry 3. 1933

50. — The Rorschach method and the organisation of personality. II. Balance in personality. Amer. J. Psych. 13, 1933.

51. — The Rorschach method and personality organisation. III The psychological and the social personality Amer. J. Orthopsychiatry 4. 1934

52. — The Rorschach test as applied to a feebleminded group. Arch. of psychology, 1932.

53. — The Rorschach Test in a Case of Character Neurosis. Amer. J. Orthopsy., 1944, 14, 230—236.

54. — The Rorschach Test in Men Discharged from the Armed Forces. War Psychiatry. Proceedings of the Second Brief Psychotherapy Council Chicago: Institute for Psychoanalysis; 1944. Pp 55.

55. — The Rorschach test in problem children. Amer. J Orthopsychiat, 1931, 1, 501—509.

56 — The Rorschach Test in Psychopathology J. Consult. Psychol., 1943, 7, 103—111.

57. — Thoughts on an impending anniversary. Amer J. Orthopsychiat., 1939, 9, 806—808

58. *Behn-Eschenburg·* Psychische Schüleruntersuchungen mit dem Formdeutversuch. Bern und Leipzig 1921.

59 *Benjamin, J D:* Discussion on «Some recent Rorschach problems» Rorschach Res. Exch., 1937, 2, 46—48.

60. — *& Franklin G Ebaugh·* The diagnostic validity of the Rorschach test. (93 ann. meet. of the Americ. Psychiatr. Assoc Pittsburgh, 10.—14. V 1937). Amer J. Psychiatry 94 (1938).

61 *Benton, A. L.* Rorschach Performances of Suspected Malingerers. J. Abnorm. Soc. Psychol, 1945, 40. 94—96

62. *Bergmann, M. S.:* Homosexuality on the Rorschach Test. Bull Menninger Clin, 1945, 9, 78—83

63. *Bidsch, H.:* Die Technik der Charakterbeurteilung Industr Psychotechn, 1934, 11, 289—302.

64. *Bigelow, R. Barry* The evaluation of aptitude for flight training. the Rorschach method as a possible aid J of Aviation Medicine, Dec. 1940.

65. *Billig, O ·* The Rorschach Test; an Important Aid in the Personality Diagnosis N. C. Med. J, 1943, 4, 46—50.

66 — *and Sullivan, D. J.* Personality Structure and Prognosis of Alcohol Addiction: a Rorschach Study. Quart. J Stud. Alcohol, 1943, 3, 554—573.

67 – and Sullivan, D. J Prognostic data in chronic alcoholism. Rorsch. Res Exch VI.
    3, 1942, 117– 127

68 Bender, H Comments concerning the Beck-Klopfer discuss on Rorschach Res Exch
    1937. 2. 43—44

69 .. Die Helldunkeldeutungen im psychodiagnostischen Experiment von Rorschach
    (zugleich ein Beitrag zur theoretischen Begrundung des Experimentes) Schweiz.
    Arch Neur 30, 1932

70 Die klinische Bedeutung des Rorschachschen Versuches. Schweiz Arch. Neurol.
    Psychiat . 1944, 53. 12 –29.

71 -- Discussion on S J Beck's «Some recent Rorschach problems» Rorsch. Res. Exch.
    II. 2, 1937. 37—42.

72 – The «light-dark» interpretations in Rorschach's experiment. Rorschach Res. Exch
    1937. 2. 37—42.

73 Binswanger Bemerkungen zu Hermann Rorschachs Psychodiagnostik Internat. Z
    Psychoannal 9, 1923

74 Binswanger, W · Über den Rorschachschen Formdeutversuch bei akuten Schizophre-
    nien Schweiz Arch. Neurol. Psychiat . 1944, 53. 101—121

75 Birzele, K . Das Reproduzieren von Bildgestalten als Hilfsmittel zur Charakterbestim-
    mung Industr. Psychotech., 1938, 15, 65—78. Psychol. Abstr.. 1939, 6466

76 Blackburn, J M . General review: methods of estimating intelligence and personality
    and their applications J. ment. Sci.. 1938 84, 1008-1053.

77 Bleuler, M · Der Rorschach-Versuch als Unterscheidungsmittel von Konstitution und
    Prozess Z Neur 151

78 — Der Rorschachsche Formdeutversuch bei Geschwistern. Z. Neur. 118.

79 — Discussion on Beck's «Some recent Rorschach problems». Rorsch. Res Exch. II,
    2, 1937, 45—46

80 — The Delimination of influences of environment and heredity on mental disposi-
    tion Character and Personality, Vol. I. June 1933 Nr. 4, S. 286.

81 — The shaping of personality by environment and heredity. Character and Per-
    sonality, 1933, 1, 286– 300.

82 — and R · Rorschach's Ink-Blot test and Racial Psychologie: Mental Pecularities of
    Morocans. Character and Personality Vol. IV December 1935. No 2.

83 --- and Wertham, Fred. Inconstancy of the Formal Structure of the Personality. Arch.
    of Neur. and Psychiatry 7. 1932.

84. Bochner, R and Halpern, F : The Clinical Application of the Rorschach Test. New
    York: Grune & Stratton, Inc. 1945. Pp. 330 2nd ed.

85. Bohm, Ewald: Der Rorschach-Test und seine Weiterentwicklung. Sonderh. «Ror-
    schachiana I» d. Schweiz. Zeitschr. f Psychol., 1945.

86 — IX Tabellarische Übersicht in Psychodiagnostik von H. Rorschach. 3. Aufl , 1937,
    Hans Huber.

87 Bonnafe, L et Tosquelles, Fr. Au sujet du test de Rorschach. Ann. méd -psychol.,
    1944, Bd. 1, S 171

88. Booth, G. C.: Comments concerning the Beck-Klopfer discussion. Rorschach Res.
    Exch . 1937, 2. 48—53.

89. — Discussion on S. J Beck's «Some recent Rorschach problems» Rorschach Res
    Exch. II, 2, 1937, 48—53

90. — Material for a comparative case study of a chronic arthritis personality: I. Psychia-
    tric report. I. 2, Nov 1936, 49.

91. -- Objective techniques in personality testing Arch Neurol Psychiat., 1939, 42, 514--530.

92. — Personality and chronic arthritis. J. Nerv. & Ment Dis., 1937, 85, 637–652

93. — & *Klopfer, B.* · Personality studies in chronic arthritis Rorschach Res. Exch, 1936--1937, 1, 40--49.

94. *Borges, J. C. C.* (The Rorschach test in epilepsy., Neurobiologia, Pernambuco, 1938, 1, 29--85. Psychol. Abstr., 1939, 5012

95. *Boss, Medard* Psychologisch-charakterologische Untersuchungen bei antisozialen Psychopathen mit Hilfe des Rorschachschen Formdeutversuchs. Zeitschrift f. d ges. Neur. und Psych Bd 133, H 3/4, 1931, S. 544.

96. *Boszörményi, Georg & Merei, Franz.* Zum Problem von Konstitution und Prozess in der Schizophrenie auf Grund des Rorschach-Versuches. Schw Arch Neur. 45, 1940.

97. *Boven, W.:* La Science du caractere Delachaux et Niestlé 1931

98. *Bovet, Th :* Der Rorschachversuch bei verschiedenen Formen von Epilepsie Schweiz. Arch. Neur 37 (1936).

99. *Boynton, P L., and Walsworth, B M :* Emotionality Test Scores of Delinquent and Non-Delinquent Girls. J Abnorm. Soc Psychol. 1943, 38, 87—92.

100. *Bradway, K. P, Lion, E. G, and Corrigan, H G.,* The use of the Rorschach in a psychiatric study of promiscuous girls. Rorsch. Res. Exch X, 3, 1946, 105—110.

101 *Brambilla, Silvio* Sulla demenza postencefalitica. Il metodo di Rorschach applicato allo studio del parkinsonismo postencefalitico. Arch. di psicol., 1941, Bd. 2, S. 842.

102 *Brander, T.,* Bidrag till kännedomen om den kroppsliga och psykiska utrecklingen hos tvillingar. Finska Läk. Sällsk. Handl, 1935, 77, 195—265

103. *Bratt, N.:* Noget om det Rorschachske formtydningsforsog og dets praktiske anven delse. Ugeskr. Laeg., 1938, 100, 534—537.

104. *Braunshausen, N* · L'étude expérimentale du caractère. Méthodes et résultats Uccle-Brussels: Centre Nat Educ, 1937, Pp. 198

105. *Brendgen, F.* · Über den Wert der Tiefenpsychologie für die Berufsberatung Z ges Neurol. Psychiat, 1938, 161, 498—511

106. *Brenman, M, and Reichard, S* Use of the Rorschach Test in the Prediction of Hypnotizability. Bull Menninger Clin, 1943, 7, 183—187

107. *Brosin, H W and Fromm, E O* · Rorschach and color blindness. Rorschach Res Exch., 1940, 4, 39—70.

108. — Some principles of Gestalt psychology in the Rorschach experiment. Rorsch. Res. Exch. VI, 1, 1942, 1—15.

109. *Brown, R R* · The Effect of Morphine upon the Rorschach Pattern in Post-Addicts Amer J. Orthopsy, 1943 13, 339—343. Also in Psychol Bull., 1942, 39, 512 - 513

110. *Brown, J. F. & Orbison, W D* A program for the experimental psychological investigation of convulsion therapy Bull. Menninger Clinic. 1938, 2, 151—154

111. *Bruno, A. M. L..* Movimiento Rorschach no Brasil. An. Paulist de Med Cir, 1944, 47, 377—401

112 — Psicograma de Rorschach: Ficha para seu registo. Arq. Policia Civil, S Paulo, 1942, 4, 185.

113. *Brussel, J. A., Grassi, J K, and Melnicker, A.* The Rorschach Method and Post-concussion Syndrome Psychiat. Quart., 1942, 16, 707—743

114. *Bryn, D.:* The problem of human types: comments and an experiment. Character & Pers., 1936, 5, 48—60.

115. *Buckle, D+F, and Cook, P H*· Group Rorschach method. Techn. of Ro sch. Rec. Exch. VII, 4 1943, 159—167.

116. *Buhler C* Father and son Rorsch. Res. Exch VII, 4 1943, 145—159.

117 *Burgemeister, B B, und Tallman, G.* Rorschach patterns in multiple sclerosis Ro sch. Res Exch. IX, 3. 1945, 111—122.

118. *Burger-Prinz* Bumkes Handbuch der Geisteskrankheiten IX, S 84 1932

119 *Burt, C.* The subnormal Mind, Oxford University Press, 1935 Pp 331

120. *Bustamente, M* Historiales clinicos de neurosis obsesiva. Conclusion. Arch. Neuro biol, 1934, 14, 927—978

121. *Cameron, D C*· The Rorschach Experiment — X ray of Personality Dis. Nerv. syst. 1942, 3, 374—376.

122. *Cantril, H. and Allport* Recent Application of the Study of Values J Abnorm and Soc. Psychol 1934.

123. *Cardona, Filippo* Il test di Rorschach nella diagnostica psichiatrica Clin d. Malatt. Nerv. e Ment. Univ. Firenze. Riv Pat nerv. 49 (1937).

124. *Carvathal Ribas, J..* Psico-diagnostico de Rorschach Rev. Clin. S. Paulo, 1942, 11, 31—34.

125. *Cavagnac, C.*· Psychologische Untersuchungen mittels des Rorschach-Tests an Schizophrenen, die nach der Methode von Fiambe ti mit Acetylcholin behandelt worden waren (italienisch) Arch di sci d cerebrazione e dei psichismi, 1946, Bd 1/2, S. 163 Ref.: Ann. méd.-psychol, 1947, Bd 2, S 599.

126. *Cavalcanti Borges, J. C* Da psicologia de epilepticos genuinos. Respostas de cói primaria no psicodiagnostico de Rorschach Rev Med. de Pernambuco. 1936, 6, 185—187.

127. — O teste de Rorschach em epilepticos. Neurobiologia, 1938, 1, 29—35

128. *Cerqueira, Luiz* Psicodiagnóstico de Rorschach. Bahia-Tip. Moderna, 1945, pages 106. (Enthält 21 Titel der Rorschach-Literatur, die von 1934—1943 in Brasilien erschienen ist.)

129. *Challmann, R. C* The Validity of the Harrower-Erickson Multiple-Choice Test as a Screening Device. J Psychol., 1945, 20, 41—48.

130. *Christoffel:* Psychoanalyse und Psychiatrie. Schweiz. Med. Wochenschrift 54. 1924.

131. — Affektivität und Farben, speziell Angst und Halbdunkelerscheinungen, Z. Neur. 82, 1923.

132. *Clapp, H S..* Clinical validation of a Rorschach interpretation: The case of Lillian K; I. Rorschach record. Rorsch. Res. Exch. II, 4, 1938, 153—155.

133. *Clardy, E. R.; Goldensohn, L N, and Levine, K.:* Schizophreniclike Reactions in Children: Preliminary Report: Studies by Electroencephalography, Pneuemoencephalography, and Psychological Tests Psychiat. Quart., 1941, 15, 100—116.

134 *Coffin, T E:* Motivation and stimulus-structuration in the process of suggestion. Psychol Bull., 1939, 36, 662.

135. *Collin, A G.:* Review· European Rorschach findings. Rorsch. Res Exch. VII, 4, 1943, 169—181.

136. *Collins, L:* Review of K H Stauder's «Konstitution und Wesensänderung der Epileptiker.» Rorsch. Res. Exch VIII, 1, 1944, 38—40.

137. *Cook, P. H.:* Mental Structure and Psychological Field: Some Samoan Observations. Character and Pers., 1942, 10, 296—308.

138. — The application of the Rorschach test to a Samoan group Rorsch. Res. Exch. VI, 2, 1942, 51—60.

139. *Copelman, L. S.:* Psihodiagnosticul Rorschach in lumina activitatii dinamice a scoartei cerebrale. Bucuresti: Societatea Romana de cercetari psihologice, 1935. Pp. 48.

140. *Cordon, R. G. and Norman* Some Psychological Experiments on Mental Defectives in Relation to the Perceptual Configurations which may underlie Speech. Part. II. Brit J. Psychol., 1932 XXIII, p 85—113.

141. *Costa, i* Le tavole del Rorschach quale mezzo di ricerca per la psicologia normale e patologica. Arch ital Psicol., 1939, 17, 17—28.

142. *Cowin. Marion.* Reporting Group Discussion· What constitutes a single response? Rorschach Res Exch, 1936, 1, 4

143. -- The use of the Rorschach in schools Rorsch. Res Exch. IX, 3, Sept. 1945, 130—133

144. -- (reporter) What constitutes a single response? Rorsch Res. Exch. I. 1. 1936. 4

145. *Cranford, V., and Schirn, R V :* Understanding the Alcohol Patient. Part I J Clin. Psychopath. and Psychother, 1944 6, 323—334.

146. *Dalla Volta, Amedeo* Ricerche sulla prova di H.Rorschach con particolare riferi mento all'antropologia criminale. Arch. di antropol crim, 1941, Bd 61, S 227.

147. *Dashiell, J F.* Some rapprochements in contemporary psychology. Psychol. Bull. 1939. 36, 1--24

148. *Davidson, H. H..* Personality and Economic Background: A Study of Highly Intelligent Children. New York: King's Crown Press: 1943. Pp. 189

149. – *& Klopfer, B ·* Rorschach statistics, Part I: Mentally retarded, normal, and superior adults Rorschach Res. Exch, 1937—38, 2, 164—169.

150. — Rorschach statistics, Part II· Normal children Rorschach Res Exch, 1938. 3, 37—43

151. *Day F, Schachtel, Hartoch A & E.:* A Rorschach study of a defective delinquent. J Crim. Psychopath., 1940, 2, 62—79.

152. *De Oliveira, W. I · O* Psicodiagnóstico de Rorschach em epilepticos. Rio de Janeiro: Companhia Editora Americana; 1945 Pp 93.

153. *Diethelm, O :* The personality concept in relation to graphology and the Rorschach test. Proc. Ass Res. nerv ment.. Dis., 1934, 14, 278—286.

154. *Dimmick, G. B .* An application of the Rorschach ink-blot test to three clinical types of dementia praecox. J. Psychol, 1935—1936, 1, 61—74.

155. *Drohocki, Z ·* Psychologiczne badania nad epilepsja przy pomocy metody Rorschacha. Nowiny Psychjatryczne, 1928, 1, 32—33

156. — Die typologische Bedeutung der Orientierung mittels Farben oder Gestalt. Polskie Arch. Psychol 5 1932. Ref. Zbl. 68, S. 604.

157. — Znaczenie typologiczne orjentacji przypomocy barwy lub ksztaltu. Pol. Arch. Psychol., 1932, 5, 406—426.

158. *Drope, Detlef* Kritische Gedanken über Rorschach-Versuch und Handschriftenkunde. Arch. f Psychol 104 (1939).

159. *Dubitscher·* Die Persönlichkeitsentwicklung des Schulkindes im Rorschachschen Formdeutversuch Z Kinderforsch. 41, 1933.

160. — Der Rorschachsche Formdeutversuch bei erwachsenen Psychopathen sowie psycho-pathischen und schwachsinnigen Kindern. Z. Neur. 142. 1932

161. — Der Rorschachsche Formdeutversuch als diagnostisches Hilfsmittel Z. Neur 138 (1932).

162. *Dublineau, J.:* De quelques liaisons psycho-cliniques dans le test de Rorschach Ann. méd.-psychol, 1944, Bd 2, S. 581.

163. — Essai d'une etude chiffree du comportement verbo-moteur dans le test de Rorschach Ann. med.-psychol. 1944, Bd 2. S. 305.

164. — Le test de Rorschach et le problème typologique. Ann. med psychol. 1944. Bl 2. S. 348.

165 — Le test de Rorschach, interprétation métnodologique Ann. méd.-psychol. 1944, Bd 2. S 502

166. — *Puech et Luquet.* Mod.fications de la structure psychologique, suivies par le test de Rorschach chez une obsedee avant et après lobotomie Ann. med.-psychol.. 1947, Bd 2, S 284

167. *Du Bois, C. and Oberholzer, E:* Rorschach Tests and Native Personality in Alor, Dutch East Indies Trans. N. Y. Acad Sci.. 1942, 4. 168—170.

168 *Du Bois, C.* The People of Alor; a Social Psychological Study of an East Indian Island. Minneapolis: University of Minnesota Press; 1944. Pp 654.

169 *Due, F. O, and Wright, M. E ·* The use of content analysis in Rorschach interpretation· I. Differential characteristics of male homosexuals. Rorsch. Res. Exch. IX, 4. 1945, 169—177.

170. *Dunbar, F* Psychosomatic Diagnosis. New York: Pau. B. Hoeber. Inc.; 1943. Pp. 741.

171. *Dunmore, H:* An evaluation of Beck's norms as applied to young children. Psychol. Bull 36, 629.

172 *Dworetzki, Gertrude* Le test de Rorschach et l'evolution de la perception Etude experimentale. (Laborat. de Psychol Univ. Genève.) Arch de Psychol. Genf, 27 (1939).

173. — Etude sur la répétition du test de Rorschach Genève, mai 1936.

174 *Earl, C. J C:* A note on the validity of certain Rorschach symbols. Rorsch. Res. Exch. V, 2, 1941. 51—61

175. *Endacott, J L.·* The Results of 100 Male Juvenile Delinquents on the Rorschach Ink Blot Test. J. Crim. Psychopath., 1941. 3, 41—50.

176 *Endara, J.* A proposito de los examines biopsicologicos en delincuentes: Arch. Criminol Neuropsiquiat., 1938, 2, 229—234.

177 — Die Rorschachsche Psychodiagnostik und Verbrechen Psychogramme zweier rückfälliger Mörder Psiquiatr y Criminol. 2, Nr. 7, 1937 (Spanisch). Ref Zbl. Neur. 88, 1938.

178. — Psicodiagnóstico de Rorschach y delincuencias clasificacion de las respuestas. An Inst Psicol Univ. B. Aires, 1938, 2, 207—232.

179. — Psicodiagnóstico de Rorschach y delincuencia Psicogramas de dos homicidas reincidentes Psiquiat. y Criminol., 1937. 2, 45—50.

180. — Psicodiagnóstico de Rorschach y sus aplicaciones clinicas. Arch. Criminol Neuropsiquiat. Quito, 1940—41, 4—5, 90—111.

181. *Enke:* Die Konstitutionstvpen im Rorschachschen Experiment. Z. Neur. 108. 1927.

182. — Die Bedeutung des Rorschachschen Formdeutversuchs für die Psychotherapie. Sitzgsber d Ges. f. Naturwiss, Marburg. Zbl. Neur. 50. 1928.

183. *Epstein, H L., and Apfeldorf, M* The use of the Rorschach in a groupwork agency. Rorsch. Res. Exch. X, I, 1946, 28—36.

184. *Eyrich, M.* Über Charakter und Charakterveränderung bei kindlichen und jugendlichen Epileptikern Zsch f d. ges. Neur. u Psychiat., 1932, 141, 640—644.

185. *Fankhauser.* Die Affektivität als Faktor des seelischen Geschehens. Bern u Leipzig 1926.

186 — Über die theoretische Grundlage der Rorschachschen Psychodiagnostik Schweiz. Verein r Psychiatrie Zürich 1923

187. — Über Wesen und Bedeutung der Affektivität. Eine Parallele zwischen Affektivität und Licht- und Farbenempfindung. Monographien aus dem Gesamtgebiete der Neur. u Psych. 19 (1919).

188. *Fateisen, H. F., and Klopfer, B.* A survey of psychologists' opinions concerning the Rorschach method. Rorsch. Res. Exch. IX, 1, 1945, 23—29.

189. *Fleischer, R. O., & Hunt, J McV.* Another method of recording the area of the blot interpreted in the Rorschach test. (To be published)

190. *Fluegel, J. G.*. Int. Z. für Psychoanalyse, 129, 142 (1922)

191. *Fosberg, I. A* An experimental study of the reliability of the Rorschach psychodiagnostic technique. Rorsch. Res. Exch. V, 2, 1941. 72—84.

192. — How do subjects attempt fake results on the Rorschach test? Rorsch. Res. Exch VII. 3, 1943. 119—121

193. — Rorschach reactions under varied instructions. Rorschach Res. Exch, 1938. 3. 12—31.

194. *Fraenkel, D:* Explication de l'ivresse de haschisch par le test de Rorschach. Hyg Ment., 1935. 30, 66—68.

195 — Der Rorschachsche Formdeutversuch als different aidiagnostisches Mittel fur Gutachter. — Ärztl. Sachverständigen-Zeitung. Nr. 2, 1932.

196. — *und Benjamin:* Die Kritik der Versuchsperson beim Rorschachschen Formdeutversuch. Schweiz. Arch. Neur. 33 1934.

197. *Franco, Franco de:* Cento fanciulli siciliani di 8—12 anni esaminati col reattivo di Rorschach. Arch. di psicol., 1942, Bd 3, S. 329

198 — Vergleichen Psychologie der Geschlechter in der Praeadoleszenz mittels der Rorschach-Methode (italienisch). Arch. di psicol., neurol. e psichiat, 1943. Bd. 4, S. 15.

199. *Frank, L. K.* Comments on the proposed standardization of the Rorschach method. Rorschach Res. Exch, 1939, 3, 101—105.

200. — Projective methods for the study of personality. J. Psychol., 1939, 8, 389—413. And Trans. N. Y Acad. Sci., 1939, 1, 129—132.

201. — *and Others.* Psychosomatic Disturbances in Relation to Personnel Selection. Ann. N. Y Acad. Sci., 1943. 44, 541—624.

202. — The Rorschach Method. J Consult. Psychol., 1943, 7, 63—66.

203. *Freeman, H., Rodnick, E H.; Shakow, D., and Lebeaux, T..* The Carbohydrate Tolerance of Mentally Disturbed Soldiers. Psychosom. Med., 1944, 6, 311—317

204 *Fuchs, Christel:* Hohe Intelligenz; Versuch ihrer experimentellen Erfassung mit dem Rorschachtest. Zeitschr. f Psychol., 1942, Bd. 152, S. 30.

205. *Funkhouser, J. B., and Kelley, D. M.* The Rorschach Ink-Blot Method Virginia Med. Mon., 1942. 69, 139—144.

206. *Furrer·* Über die Bedeutung der «B» im Rorschachschen Versuch. Imago 11. 1925.

207. — Der Auffassungsvorgang beim Rorschachschen psychodiagnostischen Versuch. Diss. Zürich 1930.

208. *Gair, M:* Rorschach characteristics of a group of very superior seven year old children Rorsch. Res. Exch. VIII, 1, 1944, 31—37.

209. *Gann, E* Reading Difficulty and Personality Organization. New York: King's Crown Press: 1945. Pp. 149.

210. *Ganz, Elisabeth, und Loosli-Usteri, Marg:* Le test de Rorschach appliqué à 43 garçons anormaux Arch. de psychol. Genève 25. 1934

211. *Gardner, George E* Rorschach test replies and results in 300 normal adults of average I. Q. Amer J. Orthopsychiatry 6, 32- 62 (1936)

212. *Geil, G. A.* The similarity in Rorschach patterns of adult criminal psychopaths and pre-adolescent boys. Rorsch Res Exch. IX, 4, 1945 201—296

213. *Giehm.* Experimentell-psychologische Ermittlang des aktuellen Kernproblems einer Personlichkeit Z. Neur. 150. 1934.

214. *Giese* Psychoanalytische Psychotechnik Imago 10 1924

215. *Gobber, K H* Blutgruppe und Typus Z. angew. Psychol., 1937, 33, 19— 47.

216. *Goldfarb, W* A definition and validation of obsessional trends in the Rorschach examination of adolescents Rorsch. Res Exch. VII. 3, 1943, 81—108

217. — Effects of Early Institutional Care on Adolescent Personality. Rorschach Data. Amer. J. Orthopsy., 1944, 14, 441—447.

218. — Organization Activity in the Rorschach Examination. Amer J. Orthopsy., 1945, 15, 525— 528

219. — Personality trends in a group of enuretic children below the age of ten Rorsch. Res. Exch. VI, 1 1942, 28— 38

220. — The animal symbol in the Rorschach test and an animal association test. Rorsch. Res Exch IX, 1, 1945, 8—22

221. — The Effects of Early Institutional Care on Adolescent Personality. Child Developm., 1943, 14, 213- 223.

222. — *and Klopfer, B* Rorschach characteristics of «Institution Children». Rorsch. Res. Exch. VIII. 2, 1944, 92-- 100

223. *Goldkuhl E :* Rorschach-Test bei Epilepsie, nebst einer grundsätzlichen Untersuchung. Upsala lakaref. forh , 1946. Bd. 51, S 283

224. *Goldmann, G S., and Bergman, M. S .* A Psychiatric and Rorschach Study of Adult Male Enuresis. Amer. J. Orthopsy., 1945, 15 160—166.

225. *Goldstein, K :* Personality studies of cases with lesions of the frontal lobes: I. The psychopathology of Pick's disease Rorsch Res. Exch. I, 3, 1937, 57—64.

226. — *and Rothmann, E .* Physiognomic phenomena in Rorschach responses. Rorsch. Res. Exch IX. 1, 1945, 1—7.

227. *Gotor, P :* El psicograma de Rorschach en la epilepsia. Rev. clin. españ. 1946, Bd. 21, S 138.

228. *Gozzano, M :* Relazione sul tema II: «Lo studio della personalità del dehnquente.» Atti I. Cong., int Criminol., Roma, 1939, 3, 315—319, Psychol. Abstr., 1939, 3147.

229. *Graf, O :* Experimentelle Psychologie und Psychotechnik Fortschr. Neurol. Psychiat., 1936, 8. 437—454.

230 *Graham, V. T..* Psychological studies of hypoglycemia therapy. J. Psychol , 1940, 10, 327—358.

231. *Grassi, J R :* Contrasting Schizophrenic Patterns in the Graphic Rorschach. Psychiat. Quart., 1942, 16, 646—659.

232. — *and Levine, K. N .* The Graphic Rorschach Manual. Psychiat. Quart., 1943, 17, 258—281

233 *Greulich V W., Day. H G., Lachmann, S. E., Wolfe, J B , & Shuttleworth, F K.* A handbook of methods for the study of adolescent children. Monograph of the Society for Research in Child Development, Vor. 3, No. 2, 1938

234 *Guggenheim, Lili* Liste d'interprétations donnees par des sujets adultes, compilée d'après les travaux de Rorschach ainsi que de ceux de ses successeurs (ronée-graphie) En vente à l'Institut J. J Rousseau, 52, rue des Pâquis. Genève.

235. *Guilford, J P ·* Introversion — Extroversion. Psychol Bull . 1934, 31, 331—354.

236 *Guirdham, A* Discussion on S. J Beck « «Some recent Rorschach problems» Rorsch Res Exch. II, 2. 1937. 72 --73.

237. — On the value of the Rorschach Test Reprinted from the «Journal of Mental Sciences», Octobre 1935

238. — (Quotation from a letter in Klopfer-Beck discussion) Rorschach Res. Exch. 1937. 2, 72- 73

239. - Simple psychological data in melancholia J. Ment. Sc.., 1936, 82. 649—653

240 -- The Diagnosis of depression by the Rorschach test. The British Journal of medical psychology 1936

241 — The Rorschach Test in Epileptics. Reprinted from the «Journal of Mental Science», Octobre 1935

242 Weitere Beobachtungen nach Rorschachs Testmethode (Bailbrookh Bath. England Schweiz Arch Neur 41 (1938).

243. *Guttman, E :* Artificial Psychoses produced by mescaline. J. Ment Sci , 1936, 82. 203— 221.

244. *Hackebusli, J Blenkorski, & Fundyler. R* An attempt at a study of the development of personality with the aid of hypnosis In Russian. Trudy psichonevr., Inst Kiev , 1933, 2, 236—272. Psychol. Abst. 1933, 5800.

245 *Hackfield. A W* An objective interpretation by means of the Rorschach test of the psychobiological structure underlying schizophrenia, essential hypertension, Graves' syndrome etc. A Preliminary report. Amer. J. Psychiatry 92. 1935.

246 *Hafyter, C* Der psychische Infantilismus im Rorschachtest. Zeitschr. f. d ges. Neurol. u Psychiat 1942, Bd. 174, S 139.

247 *Hellonell, A. I..* Acculturation processes and personality changes as indicated by the Rorschach technique Rorsch. Res. Exch VI, 2, 1942, 42—50.

248 - «Popular» responses and cultural differences: An analysis based on frequencies in a group of American Indian subjects Rorsch. Res. Exch. IX, 4, 1945, 153—168.

249 - Rorschach as an aid in the study of personalities in primitive societies (Abstract). Rorsch Res. Exch. IV, 3, 1940, 106.

250 - The Rorschach Technique in the Study of Personality and Culture Amer Anthrop , 1945. 47, 195—210

251 — The Rorschach test as a tool for investigating cultural variables and individual differences in the study of personality in primitive societies. Rorschach Res Exch , 1941, 5. 31—34

252 *Halvorson, H .* Eine Korrelation zwischen Rorschachtest und Graphologie. Z. f. angew. Psychol 84, 40 (1931).

253 *Hanfmann, E ·* A Study of Personal Patterns in an Intellectual Performance. Character and Pers , 1941, 9, 315—325.

254 — Personal patterns in the process of concept formation Psychol. Bull., 1940. 37, 515 Abstract.

255 *Harrimann, P L .* Notes on publicity. Rorsch Res Exch. VI, 3, 1942. 137

256. — Review of S J Beck's «Rorschach's test»: «I. Basic processes». Rorsch. Res. Exch. IX, 1, 1945, 41—45

257 — Review of S. J. Beck's «Rorschach's test: II A variety of personality pictures» Rorsch Res. Exch. X, 1, 1946, 37—39.

258. — The Rorschach test applied to a group of college students. Amer. J. Orthopsychiat. 1935, 5, 116—120

259. *Harrison, R* The Thematic Apperception and Rorschach Methods of Personality Investigation in Clinical Practice J. Psychol., 1943. 15, 49 74

260 *Harrower, G. J* Medical Technologists' Group Personality Estimate Canad J Med Technol , 1942, 4, 177—178.

261. — *and Cox, K. J* The Results Obtained from a Number of Occupational Groupings on the Professional Level with the Rorschach Group Method Bull Canad Psychol Assn , 1942, 2, 31—33

262 *Harrower, M R. (Harrower-Erickson)* A Multiple-Choice Test for Screening Purposes (for Use with the Rorschach Cards or Slides). Psychosom. Med , 1943, 5, 331 -341; Also in American Society for Res. in Psychosom Probl., Proceedings of the Military Session, May 9, 1943. pp. 9— 19.

263 — Clinical Use of Psychological Tests McGill Med. J. 1941. 11. 105-109.

264 — Developments of the Rorschach test for large scale application. Rorsch Res. Exch. VIII. 3, 1944, 125—140)

265. — Diagnosis and prognostic value of the Rorschach Test in neurological cases. Psychol. Bull., 1939, 36. 662.

266 — Diagnosis of Psychogenic Factors in Disease by Means of the Rorschach Method. Psychiat. Quart., 1943, 17, 57—66.

267. — Directions for administration of the Rorschach group test. Rorsch. Res Exch. V, 3, 1941, 145—153

268 — Group test techniques: A discussion of an eclectic group method. Rorsch. Res. Exch. VI, 4, 1942, 147—152.

269. — Large Scale Investigation with the Rorschach Method. J. Consult. Psychol., 1943, 7, 120—126.

270. — Personality changes accompanying cerebral lesions: I. Rorschach studies of Patients with cerebral tumors Arch. Neurol. Psychiat.. Chicago, 1940. 43. 859—890.

271. — Personality Changes Accompanying Organic Brain Lesions: III. A Study of Pre-adolescent Children. J. Genet. Psychol., 1941, 58, 391—45

272. — Personality Testing in Penal Institutions Probation, 1943, 22, 1—6.

273. — Psychodiagnostic Inkblots. New York. Grune & Stratton, Inc.; 1945. Manual and ten plates

274 — The contribution of the Rorschach Method to wartime psychological problems. J. Ment. Sci , 1940, 86, 366—377.

275. — The Patient and His Personality. McGill Med. J., 1941. 11, 25— 40.

276 — The Rorschach Method in the Study of Personality. Ann. N. Y Acad. Sci., 1943, 44, 569—583.

277 — The Rorschach Test J. Assn. Amer. Med. Coll , 1944. 19, 193—200.

278. — The Use of the Multiple Choice Test (Rorschach) in the Military Services. War Psychiatry. Proceedings of the Second Brief Psychotherapy Council. Chicago: Institute for Psychoanalysis; 1944 Pp. 55.

279. — The value and limitations of the so-called «neurotic signs» Rorsch. Res. Exch. VI. 3, 1942, 109—114.

280. — *and Miale, F. R.* Personality changes accompanying organic Brain Lesions. Pre- and Post-Operative study of two pre-adolescent children. Rorschach Res. Exch., 1940, 4, 8—25.

281 — *and Steiner, M E.:* Large Scale Rorschach Techniques: a Manual for the Group Rorschach and Multiple-Choice Test. Springfield, Illinois Charles C. Thomas; 1945, Pp. 149.

282. — Modification of the Rorschach method for use as a group test. Roisch Res. Exch. V, 3, 1941, 130—144.

283. — *Washburne, A C , and Jacob, J S L :* A Preliminary Screening Test for Disturbances in Personality. Bull. Canad Psychol. Assn., 1944, 4, 4—6

284. *Hens, Szymon.* Phantasiepiufung mit foimlosen Klecksen bei Schulkindern normalen Erwachsenen und Geisteskianken. (Diss. Zurich 1917 ·

285. *Hertz, H .* Binder's shading responses Rorschach Res. Exch , 1937—38, 2, 79—89.

286 *Hertz, M. R , and Baker, E* Personality changes in adolescence as revealed by the Rorschach method. «Control» patterns Paper read before the Midwestern Psychological Association, Ohio University, Athens, Ohio. April, 1941.

287. *Hertz, Marguerite R ·* A comparison of three «blind» Rorschach analyses. Developmental Health Inquiry of the Associated Foundations Westein Reserve University Cleveland. Reprinted from The American Journal of Orthopsychiatry, Vol. IX, April 1939.

288. — Comments on the standardization of the Rorschach gioup method. Rorsch Res. Exch. VI, 4, 1942. 153—159.

289. — Discussion on «Some Recent Rorschach Problems» Rorschach Res. Exch., 1937—38, 2, 53—65

290. — Evaluation of the Rorschach Method and Its Application to Normal Childhood and Adolescence Character and Pers., 1941, 10, 151—162.

291. — Frequency Tables to be Used in Scoring, the Rorschach Ink-blot Test. Brush Foundation, 1936, Western Reserve Univ . Cleveland. Ohio.

292. — Modification of the Rorschach Ink-Blot Test for Large Scale Application. Amer. J. Orthopsy., 1943, 13, 191—212.

293. — On the standardization of the Rorschach method. Reproduced from the Roischach Exchange, 1939, Vol III. 3.

294. — Percentage charts for use in computing Roischach scores. Brush Foundation and the Department of Psychology, 1940, Western Reserve University.

295. — Personality changes in 35 girls in various stages of pubescent development based on the Rorschach Method. Paper read before the Midwestern Psychological Association, Ohio University, Athens, Ohio, April, 1941

296. — Personality Patterns in Adolescence as Portrayed by the Rorschach Ink-Blot Method: III. The «Erlebnistypus» (a Normative Study). J. Gen. Psychol., 1943, 28, 225—276.

297. — Personality Patterns in Adolescence as Portrayed by the Rorschach Ink-Blot Method: 1 The Movement Factors. J. Gen. Psychol., 1942, 27, 119—188.

298. — Personality Patterns in Adolescence as Portrayed by the Rorschach Method: IV. The «Erlebnistypus» (a Typological Study). J. Gen. Psychol., 1943, 29, 3—45.

299. — Problems on the validity of the Rorschach Method. Amer. J. Orthopsychiat. to be published; Rorschach Res. Exch., 1940, 104—105-Abstract

300. — Recording the responses to the Rorschach Ink-blot Test. To be published

301. — Review of M. R. Harrower-Erickson and M. E Steiner's «Large scale Rorschach techniques». Rorschach Res. Exch. IX, 1, 1945, 46—53.

302. — Rorschach Norms for an Adolescent Age-Group. Developmental Health Inquiry of the Associated Foundations. Western Reserve University Reprinted fiom Child Development, Vol. 6, No. 1, March, 1935.

303. — Rorschach: Twenty years after Rorsch Res Exch. V, 3, 1941, 90—129.

304 — Scoring the Rorschach ink-blot test The Journal of Genetic Psychology 1938, 52. Development Health Inquiry. Western Reserve University.

305. — Scoring the Rorschach test with specific reference to «normal details» category. Amer J Orthopsychiatry 8, 100—121. 1938.

306 — Some personality changes in adolescence as revealed by the Rorschach Method. Psychol. Bull , 1940, 37, 515—516-Abstract. To be published by Carl Murchison

307 — The method of administration of the Rorschach ink-blot test. Child Developm.. 1936, 7, 237—254

308. — The normal details in the Rorschach ink-blot test. Rorschach Res. Exch , 1936—37, 1, 104—121.

309. — The «popular» response factor in the Rorschach scoring. J. Psychol. 6 (1938).

310 — The Reliability of the Rorschach ink-blot test. Western Reserve University. Offprinted from The Journal of Applied Psychology, Vol No. 3, June 1934.

311 — The role of the Rorschach method in planning for treatment. Rorsch. Res Exch. IX, 3, 1945, 134—146.

312. — The Rorschach ink-blot test: Historical Summary Department of Psychology Western Reserve University. Developmental Health Inquiry of the Associated Foundations, Western Reserve University. Offprinted from Psychological Bulletin. Vol 32, No 1, January 1935.

313. — The Rorschach Method. Science or Mystery J. Consult. Psychol., 1943, 7, 67—79.

314. — The scoring of the Rorschach ink-blot method as developed by the Brush Foundation. Rorsch. Res. Exch V, 1, 1942, 16—27.

315 — The shading response in the Rorschach ink-blot test: a review of its scoring and interpretation. J. gen. Psychol., 1940, 23, 123—167

316. — The Validity of the Rorschach Group Method. Psychol. Bull., 1942, 39, 514 (abstr.).

317 — & Baker, E : Personality changes in adolescence: Color patterns. Rorschach Res. Exch., 1941, 5, 30 — Abstract. To be published by Carl Murchison.

318. — Personality Patterns in Adolescence as Portrayed by the Rorschach Ink-Blot Method: II. The Color Factors. J. Gen. Psychol., 1943, 28, 3—61.

317. — and Ebert, E. H.· The mental procedure of 6 and 8 year old children as revealed by the Rorschach ink-blot method Rorsch. Res. Exch. VIII, 1, 1944. 10—30.

320 — & Kennedy, S.: The M Factor in estimation intelligence. Rorschach Res. Exchange, 1940, 4, 105—160 — Abstract.

321 — and Rubinstein, Boris R : A comparison of three «blind» Rorschach analyses. Amer. J. Orth. (1939).

322. — & Wolfson, R.. A Rorschach comparison between best and least adjusted girls in a training school. Rorschach Res. Exch , 1939, 3, 134—150.

323 Hertzman, M.: A comparison of the individual and group Rorschach tests. Rorsch. Res Exch. VI, 2, 1942, 89—108

324. — Recent research on the group Rorschach test. Rorsch. Res. Exch. VII, 1, 1943, 1—6.

325. — and Margulies, H · Developmental Changes as Reflected in Rorschach Test Responses. J Genet. Psychol , 1943, 62, 189—215.

326. — Orlansky, J , and Seitz, C. P · Personality Organization and Anoxia Tolerance. Psychosom. med., 1944, 6, 317—331.

327. — and Seitz, C P.· Rorschach Reactions at High Altitudes J. Psychol., 1942, 14, 245—257.

328. Hirning, L. C.: Case studies in schizophrenia. Rorschach Res. Exch., 1939, 3, 66—90.

329. — Report of the Research Committee. Rorsch. Res. Exch., 1942, 6, 177.

330. *Hitch, K. S.* A Rorschach Diagnosis of Cerebral Arteriosclerosis Psychiat Quart., 1943. 17, 81—86.

331. — Rorschach Examinations 'n Acute Psychiatri' Admissions. J. New Ment Dis., 1943. 97, 27—39.

332 *Hoel, H.* Pseudodebilitet. Svenska Lakartidn., 1938, 35, 1521—1533. Psychol Abst. 1939, 900.

333. *Holtzman, G G , and Holzman, E E.·* An evaluation of personality analysis in the general practice of medicine Rorsch Res. Exch V, 2, 1941, 67—71.

334. *Hunt, T* The application of the Rorschach Test and a word-association test to patients undergoing prefrontal lobotomy. Psychol. Bull , 1940, 37, 546. — Abstract.

335. *Hunter, M* A study of the Rorschach «Erlebnistypus» of Comparable White and Negro subjects Thesis for Degree of Doctor of Philosophy, Columbia University Privately published.)

336. — Responses of comparable white and negro adults to the Rorschach test J Psychol, 1937, 3, 173—182.

337. — The pratical value of the Rorschach test 'n a psychological clinic Amer. J Orthopsychiatry 9 (1939)

338. *Hutt, Max L.* The Use of Projective Methods of Personality Measurement in Army Medical Installations J Clin. Psychol., 1945, 1, 123—140.

339. — *and Shor, I ·* Rationale for routine Rorschach «testing-the-limits». Rorsch. Res. Exch X, 2, 1946. 70—76.

340 *Hylkema, G. W* De Rorschach-test bij schizophrenen Ned. Tijdschr. Psychol , 1938, 6, 1—15.

341. — Der Rorschach-Test bei Schizophrenen. Nederl Tijdschr. Psychol. 6 (1938).

342. — De Veranderingen in het Rorschach Protocol in het Verloop van de moderne Schizophreniebehandeling Een Casuistisch Onderzoek Diss. Amsterdam 1938.

343. *Ingebregtsen, E.:* Some experimental contributions to the psychology and psychopathology of stutterers Amer J Orthopsychiat , 1936, 6, 630—649.

344. *Inti Luna, R.:* Ensayo de la prueba de Rorschach en 104 niños. Rev. Neuro-Psiquiat, Lima, 1941, 4, 249—262.

345. *Ionasiu, L , Lungu, C., Iosif, S , & Cupcea, S* Contributiuni la studiul experimental al perceptiei vizuale la bolnavii mentali. Bul. Spital Boli mint. nerv. Sibiu, 1936, 28—35.

346. *Ionescu Sisesti, N., & Copelman, L* Le profil mental des parkinsoniens Anal. Psihol , 1938, 5, 156—165.

347. — *Copelman, L , and Tumin, L ·* Profilul mintal al parkinsonienilor post-encefalitici Anal. Psihol., 1939, 6, 180—186

348. *Jacob, Z .* Some suggestions on the use of content symbolism. Rorsch. Res Exch VIII, 1, 1944, 40—41

349. *Jacobson, W. T..* A study of personality development in a high school girl Rorschach Res. Exch., 1937, 2, 23—35.

350 — Charaktertypische Arten des Deutens von Helldunkelbildern. (Versuche an dem nach Struve abgewandelten Rorschachtest.) Z. Psychol. 140, 1937

351. *Jacobson, L .* Evaluation of Beck's Rorschach Norm as Applied to Children Tr. Kansas Acad Sc., 1938, 41, 257—258.

352. *Janis, M G., and Janis, 1 L.* A supplementary test based on free associations to Rorschach responses. Rorsch. Res. Exch X, 1, 1946, 1—19

353 *Jarrin, C. A.* Delito y estructura caracterologica. Arch Crim., Neuropsiquiat, epi.to. 1938. 2, 242—261

354 *Jastak J.* Rorschach performances of alcoholic patients Delaware St. Med. J. 1940, 12, 120—123

355. *Jensen, M B, and Rotter, J B.*. The Validity of the Multiple-Choice Rorschach Test in Officer Candidate Selection. Psychol. Bull, 1945, 42 182- 187.

356. *Jislin, S G* Z. Neur 98, 1925

357. *Juarros, G* · Die Methode von Rorschach und ihre neuen Arwendungen Rev Criminologia 22. 1935 (Spanisch) Ref. Zbl Neur. 80, S. 161

358. — *und Soriano, M*. Die Rorschachsche Diagnostik bei anormalen Kindern Siglo med. 80 (1927) (Spanisch).

359. -- Vergleich der Resultate der Rorschachschen Behandlung bei normalen und anormalen Kindern (Spanisch) Ref Zbl 55 1930.

360. *Just, E* Les Do dans le test de Rorschach Travail inedit de l Institut J.-J Rousseau. 1934.

361. — Le test de Rorschach appliqué à vingt malades appartenant à la categorie des psychoses simples, la démence précoce et ses sous-groupes Travail de diplome inédit de l'Institut J -J. Rousseau.

362 *Kadinsky, D* · Human whole and detail responses in the Rorschach test. Rorsch Res. Exch. X, 4, 1946, 140—144

363 *Kamman, G R* The Rorschach Method as a Therapeutic Agent Amer. J. Orthopsy., 1944. 14, 21—28.

364 *Kaplan, A. H., Miale, F. R., & Clapp, H*. Clinical validation of a Rorschach interpretation I Rorschach record. II. Rorschach interpretation. III. Summary of case history. IV Comparison between Rorschach interpretation and clinical findings. Rorschach Res. Exch., 1937—38, 2, 153—163.

365. *Katz, H*. Untersuchungen an insulinbehandelten Schizophrenen mit dem Rorschachschen Formdeutversuch. Mschr. Psychiat. Neurol., 1941, 104. 15—33.

366. *Kay, L. W., and Vorhaus, P G.* Rorschach reactions in early childhood. Part II Intellectual aspects of personality development. Rorsch. Res. Exch. VII, 2, 1943. 71—78.

367. *Kelley, D M* Announcement of the Rorschach Institute. Rorsch. Res. Exch. III, 3. 1939. 92—100.

368. — A note on the membership requirements of the Rorschach Institute. Rorsch. Res. Exch V, 4, 1941, 206—207.

369. — A questionnaire for a study and possible standardization of the technique of the Rorschach method Rorsch. Res. Exch. V, 2, 1941, 62—66.

370. — Preliminary studies of the Rorschach records of the Nazi War criminals. Rorsch. Res. Exch X, 2, 1946, 45—48

371. — Report of the first annual meeting of the Rorschach Institute, Inc., Rorschach Res. Exch.. 1940, 4, 102—103.

372. — Requirements for Rorschach training Rorsch Res. Exch. VI, 2, 1942, 74—77

373. — Survey of the training facilities for the Rorschach Method Rorschach Res Exch, 1940, 4, 84—87

374. -- The Rorschach method as a means for the determination of the impairment of abstract behavior. Rorsch. Res Exch V, 2, 1941, 85—88.

375. - *and Barrera, S. E.*: The present state of the Rorschach method as a psychiatric adjunct. Rorschach Res Exch, 1940, 4, 30—36.

376. - & *Klopfer, B.* Application of the Rorschach method to research in schizophrenia. Rorschach Res. Exch. 1939. 3, 55—66.

377 -- & *Levine, K.* Rorschach studies during sodium amytal narcoses (Abstract) Rorschach Res. Exch. 1940 4, 146.

378 - *Levine, K., Pemberton, W., and Lillian, K. K.* Intravenous sodium amytal medication as an aid to the Rorschach Method. Psychiat. Quaterly, 1941, 15, 68—73.

379. - *and Margulies, H.* Rorschach case studies in the convulsive states. Rorschach Res. Exch., 1940, 4, 157—190.

380. -- *Margulies, H., and Barrera, S E.* The stability of the Rorschach method as demonstrated in electric convulsive therapy cases. Rorschach Res. Exch., 1940, 5, 35—43

381. - *and Rioti, E.* The Geneva approach to the Rorschach method. Rorschach Res. Exch., 1939, 3, 195—201.

382 *Kemple, C.:* Contributions of the Rorschach Test to Psychosomatic Diagnosis Chapter XI, Section IV, in Psychosomatic Diagnosis, by Dunbar. F. New York. Paul B. Hoeber, Inc.

383. — Rorschach Method and Psychosomatic Diagnosis: Personality Traits of Patients with Rheumatic Diesease. Hypertensive Cardiovascular Disease, Coronary Occlusion, and Fracture. Psychosom Med., 1945, 7, 85—89.

384. -- The Rorschach method in psychosomatic problems. 1. A case of hypertensive cardiovascular disease Rorsch. Res. Exch. X, 4, 1946, 130—139.

385. *Kendig, I V* Projective Techniques as a Psychological Tool in Diagnosis. J. Clin. Psychopath. and Psychother., 1944, 6, 101—110.

386. *Kerr, M.* The Rorschach test applied to children Brit J. Psychol 23 1934.

387. — Temperamental differences in twins. Brit. J. Psychol., 1934, 27. 51—59.

388. *Kimble, G. A..* Social Influence on Rorschach Records. J. Abnorm. Soc. Psychol., 1945, 40, 89—93.

389. *Kisker, G. W :* A Projective Approach to Personality Patterns during Insulin Shock and Metrazol-Convulsive Therapy. J. Abnorm. Soc. Psvchol., 1942, 37, 120—124.

390. -- The Rorschach Analysis of Psychotics Subjected to Neurosurgical Interruption of the Thalamo-Cortical Projections. Psychiat Quart., 1944, 18, 43—52.

391 *Klebanoff, S. G* A Rorschach study of operational fatigue in army air forces combat personnel. Rorsch Res. Exch. X 4, 1946, 115—120.

392. *Klopfer, B..* Discussion of M. R. Hertz's «The normal details in the Rorschach ink-blot test». Rorsch Res. Exch. I, 4, 1937. 119—120.

393 — Discussion on «Some Recent Rorschach Problems». Rorschach Res. Exch., 1937, 2, 66—68.

394 — Instruction in the Rorschach Method. J. Consult. Psychol , 1943, 7, 112—119.

395 — Material for a comparative case study of a chronic arthritis personality· II. Rorschach interpretation. Rorsch Res. Exch. I, 2, 1936, 50—51.

396. — Personality aspects revealed by the Rorschach method Rorschach Res. Exch., 1940, 4, 26—29.

397. — Personality Diagnosis in Children. Chapter V in Modern Trends in Child Psychiatry. Edit. by Lewis, N. D C. and Pacella, B. L. New York: Internat. Univ. Press. Inc.; 1945.

398. — Personality diagnosis in early childhood· The application of the Rorschach Method at the pre-school leval. Psychol. Bull , 1939, 36, 662 — Abstract.

399. — Personality differences between boys and girls in early childhood. Psychol. Bull., 1939, 36, 538. — Abstract.

400 — Personality studies of cases with lesions of the frontal lobes. III. Rorschach study of a bilateral lobotomy case. B. Rorschach Interpretation. Rorschach Res. Exch., 1936—37, 1, 83—88.

401 — Should the Rorschach method be standardized? Rorschach Res. Exch., 1939. 3 47—54

402 *Klopfer, B. G.* The efficacy of group therapy as indicated by group Rorschach records. Rorsch. Res. Exch. IX, 4 1945, 207—209.

403 *Klopfer, B.* The present status of the theoretical development of the Rorschach method. Rorschach Res. Exch. 1936—37, 1, 142—148.

404 — The shading responses Rorschach Res Exch., 1937—38 2, 76—79.

405 — The technique of the Rorschach performance. Rorschach Res. Exch., 1937, 2, 1—14.

406 — *Burchard, M. L., Kelley, D. M., and Miale, F. R.* Theory and technique of Rorschach interpretation Rorschach Res. Exch., 1939. 3, 152—194.

407. — *and Davidson, H. H.* Form-Level Rating; a Preliminary Proposal for Appraising Mode and Level of Thinking as Expressed in Rorschach Records. Rorsch. Res. Exch., 1944 8, 164—177

408 — *and Davidson, H. H.* Record Blank for the Rorschach method of personality diagnosis Rorschach Institute, Inc., New York, 1938.

409. — *Davidson, H., Holzman, E., Kelley, D., Margulies, H., Miale, F., and Wolfson, R.* The technique of Rorschach scoring and tabulation. Rorschach Res. Exch., 1940. 4, 75—83

410. — *and Henning, L. C.* «Signs», «Syndromes», and Individuality Patterns in Rorschach Reactions of Schizophrenics Psychol Bull., 1942, 39, 513 (abst.)

411 — *Krugman, Morris; Kelley, Douglas M.. Murphy, Lois Barclay; and Shakow, David:* Shall the Rorschach method be standardized? Amer. Orthopsychiatry 9 (1939)

412. — *Margulies, H., Murphy, L. B., and Stone, L. J.* Rorschach reactions in early childhood. Rorsch. Res Exch. V. 1, 1941, 1—23

413 — *and Miale, F. R.* An illustration of the technique of the Rorschach interpretation: the case of Anne T. Rorschach Res. Exch., 1937—38, 2, 126—158.

414 — *and Sender S.* A system of refined scoring symbols. Rorschach Res. Exch., 1936—37, 1, 19—22

415. — *and Tallman, G.* A further Rorschach study of Mr. A. Rorschach Res. Exch., 1938, 3, 31—36

416. *Kluever, H.* An Analysis of Recent Work on the Problem of Types. J. Nerv. and Ment. Dis 1925

417. *Kogan, W.* Shifts in Rorschach patterns during a critical period in the institutional experience of a group of delinquent boys. Rorschach Res. Exch., 1940, 4, 131—133.

418. *Krafft, M. R., and Vorhaus, P. G..* The application of the Rorschach method in a family case work agency Rorsch. Res Exch. VII. 1, 1943. 28—35.

419. *Krafft, M R.:* Value of the Rorschach test to case work. Smitk Coll. Stud. Soc. Work, 1940, 11, 153—154. — Abstract.

420 *Kretschmer, E.* A Text-book of Medical Psychology. (Trans from the fourth German ed.) Oxford University Press, 1934, pp 274.

421 — Bumkes Handbuch der Geisteskrankheiten I, 681. 1928.

422. — Diskussionsbemerkung Zbl Neur 45. 1927.

423 — Experimentelle Typenpsychologie. Z. Neur. Bd. 113, 1928

424 — Medizinische Psychologie. Leipzig 1926.

425 — & *Enke, W* Die Persönlichkeit der Athletiker Leipzig 1936.

236

426. *Kroh, O* Experimentelle Beiträge zur Typenkunde Hrsg. v Kroh Zsch f Psychol Ergbde. 14. 22 und 24.

427 - Psychologie der Oberstufe 3 und 4 Aufl. 1933

428 *Kronfeld* Lehrbuch der Charakterkunde. Berlin 1932.

429 *Krugman, J T* A clinical validation of the Rorschach with problem children. Ro. sch Res Exch VI 2 1942. 61 - 70.

430. - Out of the inkwell: the Rorschach method Rorschach Res. Exch. 1940 4, 91—101 Also in Character and Personality, 1940, 9. 91—110.

431 — The Rorschach in Child Guidance J. Consult Psychol.. 1943. 7, 80—88

432. *Kubo, Y* A study of feeble-minded children Jap J appl Psychol, 1934, 3, 117—120

433 *Kuhn, R.:* Der Rorschachsche Formdeutversuch in der Psychiatrie Monatsschr. Psych Neur. 103. 1940.

434. - Über Maskendeutungen im Rorschachschen Versuch Monatsschr f Psychiat. u. Neurol. 1943, Bd 107, S. 1.

435. — Über Maskendeutung im Rorschachschen Versuch Monatsschr. f. Psychiat. u. Neurol 1944. Bd 109, S 169.

436. - Über Rorschachs Psychologie und die psychologischen Grundlagen des Form deutversuches Schweiz Arch. Neurol Psychiat, 1944. 53, 29—47.

437. *Lagache, D* La rêverie imageante. Conduite adaptive au test de Rorschach Bull d'orientat professionnelle. Dez. 1943 Ref.· Arn. méd.-psychol.. 1944, Bd. 1, S. 301.

438 *Laignel-Lavastine, Mme., Minkowska, Bouvet et Follin* Le test de Rorschach appliqué à l'examen clinique. Ann. med -psychol , 1940, Bd 2. S 289

439 — Le test de Rorschach appliqué à l'examen clinique Ann méd -psychol., 1941. Bd. 2, S. 1.

440 *Laignel-Lavastine, Minkowska, Bouvet et Neuveu·* Le test de Rorschach et la psychopathologie de la schizophrénie Congr. d. med aliénistes et neurol de France et d. pays de langue franç, Montpellier. 28.—30. X 1942 Ref : Ann. med.-psychol., 1943, Bd 1, S. 481.

441. *Landis, C., and Bolles, M M*. Personality and Sexuality of the Physically Handicapped Woman New York Paul B. Hoeber, Inc : 1942. Pp 171

442. *Layman, J. W·* A quantitative study of certain changes in schizophrenic patients under the influence of sodium amytal. J gen Psychol, 1940, 22, 67—86

443 *Leme Lopes, J.:* Las Interpretacoes Claro-escuro no Psicodiagnóstico de Rorschach e os Estados de Ansiedade. Rio de Janeiro Imprensa Nacional: 1943 Pp. 191

444 — O psico-diagnóstico de Rorschach na consulta medico-psicologica. Bol Inst. de Puericult., 1938, 1, 63—94.

445 *Levine, K. N:* A Comparison of Graphic Rorschach Productions with Scoring Categories of the Verbal Rorschach Record in Normal States, Organic Brain Disease, Neurotic and Psychotic Disorders. Arch. Psychol (New York), 1943, No 282, Pp 63.

446 — *and Grassi, J R*. The relation between blot and concept in Graphic Rorschach responses. Rorsch Res Exch. VI, 2, 1942, 71—73.

447 — *Grassi, J. R , and Gerson, M. J* Hypnotically induced mood changes in the verbal and graphic Rorschach· A case study. Rorsch. Res. Exch. VII, 4, 1943, 130—144.

448. — *Grassi, J R , and Gerson, M. J* Hypnotically induced mood changes in the verbal and graphic Rorschach· A case study. Part II: The response records Rorsch Res. Exch. VIII, 3, 1944, 104—124.

449. *Levit, L.:* Consideraciones sobre el «Psicodiagnostics» de Rorschach. Rev. Med. de Rosario, 1939, 29, 772—785.

450 *Levy, David and Beck:* The Rorschach test in manic depressiv psychosis. Vol. XI. Research Publications of the Association for research in nervous and mental diseases. 1931.

451 *Limares, M A.:* Untersuchungen mit der Rorschachschen Psychodiagnostik bei normalen spanischen Kindern. Arch Neur 12 (Spanisch)

452. *Lindner, R M:* A further contribution to the group Rorschach. Rorsch. Res. Exch. VII. 1, 1943 7— 15.

453 — Content Analysis in Rorschach Work Rorsch Res. Exch X, 4 1946. 121—129.

454 — Some Significant Rorschach Responses J. Crim. Psychopath., 1944, 5, 775—778

455 — The Rorschach Test and the Diagnosis of Psychopathic Personality. J. Crim Psychopath., 1943, 5, 69—93.

456 — *and Chapman, K W* An eclectic group method. Rorsch. Res. Exch. VI, 4, 1942. 139—146

457 — *Chapman, K. W, and Rinch, E C.:* The Development of a Group Rorschach Technique in a Federal Penal Institution with Special Reference to the Problem of Psychopathic Personality. Psychol. Bull. 1942, 39, 313—314.

458. *Line, W. and Griffin, J D. M.* Some results obtained with the Rorschach test, objectively scored Amer J. Psych 92 (1935)

459 — *and Griffin, J. D M.* The objective determination of factors underlying mental health Amer J. Psychiat, 1935, 91, 833—842.

460. *Linn, L:* The Rorschach test in the evaluation of military personnel Rorsch. Res. Exch. X 1, 1946, 20—27

461 *Loderer, Clara* Die intellektuelle Entwicklung im Spiegel des Rorschachschen Formdeutversuches. Nervenarzt, 1942, Bd. 15, S. 312.

462 *Loosli-Usteri, Marguerite* Der Rorschach-Test als Hilfsmittel des Kinderpsychologen Schweiz Zeitschr. f Psychol., 1942, Bd 1. S. 86.

463 — Discussion on S J Beck's «Some recent Rorschach problems». Rorsch Res. Exch. II, 2, 1937. 73—74

464 — La notion du hasard chez l'enfant. Arch de psych. 23. 1931.

465 — Le diagnostic individuel chez l'enfant du moyen au Test de Rorschach Paris 1938.

466 — Les interprétations dans le test de Rorschach. Interprétations kinesthétiques et interprétations-couleur. Arch de Psychol. Geneve 23 1932

467. — Le test de Rorschach appliqué à différents groupes d'enfants de 10 a 13 ans. Arch de Psychol. 22 1929.
Siehe auch *Ganz.*

468. *Löpfe.* Über Rorschachsche Formdeutversuche mit 10- bis 13jährigen Knaben. Z. angew. Psych 26. 1925.

469. *Lucke, Brother:* The Rorschach Method Applied to Delinquent and Non-Delinquent Boys; Summary of Research. Bull Canad. Psychol. Assn., 1943, 3, 52—53, also in French in Bull. 5, L'institut Pédagogique Saint-Georges, 1942, University of Montreal.

470. *Lynn, J. G, Levine, K N, and Hewson, L W:* Psychologic Tests for the Clinical Evaluation of Late «Diffuse Organic», «Neurotic», and «Normal» Reactions after Closed Head Injury Assn for Research in Nerv and Mental Dis., 1945, 24, 296—378.

471. *MacCalman, D. R.:* The Rorschach test and its clinical application. J. ment. Sci., 1933, 79, 419—423

472. *Madow, L* Can the Rorschach ink-blot test be used to predict hypnotizability? Master's thesis, The Ohio State University, 1938.

473. *Mahler-Schönberger, M & Silberpfennig, I.:* Der Rorschachsche Formdeutversuch als Hilfsmittel zum Verständnis der Psychologie Hirnkranker. (Psycho-Neurol Klin. Univ. Wien.) Schweiz. Arch. Neur. 40 (1938).

474. *Mall, G D :* Konstitution und Affekt. Z. Psychol. Erg. Bd. 25 1936

475. *Mandowsky, C.:* Über die Bedeutung des Rorschachschen Formdeutversuchs. Die Biologie der Person (ed. T. Brugsch and F. H. Lewy), 1931, II. 1044—59.

476. *Mangiacapra, Armando:* Il reattivo di Rorschach nello studio delle tendenze morali. Cervello, 1942, Bd. 21, S. 219.

477. *Mann, I., and Archibald, D.:* A Study of a Selected Group of Women Employed on Extremely Fine Work. Brit. Med. J., 1944, 1, 387—390.

478. *Margulies, H ·* Rorschach Responses of Successful and Unsuccessful Students Arch. Psychol. (New York), 1942, No. 271. Pp. 61.

479 *Marinescu, G , Kreindler, A., & Copelman, L.·* Essai d'une interprétation physiologique du test psychologique de Rorschach Son application à l'etude de la dynamique cérébrale des jumeaux. An Psiho., 1934, 1, 14—26.

480. *Marinesco, C. A , Kreindler et Copelmann, L :* Le test de Rorschach et la dynamique de l'écorce cérébrale d'après les lois des réflexes conditionals de Pavlov. Ann. méd. psychol. 93 1935.

481. *Mayer-Gross.* Bumkes Handbuch der Geisteskrankheiten I, 492/93. 1928.

482. *Maza, A. Linares:* Diagnóstico de niños anormales y superdotados. Rev. de Ped., 1931, 10, 412—17, 456—64.

483. — Investigaciones con el psicodiagnóstico de Rorschach en niños normales españoles. Arch. de Neurobiol., 1932, 12, 693—738.

484. *Mazkevic* Zur Methodik des Auffindens der latenten pathologischen Komplexe nach der Methode von Rorschach. (Russisch.) Ref. Zbl. Neur. 61. 1931.

485. *Meier-Müller, H ·* Die psychologischen Anforderungen des Fliegerberufes. Samml. d. Ref. geh. am Sportärztlichen Zentralkurs 1937 Bern.

486. *Meltzer, H ·* Personality differences among stutterers as indicated by the Rorschach test. Amer. J. Orthopsychiat., 1934, 4, 262—282.

487. — Personality Differences Between Stuttering and Non-Stuttering Children as Indicated by the Rorschach Test. J. Psychol., 1944, 17, 39—59.

488. — Talkativness in stuttering and non-stuttering children. J. genet. Psychol.. 1935, 46, 371—90.

489. *Miale, F. R :* Clinical validation of a Rorschach interpretation: The case of Lillian K: II. Rorschach interpretation. II, 4, 1938, 156—159

490. — The Rorschach Forum at the sixteenth annual meeting of the American Orthopsychiatric Association, Feb. 23. 1939, New York City Rorschach Res. Exch. 1939, 106—19.

491. — *Clapp, H., & Kaplan, A H :* Clinical validation of a Rorschach interpretation. Rorschach Res Exch., 1938, 2. 153—162.

492. — *Harrower-Erickson, M R ·* Personality structure in the Psychoneuroses. Rorschach Res. Exch., 1940, 4, 71—74

493. *Michael, J. C., and Buhler, C* Experiences with Personality Testing in a Neuropsychiatric Department of a Public General Hospital. Dis. Nerv. Syst, 1945, 6. 205—211.

494. *Miller, J. S., and Gair, M..* A Traumatic Neurosis of World War I 23 Years After. Psychiatric and Rorschach Investigations J. Nerv. Ment. Dis., 1943, 97, 436—446.

495. *Minkowska* Dessins d'enfants. tests de Rorschach et typologie constitutionnelle 45ᵉCongr d aliénistes et neurol. de France et d. pays de langue franç. Niort, 21—26 VII 1947. Ref: Ann. med.-psychol. 1947. Bd. 2. S 309.

496. — La methode genéalogique et le test de Rorschach, leur application à la typologie constitutionnelle. 45ᵉ Congr d. aliénistes et neurol. de France et d. pays de langue franç. Niort, 21—26. VII 1947. Ref. Ann med.-psychol, 1947. Bd 2. S. 308.

497. — L epilepsie essentielle. sa psychologie et le test de Rorschach. Ann. méd.-psychol. 1946, Bd. 2. S 321

498. — Le test de Rorschach dans l'épilepsie essentielle. Ann. med psychol. 1944. Bd 2, S 545.

499. *Mira, L. E.:* Concerning the value of Rorschachs psychodiagnostic. Progressos de la Clinica 808 (1925) (Spanisch).

500 *Mohr, P :* Die Inhalte der Deutungen beim Rorschachschen Formdeutversuch und ihre Beziehungen zur Versuchsperson. Schweiz Arch. f. Neurol. u. Psychiat., 1941, Bd. 47, S. 237.

501 — Die schwarze und sehr dunkle Tönung der Rorschachschen Tafeln und ihre Bedeutung für den Versuch. Schweiz. Arch Neurol. Psychiat, 1944, 53, 122—123.

502. *Monnier, Marcel·* La technique actuelle du test psychodiagnostique de Rorschach (Revision et critique) Ann. méd.-psychol. 96, I. (1938).

503. — Le test psychologique de Rorschach. Encéphale 29. 1934.

504. *Mons, W E R* Air Raids and the Child. Brit. Med. J., 1941, 2, 625—626.

505. *Morgan, Ch., and Murray, H..* A method for investigating fantasies The thematic apperception test. Arch. of Neur. 34. 1935.

506. *Morgenthaler, W :* Einführung in die Technik der Psychodiagnostik. (S. vorn S. 217.)

507 *Morhardt, P. E.·* Nouvelle méthode d'examen mental, le psycho-diagnostic de Rorschach. Presse méd, 1941, Jg. 49, S. 30.

508. *Morris, W W* Prognostic Possibilities of the Rorschach Method in Metrazol Therapy. Amer. J. Psychiat., 1943, 100, 222—230.

509 — Prognostic Possibilities of the Rorschach Method in Metrazol Therapy. Arch. Neurol. Psychiat., 1943, 49, 927—928.

510 *Müller, Max:* Der Rorschachsche Formdeutversuch, seine Schwierigkeiten und Ergebnisse. Z. Neur. 118. 1929.

511. — Zur Psychologie eines Mordversuchs Schweiz. Z. f. Strafrecht 38. 1925.

512. *Munroe, R :* An Experiment in Large Scale Testing by a Modification of the Rorschach Method. J. Psychol., 1942, 13, 229—263.

513 — An experiment with a self-administering form of the Rorschach and group administration by examiners without Rorschach training. Rorsch. Res. Exch X, 2, 1946, 49—59.

514. — Considerations on the place of the Rorschach in the field of general psychology. Rorsch. Res. Exch. IX, 1, 1945, 30—40.

515. — Discussion of the Paper, «The Rorschach Method in the Study of Personality». Ann. N Y. Acad. Sci, 1943, 44, 583—588

516. — Inspection technique: a method of rapid evaluation of the Rorschach protocol. Rorsch Res Exch. VIII, 2, 1944, 46—70.

517. — Inspection technique: a modification of the Rorschach method of personality diagnosis for large scale application. Rorsch. Res. Exch. V, 4, 1941, 166—191.

518 — Objective method and the Rorschach blots. Rorsch. Res. Exch. IX, 2, 1945, 59—73.

519 — Prediction of the Adjustment and Academic Performance of College Students by a Modification of the Rorschach Method. Appl. Psychol. Monog., Stanford University Press, 1945, No. 7, Pp 104.

520 — The Rorschach Test: A Report of Its Use at Sarah Lawrence College J Higher Educ. 1945, 16, 17—23

521 - The use of the Rorschach in college guidance Rorschach Res. Exch, 1940, 4, 107 - 130

522 — Three Diagnostic Methods Applied to Sally J Abnorm Soc. Psychol. 1945, 40, 215—227.

523. — Use of the Rorschach Method in College Guidance J. Consult Psychol. 1943, 7, 89—96.

524. — Lewinson, T. S, and Waehner, T S.. A Compa.ison of Three Projective Methods. Character and Pers., 1944, 13, 1—21.

525 Munz· Die Reaktion des Pyknikers im Rorschachschen psychodiagnostischen Versuch Z Neur. 91. 1924.

526. Murphy, L. B · Personality Development of a Boy from Age Two to Seven. Amer. J. Orthopsy., 1944, 14, 10—21.

527. Murray, H. A: Explorations in personality, a clinical and experimental study of fifty men of college age. New York: Oxford Univ Press, 1938, Pp. XIV & 761.

528. Myers, M C · The Rorschach Method Psychol. Bull.; 1941. 38, 748 (abstract).

529. Nadel, A. B A qualitative analysis of behaviour following cerebral lesions. Arch. Psychol., No. 224. New York: April 1938.

530. - Rorschach personality studies before and after operation for brain tumor. Psychol Bull., 1937, 34, 523—24. — Abstract.

531. Neymann and Kohlstedt: New Diagnostic Test for Introversion-Extraversion. J. Abnor. and Soc. Psychol. 1929.

532. Oberholzer, E.· Rorschach's Experiment and the Alorese. Chapter 22 in «The People of Alor» by Du Bois, C. Minneapolis University of Minnesota Press 1944.

533. - Rorschach's experiment in traumatic mental disorders Paper read before the annual meeting of the American Psychiatric Association, Chicago, 1939.

534. — Zur Auswertung des Formdeutversuches fur die Psychoanalyse Internat. Z. psychoanal. 10. 1924 (s. a. vorn S 181).

535. — Zur Auswertung des Rorschachschen Versuches bzgl. Diagnose und Krankheitsresp. Heilungsablauf. Schweiz. Arch. Neur 24 1929.

536. — Zur Differenzialdiagnose organisch-psychischer und psychogen bedingter Störungen nach Schädel- und Hirntraumen vermittels des Rorschachschen Formdeutversuches Bericht am I. internat neurologischen Kongress in Bern 1931.

537. — Zur Differenzialdiagnose psychischer Folgezustände nach Schädeltraumen mittels des Rorschachschen Formdeutversuchs. Vorläufige Mitteilung an Hand der Ausweitung. eines Einzelbeispiels Z. Neur. 136. 1931

538. Oeser, O A. Some Experiments on the Abstraction of Form and Colour· Part II, Rorschach Tests. Brit J. Psychol. 1932.

539 Ombredane, A., Suarès & Canivet. Sur le mécanisme des crises d'angoisse vespérales et nocturnes de l'enfant. Groupement franc Etud. Neuro-psychopath. infant., 1938, 1, No. 3, 49—61.

540. Oppenheimer, E., u Spejer, N.: Resultate der Rorschach-Probe bei einem Fall von Dementia paralyctia vor und nach der Malariakur. (Psychiatr. Inricht. «Het Apeldoornsche Bosch», Apeldoorn.) Psychiatr. Bl 41 u dtsch. Zusammenfassung (1937).

541 *Parson, C. J.·* Children's Interpretations of Ink-Blots (A Study in some charac teristics of children's imaginations'. 1917.

542. *Parsons, F. H.,* Eight Cases of Section of Corpus Callosum in Individuals with a History of Epileptic Seizures: Psychological Tests J. Gen Psychol. 1943, 29, 227—241.

'43 *Paster, S, and Grassi, J. R.* Clarification of Rorschach Responses of the Graphic Rorschach Method. J. Clin. Psychol.. 1945, 1, 28—36

544 *Patterson, M, & Magau, D C.·* An investigation of the validity of the Rorschach technique as applied to mentally defective problem children Proc. Amer Ass ment Def., 1938, 43, No. 2, 179—185.

545. *Paulsen, L.* Phantasievorgänge bei der Deutung sinnarmer Farbkomplexe. Arch ges. Psychol., 1937, 99, 1—79.

346. — (reporter) Proposed Projects. Rorsch. Res Exch. I, 1, 1936, 3.

547 — Rorschachs of School Beginners. Rorschach Res. Exch.. 1941, 5, 24—29

548 *Pemberton, W H.,* General Semantics and the Rorschach Test. Papers Amer Congr. Gen. Semant, 1943, 2, 251—260.

549. *Pescor, M. J·* Age of delinquents in relationship to Rorschach test scores Publ. Hlth. Rep., Wash., 1938, 53, 852—864.

550. — Marital status of delinquents in relationship to Rorschach test scores Publ. Hlth. Rep., Wash., 1939, Suppl. No. 153, Pp. 6

551 *Pfahler, G.·* System der Typenlehren. Habilitationsschrift. Zschr. f. Psychol. Ergbd.,15.

552 *Pfister.* Ergebnisse des Rorschachschen Versuches bei Oligophrenen Allg. Z. Psy chiatrie 82. 1925

553. — Expériences de Rorschach, faites avec 2 séries différentes de taches présentées collectivement et individuellement, Genève, juillet 1934

5524. *Picard, Pierre:* Contribution à l'étude du test psychologique de Rorschach Diss: Lyon 1941. 118 Seiten.

555 *Piotrowski, Z A.* A comparison of congenitally defective children with schizophrenic children in regard to personality structure and intelligence type Proc. Amer. Ass. ment Def., 1937, 42, 78—90.

556. — A note on the «Graphic Rorschach» and the «Scoring Samples». Rorsch. Res. Exch. VII, 4, 1943, 182—184.

557. — A Rorschach blind analysis of a compulsive neurotic. Kwart. psychol. 11 (1939).

558. — A simple experimental device for the prediction of outcome of insulin treatment in schizophrenia. Psychiat. Quart., 1940, 14, 267—273.

559 — Blind analysis of a case of compulsion neurosis. Rorsch. Res. Exch. II, 3. 1938, 89—111.

560 — Blind analysis of a case of compulsion neurosis. Rorsch. Res. Exch., 1937—38, 2, 89—111; also in Kwart. Psychol., 1939, 11, 231—264.

561. — Comments concerning the Beck-Klopfer discussion. Rorschach Res. Exch., 1939, 2, 68—69.

562 — Discussion on S. J Beck's «Some recent Rorschach problem». Rorsch. Res. Exch. II, 2, 1937, 68—69.

563. — Experimental psychological diagnosis of mild forms of schizophrenia. Rorsch. Res. Exch. IX, 4, 1945, 189—200.

564 — On the Rorschach method and its application in organic disturbances of the central nervous system. Rorschach Res. Exch., 1936—37, 1, 23—40; also Kwart Psychol., 1937, 9, 29—41.

565. — On the Rorschach Method of Personality Analysis. Psychiat Quart., 1942. 16, 480—490

566 — Personality studies of cases with lesions of the frontal lobes: II. Rorschach study of a Pick's disease case. Rorschach Res. Exch., 1936—37, 1, 65—77.

567 — Positive and negative Rorschach organic reactions. Rorschach Res Exch., 1940, 4, 147—151.

568. — Psychological difference between the schizophrenic and organic patient as revealed in the Rorschach technique. (Paper read before the annual meeting of the Rorschach Institute, 1940, New York City)

569. — Recent Rorschach literature. Rorschach Res. Exch., 1937—38, 2, 172—175.

570. — Review of R Bochner and F. Halpern's «The clinical application of the Rorschach test». Rorsch. Res. Exch. VI, 2, 1942. 78—80

571. — Rorschach manifestations of improvement in insulin treated schizophrenics Psychosom. Med., 1939, I, 508—526.

572. — Rorschach studies of cases with lesions of the frontal lobes. (Dep of Psychiatry, Columbia Univ. New York). Brit. J. med. Psychol. 17 (1937)

573. — Tentative Rorschach formulae for educational and vocational guidance in adolescence. Rorsch. Res. Exch VII, 1, 1943, 16—27.

574. — The fallacy of measuring personality by the same methods as intelligence Psychol. Bull., 1937, 34, 546—547. — Abstract.

575. — The methodological aspects of the Rorschach personality method. Kwart psychol. 9 (1937)

576. — The M, FM, and m responses as indicators of changes in personality. Rorschach Res. Exch , 1936—37, 1, 148—157.

577. — The modifiability of personality as revealed by the Rorschach method: Methodological considerations. Rorsch. Res. Exch VI, 4, 1942, 160—167.

578. — The prognostic possibilities of the Rorschach method in insulin treatment (Dep. of Psychiatry, Columbia Univ. New York). Psychiatr. Quart. 12 (1938).

579. — The reliability of Rorschach's Erlebnistypus. J. abnorm. a. soc. Psychol. 32 (1937).

580. — The Rorschach inkblot method in organic disturbances, of the central nervous system. J. nerv. Dis 86 (1937).

581. — The Rorschach method of personality analysis in organic psychoses. Psychol Bull , 1936, 33, 795. — Abstract.

582. — Use of the Rorschach in Vocational Selection. J. Consult Psychol., 1943, 7, 97—102.

583. — Candee, B , Balinsky, B., Holtzberg, S , and Von Arnold, B.: Rorschach Signs in the Selection of Outstanding Young Male Mechanical Workers. J. Psychol., 1944, 18, 131—150.

584. — and Kelley, D. M . Application of the Rorschach Method in an epileptic case with psychoneurotic manifestations. J. nerv. ment. Dis , 1940, 92, 743—751.

585. Porot, Maurice: Le test de Rorschach dans l'anorexie mentale. Soc méd. d. hôp. d'Alger, 14. XII. 1946. Ref.: Presse méd., 1947, Jg. 55, S. 180.

586. — Le test de Rorschach et sa valeur pratique. Soc. méd. d. hôp d'Alger, 14. XII 1946. Ref.. Presse méd., 1947, Jg. 55, S. 180.

587. Powell, M : Relation of scholastic discrepancy to free associations on the Rorschach tests. Kentucky Person Bull , 1935, No. 14

588. Prados, M.. Rorschach studies on artists: Painters. I. Quantitative analysis Rorsch. Res. Exch. VIII, 4, 1944, 178—188.

589. Psychiatrie und Rorschachscher Formdeutversuch Verh. d Schweiz Ges. f. Psychiat Munsterlingen und Kreuzlingen, 26 u 27 VI Orell Fuessli, Zürich, 1944

590. *Rabin, A J* Rorschach Test Findings in a Group of Conscientious Objectors Amer J Orthopsy, 1945, 15 514—519

591. *Raines, G. N, and Broumhead, E* Rorschach Studies on Combat Fatigue. Dis. Nerv. Syst. 1945, 6, 250—256

592. *Rapaport, D* Principles Underlying Projective Techniques. Character and Pers. 1942, 10, 213—219

593. - *Gill, M, and Schafer, R.* Diagnostic Psychological Testing. (Two volumes.) Chicago· Year Book Publishers, 1945.

594. — *and Schafer, R:* The Rorschach Test: A Clinical Evaluation. Bull Menninger Clin., 1945, 9, 73— 77.

595. *Reistrup, Herman* Der Rorschach-Test als Hilfsmittel bei der Diagnostizierung von Milieureaktionen. Acta psychiat. et neurol., 1946, Bd. 21, S 687

596. *Ricci, Amedeo:* Studi di diagnose differenziale col reattivo del Rorschach (Istit. di Psicol Sperim, Univ Torino) Cervello 18 (1939).

597. *Richards, T. W* Epileptic seizure in the Rorschach test situation Rorsch Res. Exch. X. 3, 1946, 101—104.

598. - The Appraisal of Naval Psychiatric Casualties by the Rorschach Method. Naval Med. Bull., 1943, 41, 788—799.

599 *Richardson, L H ·* A Personality Study of Stutterers and Non-Stutterers. J Speech Disorders, 1944, 9, 152—160

600. *Rickers, M* Descriptions of the first grade normal details for the ten test-plates. Appendix of Klopfer's article in Rorschach Res. Exch., 1936, 1, 16—17.

601. *Rickers-Ovsiankina, M:* Rorschach scoring samples Worcester, Mass., Worcester State Hospital, 1938.

602. -- Some theoretical considerations regarding the Rorschach method. Rorsch. VII, 2, 1943, 41—53.

603. - The Rorschach test as applied to normal and schizophrenic subjects. Brit J. med. Psychol. 17 (1938).

604. *Rieti, Ettore·* Valore semeiologico dell'esame psicologico del malato di mente. Ann. Osp. psichiat. Prov. Genova 8 (1936)

605. *Rittmeister, J F.* Psychische Befunde bei einem Geschlecht mit myotoner Dystrophie. Schweiz Arch Neur 43 (1939)

606 *Rizzo, C* (Preliminary researches on normal Italian adults by Rorschach method) Riv Sper. Freniat., 1937, 61, 1124—1150.

607. *Robb, R W., Kovitz, B, Rapaport, D..* Histamine in the treatment of psychosis. Amer. J. Psychiat. 1940 97, 601—610.

608. *Rochlin, G N., and Levine, K N.* The Graphic Rorschach Test I. Arch Neurol. Psychiat., 1942. 47, 438 448.

609. *Roe, A:* Painting and personality Rorsch Res Exch. X, 3, 1946, 86—100

610. *Roemer, A G.* Die Innenwelt einer Persönlichkeit und das Problem ihrer wissenschaftlichen Erschliessung Psychol Rdsch. 2. 1930.

611 - Psychographische Tiefenanalyse eines Grossindustriellen und seines Stabes. Prakt Psychol. 4. 1922/23

612. - Vom Rorschachtest zum Symboltest. Zentralbl f. Psychotherapie, 10. 1938.

613. *Rombouts, J M* Untersuchungen mit undeutlichen (nebligen) Schattenbildern. Psychiat Bl 43 (1939) (Holländisch).

614. *Rorschach, H* · Psychodiagnostics, a Diagnostic Test Based on Perception. (Transl.) New York: Grune & Stratton, Inc.; 1942 Pp. 226.

615. *Rorschach, O.·* Über das Leben und die Wesensart von Hermann Rorschach. Schweiz Arch. Neurol. Psychiat., 1944, 53, 1—11

616. *Rorschach, H, und Obernolzer, E :* Zur Auswertung des Formdeutversuchs fur die Psychoanalyse Zsch. f. d. ges. Neur u. Psychiat., 1923, 82, 240—274. Also translated. The Application of the interpretation of form to psychoanalysis J Nerv Ment. Dis., 1924, 60, 225—248, 359 –379

617. Rorschach Research Exchange, Vol I—XI (1936—1947). Rorsch. Institute, Inc. New York.

618. *Rosenberg, S J., and Feldberg, T M.* Rorschach characteristics of a group of malingerers. Rorsch. Res. Exch VIII, 3, 1944. 141—158.

619. *Rosenzweig, S.·* A note on Rorschach prehistory. Rorsch Res. Exch. VIII. 1, 1944, 41—42.

620. — Outline of a cooperative project for validating the Rorschaeh test. Amer J. Orthopsychiat, 1935, 5, 121—123

621. *Ross, W. D.·* A contribution to the objectification of group Rorschach scoring. Rorsch. Res. Exch. VII, 2, 1943, 70.

622. — Anatomical perseveration in Rorschach records. Rorschach Res. Exch., 1940. 4, 138—145

623. — A Quantitative Use of the Rorschach Method. Amer. J. Psychiat, 1944, 101, 100—104

624. — Notes on Rorschach «signs» in diagnosis and research. Rorsch. Res. Exch VI, 3. 1942, 115—116.

625. — Summary and review of H. G. Van der Waals' «Rorschach investigations in neuroses, psychopathic states, and related conditions». Rorsch. Res. Exch X, 4, 1946, 168—170.

626. — The «anxiety neurosis» Rorschach record compared with the typical basically neurotic record Rorschach Res. Exch., 1940, 4, 134—137.

627. - The Contribution of the Rorschach Method to Clinical Diagnosis. J Ment. Sci, 1941, 87, 331—348

628. — The Rorschach Performance with Neurocirculatory Asthenia. Psychosom. Med., 1945, 7, 80—84.

629. — The uses of the Rorschach method in the Canadian Army Rorsch. Res Exch. VIII, 3, 1944, 159—161.

630. — *Dancey, T E, and Brown, F T :* Rorschach Scores of Parachute Troopers in Training. Bull. Canad Psychol. Assn., 1943, 3, 26—27.

631. — *and McNaughton, F. L* Objective Personality Studies in Migraine by Means of the Rorschach Method. Psychosom. Med., 1945, 7, 73—79.

632 — *and Ross, S.:* Some Rorschach ratings of clinical value. Rorsch Res. Exch VIII. 1, 1944, 1—9.

633. *Rottersman, W.*. Green Ink: Preliminary Report. J. Nerv Ment. Dis., 1944, 100, 507—510.

634. — *and Goldstein, H H* Group Analysis Utilizing the Harrower-Erickson (Rorschach) Test Amer J. Psychiat., 1945, 101, 501—503.

635. *Ruesch, J, and Finesinger, J. E.:* The Relation of the Rorschach Color Response to the Use of Color in Drawings. Psychosom. Med, 1941, 3, 370—388

363. *Rymer, C A , Benjamin, J. D , and Ebaugh, F G* The hypoglycemia treatment of schizophrenia. Jour Amer. Med. Assoc , 1937, 109. 1249—1251.

637. *Salas, José* Analyse der Psychodiagnostik nach Rorschach in einem Fall von Schizophrenie. Archivos Neurobiol. 12 1932 (Spanisch.) Ref Zbl Neur. 67. S. 86

638. — Die Klassifikation der Antworten bei der Psychodiagnostik nach Rorschach. Archivos Neurobiol. 18 1933. (Spanisch) Ref. Zbl. Neur 69. 1933

639. — El psicodiagnóstico de Rorschach. Arch. de Neurobiol., 1932, 12. 316—339.

640. *Sanders, J., Schenk, V W. D., and Van Veen, P.:* A family with Pick's disease Verh. Akad. Wet Amst , 1939, Sec 2, Part 38, No. 3, pp. 1—124.

641. *Sandford, R , Adkins, M M., & Cobb, E S* An experiment to test the validity of the Rorschach test. Psychol. Bull., 1989, 36, 662. — Abstract.

642. *Sarbin, T. R., and Madow, L. W :* Predicting the Depth of Hypnosis by Means of the Rorschach Test. Amer. J. Orthopsy., 1942, 12, 268—271

643. — Rorschach patterns under hypnosis Amer. J Orthopsychiatry 9 (1939).

644. *Sargent, H..* Projective Methods: Their Origins, Theory, and Application in Personality Research. Psychol. Bull., 1945, 42, 257—293.

645. *Saudek, R ·* A British pair of identical twins reared apart. Char. and Person, 1934, 3. 17—39.

646. *Schachtel, Anna Hartoch:* The Rorschach Test with Young Children The American Journal of Orthopsychiatry, 1944, vol. 14, pp. 1—9.

647. — *and Levi, M. B :* Character Structure of Day Nursery Children in Wartime as Seen through the Rorschach. Amer. J. Orthopsy., 1945, 15, 213—222.

648. — *Henry, Jules and Zunia·* Rorschach Analysis of Pilaga Indian Children. The American Journal of Orthopsychiatry, 1942, vol. 12, pp. 679—712.

649. — *and E .* The Rorschach Test. Chapter 10 (pp. 877—414) of the book: Child Life in School. A Study of a Seven-Year-Old Group. By Barbara Biber, Lois B. Murphy, Louise P. Woodcock, Irma S Black. With a chapter on the Rorschach Test by A. H. and E. Schachtel New York 1942. E. P. Dutton and Co. Inc.

650. — *und Ernst.* Über einige Beziehungen zwischen Graphologie und Rorschachs Psychodiagnostik. Psyche 3. 1936.

651. *Schachtel, E. G .* On Color and Affect; Contributions to an Understanding of Rorschach's Test II. Psychiatry, 1943, 6, 393—409.

652 — Review: The Rorschach Technique, by Bruno Klopfer. Psychiatry, 1942, vol. 5, pp. 604—606.

653 — Some Notes on Fire-setters and their Rorschach Tests Journal of Criminal Psychopathology, 1943, vol. 5, pp. 341—350.

654 — The Dynamic Perception and the Symbolism of Form. With Special Reference to the Rorschach Test. Psychiatry 1941, vol. 4, pp. 79—96.

655. *Schachtel, E and H. A.:* Discussion on «Some recent Rorschach Problems». Rorschach Res. Exch., 1937, 2, 70—72.

656. — *and H. A.:* The Curve of Reactions in the Rorschach Test. A contribution to the Theory and Practice of Rorschach's Psychodiagnostic Ink Blot Test. Amer. J. Orthopsychiat , 1937, vol. 7, pp. 320—348.

657. *Schachter.* (Das Rorschachsche Profil in einem Fall von hyperovariellem Syndrom) (italienisch). Il Cervello, 1946, No. 5—6.

658. — *et Cotte·* Etude neurologique rorschachienne d'un instable, débile, bègue, onychophage, gaucher et énurétique. Comité méd. d. Bouches-du-Rhône, 7. III. 1947. Ref.: Presse méd., 1947, Jg. 55, S. 485.

659. *Schade, W.* Handschrift und Erbcharakter. Z. angew. Psychol, 1939, 57, 303—381. Subtitel: An investigation of children and youths.

660. *Schenk, V. W . D.:* Der Formdeutversuch (Rorschach) bei organischen Hirnerkrankungen. (Heilanst. Rosenburg Groosduinen.) Psychiatrische en Neurologische Bladen 2. 1938.

661 — *und Coltof, F.* Veränderungen im Rorschach-Test nach Insulinbehandlung (holländisch). Psychiat. en neurol. blad., 1940, Bd. 44. S. 435

662. *Schmid, Edmund, und Schmid-Ganz, Madeleine:* Beitrag zur Frage der psychischen epileptischen Aquivalente. (Univ.-Kinderklin. Bern.) Z. Kinderpsychiatr. 6 (1939).

663. *Schmidl, F..* The Rorschach Personality in Family Case Work. The Family, 1943, 24, 83—90.

664. — The use of the Rorschach method in social work treatment of adults. Rorsch. Res. Exch. IX, 3, 1945, 123—125.

665 *Schmidt, Bruno:* Reflektorische Reaktionen auf Form und Farbe und ihre typologische Bedeutung Zschr. f. Psychol. 137.

666. *Schmidt, H. O..* Test Profiles as a Diagnostics Aid: The Rorschach. J. Clin. Psychol. 1945, 1. 222—227.

667. *Schneider, E..* Der Rorschachsche Formdeutversuch. Industrielle Psychotechnik, XII, 1935.

668. — Die Bedeutung des Rorschachschen Formdeutversuchs zur Ermittlung intellektuell gehemmter Schüler. Zeitschr. f. angew. Psychol. 32. 1928.

669. — Eine diagnostische Untersuchung Rorschachs auf Grund der Helldunkeldeutungen ergänzt. Z. Neur. 159 1937.

670. — Faul und dumm. Schweizer Erziehungs-Rundschau 1935/36.

671. — Intellektuell gehemmte Schüler im Rorschachschen Formdeutversuch. (Im Manuskript.)

672 — Inteligences noteiksana ar Rorsachu experimentu (Intelligenzprüfungen mit dem Rorschachschen Versuch). Musunakot (unsere Zukunft), Riga 1925. Nr. 11—14.

673. — Neurotische Depression und Stehlen. Zeitschr f psychoanalytische Pädagogik. Wien 1933.

674 — Psychodiagnostisches Praktikum für Psychologen und Pädagogen Eine Einführung in Hermann Rorschachs Formdeutversuch. Leipzig, Barth. 1936.

675. — Über Aufnahmeprüfungen. Die Schulreform, Bern 1930.

676. — Über Psychodiagnostik. Die Schulreform. Bern 1922. (Enthält eine Blinddiagnose durch Rorschach ausgeführt.)

677 *Scholl, R :* Die teilinhaltliche Beachtung von Form, Farbe und Grösse im vorschulpflichtigen Kindesalter. Zschr f. Psychol. 109.

678. — Untersuchungen über die teilinhaltliche Beachtung von Farbe und Form bei Erwachsenen und Kindern. Zschr f. Psychol. 101.

679. — Zur Theorie und Typologie der teilinhaltlichen Beachtung von Form und Farbe. Zschr. f. Psychol. 101.

680. *Seliger, R. V., and Cranford, V.* The Rorschach Analysis in the Treatment of Alcoholism. Med. Rec., N. Y., 1945, 158, 32—38.

681. *Selinsky, H., Klopfer, Bruno, & Emery, Marg :* Inferences drawn from Rorschach tests in convulsive states. J. Ner. Dis. 84, 1936.

682. *Sender, S :* Discussion of M R. Hertz's «The normal details in the Rorschach ink-blot test». Rorsch. Res. Exch. I. 4, 1937, 118—119.

683. — The influence of variations in Rorschach group method administration upon the scorability of the records Rorsch Res. Exch. VII. 2. 1943, 54—69.

684 — The significance of the Rorschach method for consulting psychology: B Complementary summary Rorsch. Res. Exch. I. 5, 1937. 164—166.

685 — and Klopfer, B: Application of the Rorschach test to child behavior problems as facilitated by a refinement of the scoring method Rorschach Res. Exch., 1936—1937. 1. 5—17.

686 — Klopfer, B., and Rickers, M Description of the first grade normal details for the ten test plates Rorsch Res. Exch. I, 1, 1936, 16—17.

687 Serebrinsky. B El Psicodiagnostico de Rorschach en los Homicidas. Argentina: Cordoba 1941. 198 pp.

688. — Psicodiagnostico de Rorschach e Inventario Personal de Bernreuter en los Homicidas. Rev Psiquiat. Crim.. B. Aires, 1941, 6, 602—610.

689. Shakow, D, and Rosenzweig, S The use of the tautophone («verbal summator») as an auditory apperceptive test for the study of personality. Character and Personality, 1940, 8, 216—226.

690 Shapiro, L · Le test de Rorschach Travail de comparaison entre garçons et filles. Travail de diplôme inédit de l'Institut, 1932.

691 Shapiro-Pollak· Contribution à l'étude psychologique de la puberté à l'aide du test de Rorschach. Paris: Soc. Nouv. d'Imprim., 1935. Pp. 115.

692 Shaskan, D, Yarnell, H, and Alper, K · Physical, Psychiatric, and Psychometric Studies of Post-Encephalitic Parkinsonism. J. Nerv Ment. Dis., 1942, 96, 653—662, also in Arch. Neurol. Psychiat., 1942, 48, 666—688.

693 Shuey, H A new interpretation of the Rorschach test Psych. Rev., 1933, 40, 213—15.

694. — Further discussion on «Some recent Rorschach problems». Rorschach Res. Exch., 1937—38, 2, 170—171.

695 Sicha, K, and Sicha, M A step toward the standardization of the scoring of the Rorschach test. Rorschach Res. Exch., 1936—1937. 1, 95—101.

696. Siegel, M G · The Rorschach Test as an Aid in Selecting Clients for Group Therapy and Evaluating Progress. Ment. Hyg, 1944, 28, 444—449.

697 — The use of the Rorschach test in a treatment program. Rorsch. Res. Exch. IX, 3, 1945. 126—129

698 Sill, J B · A case study comparing the performance on the Binet and on the Rorschach. Rorschach Res. Exch., 1937—38, 2, 112—124.

699 Singeisen, F. Rorschachbefunde bei chronisch Lungentuberkulösen und Herzkranken. Schw. Arch Neur. 45. 1940

700 Skalweit. Der Rorschach-Versuch als Unterscheidungsmittel von Konstitution und Prozess. Erwiderung auf den gleichlautenden Aufsatz von M. Bleuler. Z. Neur. 152. 1935

701. — Konstitution und Prozess in der Schizophrenie. Leipzig 1934.

702 — Schizophrenie. Fortschr. Neurol Psychiat., 1939, 11, 331—349

703 Soukup Der Rorschachsche Versuch und das Studium der Persönlichkeit. Casop. cesk. lek. 1931 Ref Zbl. f. Psychotherapie 1931

704. Stainbrook. E. J · A modified Rorschach technique for the description of transitory post-convulsive personality states. Rorsch. Res. Exch. V, 4, 1941, 192—203.

705. — The Rorschach Description of Immediate Post-Convulsive Mental Function. Character and Pers, 1944, 1q, 302—322.

706. - *and Segel, P S .* A Comparative Rorschach Study of Southern Negro and White High School and College Students J. Psychol., 1944, 17, 107—115

707. *Stauder, K H.* Konstitution und Wesensänderung der Epileptiker. Leipzig 1938.

708. *Starrianos, B* An investigation of sex differences in children as revealed by the Rorschach method Rorsch. Res. Exch. VI, 4, 1942, 168—175.

709 — Location of Responses. Rorsch. Res Exch., 1943, 7, 78.

710. *St. Clair W. F.,* The self-recording technique in Rorschach administration. Rorsch. Res. Exch. VII, 3, 1943, 109—118.

711. *Stein-Levinson, T* Material for a comparative case study of a chronic arthritis personality. III. Graphological analysis. Rorsch. Res. Exch. I, 2, 1937, 52—54.

712. *Steinzor, B .* Rorschach Responses of Achieving and Non-Achieving College Students of High Ability. Amer. J Orthopsy, 1944, 14, 494—504.

713. — *Stern, K , and MacVaughton, D.·* Capras' Syndrome. a Peculiar Illusionary Phenomenon Considered with Special Reference to the Rorschach Findings. Psychiat. Quart., 1945, 19, 139—168.

714. *Stern, W* Cloud pictures: a new method for testing imagination. Character and Pers., 1937, 6, 132—146

715. — Ein Test zur Prüfung der kindlichen Phantasietätigkeit. (Wolkenbilder-Test.) Z Kinderpsychiatr. 5 (1938).

716. *Sterren, H. A, von der·* «Schwierige» Kinder und Rorschachs Psychodiagnostik. (Hollandische und dtsch. Zusammenfassung.) Psychiatr. Bl. 42 (1938).

717 *Strure* Typische Ablaufsformen des Deutens bei 14—15jährigen Schulkindern. Exp. Untersuchungen mit der umgestalteten Rorschach-Methode. Z. angew. Psychol. 37 1930

718 *Suars, N.:* Le test de Rorschach chez les adolescents. Travail de diplôme inédit de l'Institut J.-J. Rousseau.

719. *Suares, N. D..* Personality development in adolescence. Rorschach Res. Exch., 1938, 3. 2—12.

720 *Sunne, D .* Rorschach Test Norms of Young Children, Child Development VII, 1936.

721. — *Thornton, G R., and Guilford:* The reliability and meaning of Erlebnistypus scores in the Rorschach test. J abnorm. a soc. Psychol. 31. 1936.

722. *Swift, J W :* Matchings of Teachers' Descriptions and Rorschach Analyses of Preschool Children. Child Development, 1944, 15, 217—224.

723. — Relation of Behavioral and Rorschach Measures of Insecurity in Preschool Children. J Clin. Psychol., 1945, 1, 196—205

724. — Reliability of Rorschach Scoring Catagories with Preschool Children. Child Developm., 1944, 15, 207—216.

725 — Rorschach responses of eight-two pre-school children. Rorsch. Res. Exch. IX, 2, 1945, 74—84.

726. *Symounds, P. M., and Krugman, M.:* Projective methods in the study of personality. Rorsch Res. Exch IX, 2, 1945, 85—101, and Rev. Educ. Res , 1944, 14, 81—98.

727. *Tallman, G :* Further results of retesting Mr. A. Rorsch. Res. Exch. III, 1, 1938, 35—36.

728 — *and Klopfer, B..* Personality studies of cases with lesions of the frontal lobes: III. Rorschach study of a bilateral lobectomy case. Rorschach Res. Exch., 1936—37, 1, 77—89

729. *Tavares Bastos, A.:* A Constatacao de Fatores Psicogenicos em Pacientes Epilepticas, ao Test de Rorschach. An Colôn Gustavo Riedel, 1943, 6, 115—145.

730 — Sòbre a Identidade de Certas Expressões nas Repostas de Casas e Pessias afins ao Test de Rorschach. An Còlon Gustavo Riedel, 1943, 6, 57—52.

731. *Thornton, G R :* A note on the scoring of movement in the Rorschach test. Amer. J. Psychol., 1936, 18, 524—525.

732. *Torrance, K* The Rorschach Method in a Correctional Institution. Ment H.th Bull III Soc Ment Hyg, 1943, 21, 14—16

733. *Tranque Garcia, F.:* Color y Claroscuro en el «Test. de Rorschach Psicotecnica. 1942, 3, 428—433.

734. *Troup, Evelyn:* A comparative study by means of the Rorschach method of personality development in twenty pairs of identical twins. Genet. Psychol Monogr 20 1638.

735. — *and Klopfer, B.* Sample case studies Rorschach Res. Exch., 1936—37, 1, 121—140.

736. *Tschudin, A.:* Chronische Schizophrenien beim Rorschachschen Versuch. Schweiz. Arch. Neurol Psychiat., 1944, 53, 79—100

737. *Tulchin, S. H :* The pre-Rorschach use of Ink-blot tests Rorschach Res. Exch., 1940 4, 1—7.

738. — *and Levy, D M ·* Rorschach Test Differences in a Group of Spanish and English Refugee Children Amer. J. Orthopsv., 1945, 15, 361—368

739 *Urbaitis, J. C., and Waterman, J* Application of the Rorschach Test to Practice in Mental Disease Hospitals. Arch. Neurol Psychiat., 1941, 45, 383—384

740. *Van Bark, B , and Baron, S ·* Neurotic elements in the Rorschach records of psychotics. Rorsch. Res. Exch. VII, 4, 1943, 166—168.

741. *Varvel, W. A .* Suggestions toward the experimental validation of the Rorschach test. Bull. Menninger Clin., 1937, 1, 220—226.

742. — The Rorschach test in psychotic and neurotic depressions. Bull. Menninger Clinic, 1941, 5, 5—12

743. — The Rorschach Test in Relation to Perceptual Organization and to Intelligence. Psychol. Bull., 1941, 38, 705. (Abstr)

744. — The Rorschach test in relation to perceptual organization and to intelligence. Psychol. Bull., 1941, 38, 705 (abstract).

745. *Vaughn, James. and Krug, Othdda* The analytic character of the Rorschach ink-blot test. Amer. J. Orthopsychiatry 8 (1938).

746. *Veit* Der Parkinsonismus nach Encephalitis epidem. im Rorschachschen Formdeutversuch Z. Neur. 110 1927.

747. — Der Rorschachsche Versuch als klinisches Hilfsmittel. Versammlung südwestdeutscher Psychiater. Zbl Neur. 45, 1927

748. *Veit, R :* Do Valor Diagnostico do «Test» de Rorschach. Rev. Neurol. Psiquiat., Sao Paulo, 1942, 8, 24.

749. *Vernon, P. E.:* A Test for Personal Values, J Abnorm. and Soc. Psychol. 1932, XXVI.

750. — Recent Work on the Rorschach Test. J. Ment. Sc. October 1935.

751. — Rorschach bibliography No. III. Rorschach Res. Exch., 1936—37, 1, 89—93.

752. — The American and the German approach to the Study of Personality. Brit. J. Psychol 1933.

753. — The matching method applied to investigations of personality Psychol. Bull., 1936, 33, 149—177

754. — The Rorschach ink-blot test. I. Brit. J. med. Psychol. 13 (1933)

755. — The Rorschach ink-blot test. II. Brit. J. med. Psychol. 13 1933.

756. — The Rorschach ink-blot test III. Brit. J med. Psychol. 13. 1933.

757. — The significance of the Rorschach test. Brit. J. med Psychol 15. 1935.

758. *Victoria, Marcos·* Demonstration des Rorschachschen Tests. Rev. otol etc y Cir neur. sud-amer. 12 (1937) (Spanisch).

759. — Presentacion del Test de Rorschach. Rev. Otol. Neuro. Oftal. y Cu. Neur. Sud-Amer. 1937, 12. 29—35

760 *Vorhaus, P G·* Non-reading as an expressing of resistance Rorsch Res. Exch X, 2, 1946. 60—69

761 — Rorschach reactions in early childhood. Part III Content and details in preschool records Rorsch Res. Exch VIII, 2, 1944, 71—91

762. *Wauls. H. G, van der.* Über die Beziehungen zwischen dem Assoziationsexperiment nach Jung und der Psychodiagncstik nach Rorschach (Psychiatr & Neurol. Klin., Wilhelmina-Gasth., Univ Amsterdam.) Schweiz. Arch. Neur. 42 (1938).

763 *Watson, G :* New trends in clinical procedures and psychotherapy. J Consult. Psychol., 1940, 4, 81—93

764. *Weber, A :* Delirium tremens und Alkoholhalluzinose im Rorschachschen Formdeutversuch. Z Neur. 159 1937

765 — Der Rorschachsche Formdeutversuch bei Kindern. Schweiz Arch. Neurol Psychiat., 1944, 53, 47—61.

766. *Weissenfeld, F..* Der Rorschachsche Formdeutversuch als Hilfsmittel zur Differentialdiagnose zwischen genuiner Epilepsie und Übererregbarkeitsepilepsie. Zeitschr. f d. ges. Neurol. u. Psychiat., 1941, Bd. 171, S. 321.

767. *Weisskopf, E A.* The Influence of the Time Factor on Rorschach Performances. Rorsch Res. Exch., 1942, 6, 128—136. Also in Psychol. Bull., 1942, 39, 51. (Abstr.)

768. *Wells, F L.:* Rorschach and the free association test. J. gen. Psychol. 13 1935.

769 *Werner, H.* Perceptual Behavior of Brain Injured, Mentally Defective Children: An Experimental Study by Means of the Rorschach Technique. Genet Psychol. Monogr., 1945, 31. 51—110.

770. — Rorschach Method Applied to Two Clinical Groups of Mental Defectives Amer. J Ment. Def. 1945, 49. 304—306

771. *Wertham, F.* Progress in Psychiatry Experimental Type Psychology. Arch. of Neurol. and Psychiat. Sept. 1930.

772 *Whitacker, A E., de* Die klinischen Anwendungsmöglichkeiten des psychologischen Rorschach-Versuches (Portugiesisch.) Rev. Neur. S Paulo 1, 1935. Ref. Zbl. Neur 81. S. 31.

773 — Die Verwendung des Rorschachschen psychologischen Tests in der gerichtlichen Psychopathologie Allgemeines über die Methode. Arch. Soc Med. leg. 2. Criminol. S. Paulo 6, 1935. (Portugiesisch.) Ref. Zbl. Neur 82 S. 330.

774 *Wittson, C. L , Hunt, W. A., and Older, H. J·* The Uses of the Multiple-Choice Group Rorschach Test in Military Screening. J. Psychol., 1944, 17, 91—94.

775 *Wolfson, R·* Scoring, tabulation and interpretation of the two sample cases. Rorschach Res Exch., 1939, 3, 14—150.

776. *Wollrab, H .* Aufschliessung der persönlichen Innenwelt. Z angew. Psychol., 1939, 58, 93—117.

777. *Wood, A., Arluck, E , and Margulies, H.:* Report of a group discussion of the Rorschach method held under the auspices of the Josiah Macy Jr. Foundation. Rorsch. Res Exch. V, 3, 1941, 154—165.

778. *Yawger, N. S·* The Rorschach Ink Blot Tests Philadelphia Med., 1943—1944, 39, 548—551.

251

779. *Zolliker, A* Schwangerschafts-Depression und Rorschachscher Formdeutversuch. Schweiz. Arch Neurol Psychiat., 1944, 53, 62–78.

780. *Zubin, J , Chute, E., and Veniar, S* Psychometric Scales for Scoring Rorschach Test Responses. Character and Pers 1943, 11, 277–301

781. *Zulliger, H :* Das Auftreten und die Bedeutung des Farbshocks beim Rorschachschen Test. Nederl Tijdschr Psychol. 6 (1938) (Hollandisch .

782. — Der Behn-Rorschach-Test. Schweiz Zeitschr. f. Psychol , 1942. Bd. 1. S 93

783. - Der Behn-Rorschach-Test Ztrlbl f. Psychother , 1942, Bd. 13, S 397

784. — Der Behn-Rorschach-Versuch (Be-Ro-Test', I. Band Text, II Band. Tafeln Arbeiten z angew Psychiatrie. Bd 6, Verlag Hans Huber, Bern, 1941.

785 — De Rorschachtest ten dienste van den opvoedkundige en de beroepskeuze Ned Tijdschr. Psychol., 1937, 3. 50—88.

786. — Der Rorschachsche Testversuch im Dienste der Erziehungberatung. Z Psychoanal. Pädag. 6. 1932.

787. — Der Rorschachsche Testversuch in der Erziehungsberatung. Psychother. Prax 3, 1936.

788. — Der Rorschachtest im Dienste der Erziehungs- und Berufsberatung Gesundheit und Wohlfahrt 14 1934.

789. — Der Rorschachtest im Dienste des Erziehers und die Berufswahl. Nederl. Tijdschr. Psychol. 5, 1937 (Holländisch)

790. — Diagnostische Schwierigkeiten bei einem «merkwürdigen Bub» und der Rorschachsche Test. Zeitschr. f. Kinderpsychiatr 1935.

791. — Die Angst im Formdeutversuch nach Dr. Rorschach. Z. Psychoanal. Pädag. 7. 1933.

792. — Die Bedeutung des Rorschachschen Formdeutversuchs für den Pädagogen. Berner Schulblatt 1932.

793. — Einbezug des Rorschachschen Testversuchs ins Arbeitsfeld des Erziehungsberaters und -helfers Psyche 2, 1935, Ref. Zbl. Neur. 78 (1936).

794. — Erscheinungsformen und Bedeutung des Farbshocks beim Rorschachschen Formdeutversuch. Z. Kinderpsychiatrie 4 (1937)

795 — Hat der Rorschachsche Formdeutversuch dem Volksschullehrer etwas zu bieten? Schweiz. Erziehungsrundschau 1935.

796. — Jugendliche Diebe im Rorschachformdeutversuch. Verlag Paul Haupt, Bern-Leipzig. 1938.

797. — Schwierige Kinder. Bd. X der «Bücher des Werdenden». Bern 1951. Verlag Hans Huber, Bern.

Index

P Ruch Daulte Biel Bienne (Schweiz)